Harold Swainson

The church of Sancta Sophia, Constantinople

A study of Byzantine building

Harold Swainson

The church of Sancta Sophia, Constantinople
A study of Byzantine building

ISBN/EAN: 9783337149253

Printed in Europe, USA, Canada, Australia, Japan

Cover: Foto ©Andreas Hilbeck / pixelio.de

More available books at **www.hansebooks.com**

THE CHURCH OF SANCTA SOPHIA CONSTANTINOPLE A STUDY OF BYZANTINE BUILDING BY W. R. LETHABY & HAROLD SWAINSON

1894
Macmillan & Co. London & New York

PREFACE

Sancta Sophia is the most interesting building on the world's surface. Like Karnak in Egypt, or the Athenian Parthenon, it is one of the four great pinnacles of architecture, but unlike them this is no ruin, nor does it belong to a past world of constructive ideas although it precedes by seven hundred years the fourth culmination of the building art in Chartres, Amiens, or Bourges, and thus must ever stand as the supreme monument of the Christian cycle. Far from being a ruin, the church is one of the best preserved of so ancient monuments, and in regard to its treatment by the Turks we can only be grateful that S. Sophia has not been situated in the more learned cities of Europe, such as Rome, Aachen, or Oxford, during " the period of revived interest in ecclesiastical antiquities." Our first object has been to attempt some disentanglement of the history of the Church and an analysis of its design and construction; on the one hand, we have been led a step or two into the labyrinth of Constantinopolitan topography, on the other, we have thought that the great Church offers the best point of view for the observation of the Byzantine theory of building.

It may be well for us to state how, in the main, we have shared our work. The one of us—by the accident of the alphabet, second named—has done the larger part of the reading and the whole of the translation required. The first has undertaken more of the constructive side of the book and the whole of the illustrations. We both visited Constantinople, and wish to thank Canon Curtis for help then and since. Mr. Ambrose Poynter has read the proofs. In our text we have thought it well to incorporate so far as possible the actual words of the writers to whom we have referred. The dates when the more ancient authors wrote are given under their names in the index; so are the years of the accession of the Emperors mentioned in the text. Although we have made full use of Salzenberg's great work in the preparation of some of our illustrations, none are mere transcripts from his book.   In some instances where scales are given to details, the scales are but rough approximations.

Much remains to be observed at S. Sophia; the Baptistery, the Cisterns beneath the church, and the Circular Building to the east are practically unknown, and any fact noted in regard to them will almost certainly be new.   But it is still more important that building customs, recipes, and traditions should be recorded.   Byzantine art still exists not only on Mount Athos but all over the once Christian East—at Damascus the builders are still Christians, and the Greek masons of Turkey, M. Choisy says, are still the faithful representatives of the builders of the Lower Empire, and their present practice is a sure commentary on the ancient buildings.

A conviction of the necessity for finding the root of architecture once again in sound common-sense building and pleasurable craftsmanship remains as the final result of our study of S. Sophia, that marvellous work, where, as has so well been said, there is no part where the principles of rational construction are not applied with "hardiesse" and "franchise."   In estimating so highly the Byzantine method of building in its greatest example, we see that its forms and results directly depended on then present circumstances, and then ordinary materials. It is evident that the style cannot be copied by our attempting to imitate Byzantine builders ; only by being ourselves and free, can our work be reasonable, and if reasonable, like theirs universal.

L'ART C'EST D'ÊTRE ABSOLUMENT SOI-MÊME.

CONTENTS

S. SOPHIA CHAPTER I

Byzantium.—Where the narrow swift-flowing Bosporus, which divides Asia from the most eastern part of southern Europe, flows into the Sea of Marmara, a crescent-shaped arm of the sea runs westward into the land, leaving a narrow promontory, which, like the prow of a boat in profile, puts out to the east. The point of this promontory is a mass of rock rising steeply from the sea: divided by a slight transverse depression from the rest of the land, it forms the first hill of the seven which were afterwards inclosed by the walls of Constantinople.

On this crest (by the present Seraglio Point), commanding the passage to the Euxine, was built, in the seventh century B.C., by colonists from Megara—with whom Dionysius couples the Corinthians—the Acropolis, the sacred city and citadel, and within certain limits the lines of its containing walls may still be traced. The lower city gathered about the slopes outside the Acropolis, and had other walls defining its landward limits. Dionysius, the ancient Byzantine writer, who describes the city before the siege of Severus, 196 A.D., says that this citadel of Byzantium was on the promontory of the Bosporus, above the bay called Keras (the Golden Horn). "At a little distance over the height is the altar of Athena Ecbasia —of the landing—where the colonists fought as for their

B

own land. There is too a temple of Poseidon, an ancient
one and hence quite plain, which stands over the sea. . . .
Below the temple of Poseidon, but within the wall, on
the level ground are stadia and gymnasia, and courses for
the young." [1] This Acropolis is roughly outlined in Fig. 1,
the evidence being the contours of the hill, remains and
records of certain walls to be mentioned later, and the
boundaries between the first four regions in Constantine's
city as given in the *Notitia*,[2] a description of the city
written in the beginning of the fifth century. The Acropolis so defined has a striking resemblance to other Greek
hill cities—Tiryns, Mycenae, Acrocorinth, and the Acropolis
of Athens. In Fig. 1 the cross shows the site of the
present Church of S. Sophia; the arrow shows the
Hippodrome, which, still existing, is the great monument of
pre-Constantinian times, and forms the key for all study
of the subsequent city ; O shows the position of the column
said to have been erected by Claudius Gothicus about
270 A.D., which stands at the north end of the Acropolis
overlooking Seraglio or Demetrius Point.

Of the ancient Greek town few positive remains have
come down to us, with the exception of the coins. A publication by the Greek Philological Society of Constantinople
mentions as among several pre-Constantinian inscriptions a
marble slab found in "the tower next to the *Zouk Tsesmé*
gate on the left as one ascends to S. Sophia," which refers
to the stadium erected by Pausanias the General in 477
B.C., " within the walls of Byzantium and below the temple
of Poseidon." [3] The coins also go back to the fifth century
B.C. The early ones show a cow standing on a dolphin,
with the letters BY. In the third century we have Poseidon
seated on a promontory, and later again a dolphin twined round
a trident—all the types having evident reference to the sea-
washed city. Another relic of ancient Byzantium is still
to be seen below the curve of the Hippodrome, where a

---

[1] 'Ανάπλους Βοσπόρου, ed. C. Wescher, 1874, p. 5.
[2] *Notitia Dignitatum*, eds. Pancirolus, Venice, 1602, and Seeck Berlin,
1876. The date given by Seeck for the *Notitia* is 411–413 A.D.
[3] 'Ελληνικὸς Φιλολογικὸς Σύλλογος ; παράρτημα, 1885.

white marble capital of good Greek Doric work lies neglected on the seaward bank of the new railway.

In additiom to the ancient buildings already mentioned, we learn froim Dionysius that the city possessed a temple of Gé Onesidora—the fruitful earth—which consisted of "an unroofed space surrounded by a wall of polished stone." Near by were "temples of Demeter and the Maiden (Persephone), with many pictures in them, relics of their former wealth." This author was also shown the sites of temples to Hera and Pluto, "the former having been destroyed by Darius, and the latter by Philip of Macedon." He also speaks of a large round tower joined to the wall of the city.

Some records or legends of the ancient city are also contained in the Paschal Chronicle.[1] After the siege Severus "built the public bath called Zeuxippus. Now in the middle of the four-porticoed[2] space stood a bronze *stele* of the sun, below which he wrote the name of the sun. The people of Thrace indeed call the place Helion, but the Byzantines themselves call this same public bath 'of Zeuxippus' after its original name, although the emperor ordered it should be called Severion. Opposite to it in the acropolis of Byzantium he built the temple of Apollo, which also faced the two other temples formerly built by Byzas—one to Artemis with the olive, and the other to Phedalian Aphrodite. And the figure of the sun was taken from the four-porticoes and placed in this temple (of Apollo). Opposite the temple of Artemis he built large kennels, and a theatre opposite the temple of Aphrodite. He bought houses and gardens from two brothers, and after pulling down the former and uprooting the latter he built the Hippodrome. Severus restored the Strategion as well. It was first named by Alexander of Macedon, who, in his campaign against Darius, reviewed his troops there before attacking the Persians."

[1] Ed. Bonn, i.,, p. 494.
[2] Lydus speaks of a fire spreading from the "Forum of Zeuxippus" to that of Constantiine (p. 265). The baths of Zeuxippus are placed at the north end of the Hippodrome by Labarte and Mordtmann.

New Rome.—It was about 328 A.D. or the following
year that Constantine decided to enlarge this city, which
had long been under the domination of Rome, and to
make it his capital. The work of building was pushed
forward with great energy, and it was consecrated in May
330. By an edict engraved on a stone erected in the
Strategium, it was called the New Rome of Constantine.
In the documents of the patriarchs of the Greek Church
the city is still called New Rome.

The quarries of easily wrought marble of large crystalline structure and soft white colour found in such abundance
in the island of Proconnesus, only a few miles away over
the sea to which it has given its name of Marmara, then as
now furnished a perfect building material ; while the still
worked quarries of Egypt and Thessaly provided imperial
purple and green. But a richer quarry was doubtless found
in the porphyry and cippolino shafts of the old temples
of many a declining city.

Constantine's city does not appear to have been so
completely Christian as the ecclesiastical writers would have
us suppose. Zosimus tells us that Constantine erected a
shrine to the Dioscuri in the Hippodrome, and he mentions
the temples of Rhea and the Tyché of the city in a large
four-porticoed forum. A whole population of bronze and
marble statues was brought together from Greece, Asia
Minor, and Sicily. The baths of Zeuxippus alone are said
to have had more than sixty bronze statues,[1] a still greater
number were assembled in the Augusteum and other
squares, and in the Hippodrome, where, according to
Zosimus,[2] Constantine placed the Pythian tripod, which had
been the central object in the temple of Apollo at Delphi.
On the triple coils of the bronze serpents in the At-Meidan
can still be read the names of the Greek states, which, after
the battle of Plataea, dedicated a tithe of the spoil to
the Delphic oracle, as described by Herodotus.[3]

An extremely valuable description of ancient Byzantium and

[1] Christodorus, a fifth-century poet.—F. Baumgarten, 1891.
[2] *Hist.* ed. Bonn, p. 97.
[3] Rawlinson's *Herodotus*, 1875, vol. iv., p. 467.

the reconstruction by Constantine is given by Zosimus, writing not much more than a century after the transformation. "Now the city lay upon the crest of a hill which forms a part of the isthmus that is made by what is called the ' Horn ' (κέρας) and the Propontis. And formerly it had its gate (πύλη) at the end of the colonnades which Severus built." . . . "And the wall on its western part descending along with the crest reached to the temple of Aphrodite, and the sea of Chrysopolis [Scutari] which is opposite ; and in the same way from the crest the wall descended northward to the harbour which is called Neorion, and from thence up to the sea which lies directly in front of the straits through which one enters the Euxine." . . . "This then was the ancient size of the city. And Constantine erected a circular forum *where formerly was the gate*, and surrounded it with porticoes of two storeys. He set up two very big arches of Proconnesian marble opposite each other ; through them one entered the porticoes of Severus or issued from the ancient city. And wishing to make the city much larger he further continued the old wall fifteen stadia, and inclosed the city with a wall which cut off the isthmus from sea to sea."

It is clear from this that the ancient land gate of Byzantium stood on the crest of the ridge close to the site now occupied by the Porphyry Column (which was set up by Constantine in the New Forum), and formed the end of a street of columns built by Severus (the *Mese*). From this gate the wall ran southwards to a temple of Aphrodite, and along the shore of the Propontis opposite Scutari. Northwards it descended to the Golden Horn at the Neorion port, and turned along the shore to Seraglio Point. Now the Neorion port was just outside the entrance to the modern Galata bridge,[1] and the account agrees perfectly with the *Notitia* in which we find the following : " The sixth ward at entering on it is level ground for a short distance, all the rest is upon the descent ; for it extends from the Forum of Constantine to the stairs where you ferry over to Sycae [Galata]. It contains the porphyry pillar of Constantine ;

[1] Mordtmann, *Esquisse topo. de Constantinople*, p. 48 and map.

the Senate House in the same place, the Neorion port ; the stairs of Sycae, &c."

It is evident that the city which Constantine found had been virtually rebuilt by Severus in the style of the East. From the days when Alexandria and Antioch were planned a city had become a whole to be designed according to rule. Essential features of such cities—of which Palmyra is the best representative—were long avenues of columns forming the main streets, and a triumphal arch with a central "golden milestone." The main street of columns at Constantinople, which we later hear of by the name of the *Mese* as forming the way from the Milion to the Forum of Constantine, cannot be any other than the "Porticoes of Severus" just mentioned. In the fifth century we find the *Mese* referred to in the building laws of Zeno. "We ordain that none shall be allowed to obstruct with buildings the numerous rows of columns which are erected in the public porticoes, such as those leading from what is called the Milion to the Capitol," any shops or booths between the columns "must be ornamented on the outside at least with marble, that they may beautify the city and give pleasure to the passers by." [1] Mordtmann shows that this great columned way occupied very nearly the line of the present Divan Yiulu ; indeed, it is hardly possible to divert the great arteries at any stage of a city's evolution, and the *Mese* itself probably followed the course of a foot-track to the gate of the Acropolis.

By building walls across the land between the Golden Horn and the sea at distances farther and farther from Seraglio Point, the city has been successively enlarged ; the great land walls, within which the shrunken city now lies, are mainly the work of Theodosius II. These, the walls of the Constantinople known to the Crusaders, are still com-

[1] *The Museum of Classic. Antiq.* 1857, p. 305. The Capitol was beyond Forum Cons. Lydus speaks of "the porticoes that pass through the city and lead to the Forum of Constantine, and the broad space is screened symmetrically with great and beautiful columns. [Some of] these porticoes are said to have been built by men from Naples and Puteoli who came to Byzantium to please Constantine." (Ed. Bonn, p. 266.)

paratively perfect; a triple line on the land side and a single line around the sea margin, some fourteen miles of walls, eight or ten to fifteen feet thick, strengthened by great towers, completely girdles the city round about. The land-wall of Constantine's city, situated between the Acropolis and the present walls, has disappeared, but its course has been traced (see Fig. 1).

Acropolis.—The topography of ancient Constantinople has engaged the attention of generations of writers, and an approximation to true results has undoubtedly been reached. First we must mention Pierre Gilles, usually called Gyllius, who, travelling to collect MSS. for Francis I., resided in the city for many years, and died in 1555. Then Du Cange, in his great work *Constantinopolis Christiana*, 1680, by a careful comparison of the authorities, certainly made discoveries in a country he had never visited. The folios of Banduri [1] followed in 1711 ; and in 1861 Labarte published a more detailed study of the Imperial quarter, chiefly based on the ample notices in the Book of Ceremonies of Constantine Porphyrogenitus. This work, *Le Palais Impérial de Constantinople et ses Abords*, shows remarkable insight and critical acumen. Buzantios in *Constantinopolis*, 1861, and Paspates in his *Byzantinae Melatae*, 1877, made several further identifications. The latter followed with *The Great Palace of Constantinople*, recently translated by Mr. Metcalfe, which goes over the same ground as Labarte ; but the excavations for the railway, which now circles Seraglio Point, had in the meantime exposed some remains, and made the examination of certain walls possible.

Although Paspates made several valuable suggestions, many of his conclusions are certainly not sustained by his reasoning ; indeed, Labarte in many points of divergence was probably much nearer the facts. Paspates' views were accepted by Mr. Bury,[2] to be followed in turn by

---

[1] *Imperium Orientale*, Paris, 1711.
[2] Bury, *A History of the later Roman Empire* (395 A.D. to 800 A.D.), vol. i., p. 57. Mr. Bury, in an excellent review of Paspates' book in

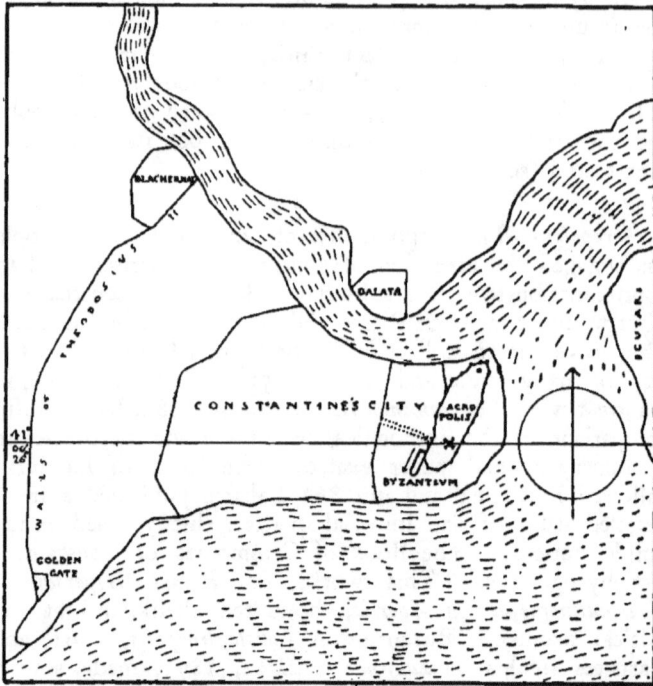

FIG. 1.—Plan of Constantinople showing its development.

Mr. Oman in *The Byzantine Empire* of the "Story of the Nations" Series. A work in Russian has recently been devoted to the study of the Palace quarter.[1] Unger's collection of topographical references in *Quellen der Byzantinischen Kunstgeschicht* is also of the greatest service.

In 1892 appeared Dr. Mordtmann's *Esquisse,* together with a large plan of the city, on which the probable identifications of the ways and buildings were laid down; this was prepared

The Scottish Review, Ap. 1894, gives up the position assigned to the Augusteum by that author.

[1] D. Byéljajev, *Byzantina,* St. Petersburg, 1891, reviewed in *Byzantinische Zeitschrift,* 1892, p. 344.

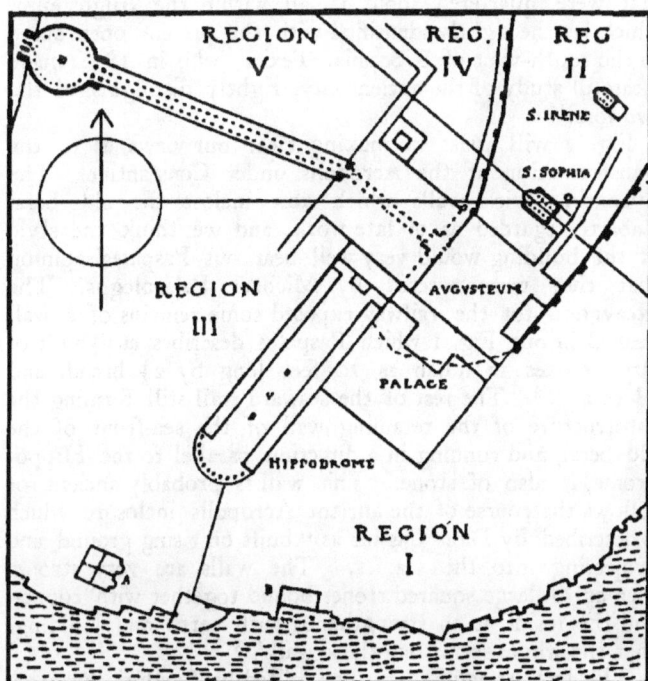

FIG. 2.—Plan of the Acropolis, &c., of Constantine's city.

at the instance of the Comte Riant, who, in his *Exuviae Constantinopolitanae*, contributed the result of much research to our knowledge of Byzantine antiquities.

Dr. Mordtmann, by a study of the whole of the city area and its entire circumvallation as we have it to-day, in comparison with the written descriptions, has laid a firmer grasp on the problem. Labarte, he points out, was chiefly misled by a confusion of the buildings in the Forum of Constantine and those in the Forum Augusteum—a mistake elaborated in some respects by Paspates. Labarte thus placed the prophyry column of Constantine, which still marks the site of the former, together with other buildings

that were quartered about it, all within the Augusteum,
which last he rightly identified with the present open space
to the south-west of S. Sophia. Texier, who in 1834 made
a careful study of the ancient city, rightly distinguished the
two fora.[1]

Fig. 2 will assist in making clear our views as to the
transformation of the Acropolis under Constantine. The
Byzantine brick walls which now inclose the old Serai
Labarte regarded as of late work, and we think the style
of the building would very well bear out Paspates' opinion
that they were erected by Michael Palaeologus. The
excavation for the railway exposed some remains of a wall
near O in our Fig. 1 which Paspates describes as "built of
large stones as much as 10 feet long by $2\frac{1}{2}$ broad, and
$1\frac{1}{2}$ thick."[2]   The rest of the seaward wall still forming the
substructure of the retaining wall of the sea-front of the
old Serai, and running in a direction parallel to the Hippodrome, is also of stone. This wall is probably ancient or
follows the course of the ancient Acropolis inclosure which
is described by Dion Cassius as "built on rising ground and
projecting into the sea. . . . The walls are very strong,
formed of large squared stones bound together with copper,
and the inside is so strengthened with earth and buildings
that the whole seems one thick wall."[3]

The late Anonymous author edited by Banduri says that
the wall of ancient Byzantium commenced at the Golden
Horn near the gate of S. Eugenius to pass along by the
Golden Milestone.[4] We place no reliance on the Anonymous
for early history, but there is much to confirm Mordtmann's
view that an ancient wall occupied this position and that the
Milion—which the Anonymous says was the land gate—
was situated upon its course and formed indeed the entrance
from the Street of Columns. This wall, which Mordtmann
says passed on the land side of the old Serai in front of the

---

[1] MSS., plans, and descriptions, in the Library of R. Inst. Brit.
Architects.

[2] Paspates, *The Great Palace*, p. 20.   Mr. Metcalfe's translation is
intended throughout.

[3] Lib. lxxiv., ch. 10.   [4] Mordtmann, *Esquisse*, pp. 4 and 5.

modern museum (Tchenli Kiosk) where there is a high retaining wall, and continued to the west of S. Sophia not far from the narthex, we consider must be that which formed the landward inclosure of the Acropolis. The fourth region of the city, Mordtmann says, was separated from the second by the rock of the Acropolis and this wall. We are confirmed in our acceptance of the other wall described by Paspates as the seaward wall of the Acropolis, not only because it is built against the steep escarpment of the rock, but by finding that in the division of the city into the wards or regions of the *Notitia* the first ward exactly comprised the space between the wall and the sea ; the second region contained the old Acropolis itself, with a triangle of lower ground at the north against the Golden Horn, where was probably the sea gate ; while the third was divided from the fourth by the great way which left the Milion gate on the old landward wall of the Acropolis. Such pre-existing features naturally formed the boundaries of the wards.

We now give from the *Notitia Dignitatum* the descriptions of the first four regions of the fourteen into which Constantine's city was divided, which will show how Constantine occupied the old areas with the royal and public quarters of his new city. Twelve regions were included within the walls, and two others were formed by the suburbs of Blachernae and Galata.

REGION I.	REGION II.
Contains the house of Placidia Augusta ; the house of most noble Marina ; the Baths of Arcadius ; 27 streets or alleys ; 118 houses ; 2 porticoes; 15 private baths; 4 public cornmills ; 15 private cornmills ; 4 terraces of steps. It is under one curator, who looks after the whole region ; it has 1 vernaculus, a slave (or messenger) for all regions ; 25 collegiati, who are selected from different Guilds (Corporati), and help at fires ; and 5 street wardens, who watch the city at night.	Gradually rises with a gentle ascent beginning from the smaller theatre, and then descends abruptly to the sea. It contains the Great Church ; the Ancient Church ; the Senate ; the Tribunal built with porphyry steps ; the Baths of Zeuxippus ; the theatre ; the amphitheatre ; 34 streets or alleys, 98 houses ; 4 large porticoes ; 13 private baths ; 4 private cornmills ; 4 terraces of steps. It had also 1 curator, 1 vernaculus ; 35 collegiati, 5 street wardens.

REGION III.

Is a plane surface in its higher part, where is the Circus, but from the end of this it descends steeply to the sea. It contains the Circus Maximus; the house of Pulcheria Augusta; the new harbour; a semicircular portico, called by the Greeks Sigma; the Tribunal of the Forum of Constantine; 7 streets; 94 houses; 5 large porticoes; 11 private baths; 9 private cornmills. It had 1 curator; 1 vernaculus; it had also 21 collegiati; and 5 street wardens.

REGION IV.

From the Golden Milliarium is prolonged, with hills rising to right and left in a valley leading to an open space. It contains the golden Milliarium; the Augusteum; the Basilica; the Nymphaeum; the Portico of Fanio; a marble ship—the monument of a naval victory—the church or martyrium of S. Mennas; the Stadium; the Scala Timasii; 32 streets; 375 houses; 4 large porticoes; 7 private baths; 5 private cornmills; 7 terraces of steps. It had 1 curator; 1 vernaculus; 45 collegiati; 5 street wardens.

Augusteum.—Thus Region I., occupying the land between the Acropolis wall and the sea, was partly reserved for palaces; Region II. coincided with the Acropolis, and had its south end devoted to the Forum Augusteum and the Christian Basilicas of S. Sophia (" the Great Church ") and St. Irene (" the Old Church."). It will be observed that in the *Notitia* the Augusteum is given to Region IV., to which it does indeed adjoin; Mordtmann [1] considers that the Augusteum, like the buildings round it, must have belonged to Region II., but suggests that there may have been a continuation of the open space farther to the west in Region IV., and some such space as this certainly seems required by several of the references.

Gyllius first made the identification of the Augusteum with the present open space on the south of S. Sophia; in this he was followed by Labarte, and Mordtmann concurs. Paspates in making the Augusteum occupy the ground along the east side of the Hippodrome stands alone against, as it seems to us, all evidence. For example, he is compelled to shift the inscribed pedestal of the statue of the Empress Eudoxia, which we cannot but believe was found in its original position (see Mordtmann, p. 64, and Paspates, p. 105, and below, p. 13). The *Mese* moreover he makes the centre of his Augusteum. Mr. Bury thought it proved that the

[1] *Esquisse Top.* p. 3.

Augusteum "was also called the Forum of Constantine," because a passage in *Cedrenus* speaks of the Senate House (τὸ σευάτον) as in the Forum of Constantine. It is perfectly clear however from the *Notitia* that there were two Senate Houses—one in the Forum mentioned in the extract we have given from the description of the sixth ward, and the other included in the second region as just quoted.[1]

In the Augusteum was erected a Senate, its front facing the west. "The Senate," says Mordtmann, "was placed where to-day stands the Tribunal of Commerce." That is, on the east side of the present place of S. Sophia against what must have been the eastern side of the Augusteum and the ancient Acropolis, on the seaward wall of which it was probably founded. In digging the foundations of the Tribunal of Commerce in 1847 the ancient pavement was found, at a depth of twelve feet, and the base of the celebrated statue of Eudoxia, with an inscription, marked it as the site of the Courts of Justice (Mordtmann, p. 64). The statue, Socrates[2] says, was "of silver, and it stood upon a lofty pedestal (*bema*), not far from the church called S. Sophia, with a road between."

The Augusteum, following the Hippodrome, does not lie four-square with the cardinal points, but almost diagonally to them : for convenience, however, we shall speak of the directions as North, South, East, and West, calling the side towards the *Mese* the west. On the north side, and following the same system of alignment, is the present S. Sophia. The palace of the Patriarch probably adjoined the church, on the north side of the square.

The royal palaces mentioned in the *Notitia* were on the south of the Augusteum. According to the *Paschal Chronicle*, written about 630 A.D., Constantine the Great made a palace beside the Hippodrome, "and the ascent from the palace to the stand of the Hippodrome was by means of the stair called the spiral" (Paspates, *Great Palace*, p. 47). This palace does

---

[1] Zosimus (p. 139) and Lydus (p. 265) say that the Emperor Julian built a Senate. So also according to Sozomen (ii. 3) and the *Paschal Chron.* did Constantine.

[2] *Hist. eccles.* lib. vi., ch. xviii.

not seem to have become of great importance until Justinian's time. The *Notitia* merely mentions the House of Placidia Augusta, and the House of the most noble Marina, the daughters of Arcadius, in the first ward ; and the House of Pulcheria Augusta in the third ; and speaks of several other royal palaces in the 9th, 10th, and 11th wards. The palace of the emperor at this time was in the 14th ward, which was outside the walls and isolated, making "the figure of a small city by itself; " this is the celebrated palace of Blachernae.

The Church.—It was in May 328 that Helena is said to have discovered the true cross and other relics at Jerusalem. And this event, which synchronizes exactly with Constantine's choice of Byzantium as his capital, was probably not without direct relation to the foundation of the church dedicated to Christ. Socrates writes, " A portion of the cross she (Helena) inclosed in a silver chest and left in Jerusalem as a memorial, but the other part she sent to the king." [1]

Theophanes, Cedrenus, Glycas, Paul the Deacon, Nicephorus Callistus, and other late historians agree in making Constantine the founder of the first Church dedicated to the Second Person of the Trinity as the Divine Wisdom ; and Cedrenus even gives a name—Euphrates—to the architect.[2] Codinus, who wrote in the fifteenth century, alone relates that Constantine purified a previously existing temple and dedicated it to Christian uses.

There is much evidence to show that the church could not have been completed by Constantine even if he had founded it, or contemplated its foundation. In the life of the emperor, the Church of the Holy Apostles, which was built near the Forum of Constantine, and in which the emperor was buried, is described at length,[3] but it does not mention S. Sophia, although the author takes pains to enumerate the Christian objects in the city—saying that there were "many Oratories and Martyria, and by the fountains in the middle of the agorae were figures in gilt bronze of the

---

[1] *Ecc. Hist.* lib. i., xvii.
[2] Du Cange, *Descriptio S. Sophiae*, ed. Bonn, p. 62.
[3] Eusebius, *De Vita Cons.* lib. iv., cap. lviii–lix.

Good Shepherd and of Daniel with the lions ; in the palace was a cross wrought in gold with many coloured precious stones." [1]

In the fifth century *Notitia*, as we have seen, S. Irene is called the Old Church and S. Sophia the Great Church.

The historian Socrates, probably the best authority, says that Constantine " built two churches, one he called Irene and the other the Apostles," [2] and he attributes S. Sophia entirely to Constantius. " The King built the great church which is called Sophia and joined it to that called Irene, which the father of the king had previously increased and beautified, and now both churches were included within one wall and had one title."

Upon its completion, it was dedicated, with magnificent cere-mony, by the patriarch Eudoxius on Sunday, February 15th, 360 A.D., " in the thirty-fourth year after its foundation." [3] This would fix its foundation in the year 326 A.D., two years after Constantine, having defeated Licinius, had begun to reign alone. Cedrenus writes, " Eudoxius consecrated a *second* time the Church of the Divine Wisdom, because after its first completion, and the dedication by Eusebius, it had fallen and been again restored by Constantius," [4] and he places this event in the twenty-second year of Constantius' reign.

Cedrenus is a late and credulous writer, and in attributing a first dedication to Eusebius—who would certainly have told us himself—he shows how untrustworthy is the whole story. Altogether we cannot do better than accept the account of Idatius and that given in the *Paschal Chronicle*, with perhaps a little suspicion on the part which refers to Constantine, " In this year (360) in the month Peritius was dedicated the great church of Constantinople, in the thirty-fourth year from the time when Constantine had laid the foundations. For the opening ceremony (*encaenia*) Constantius brought many offerings of gold, and great treasure of silver ; many tissues adorned with gold thread and stones for the sanctuary ; for

---

[1] *De Vita Cons.* lib. iii., cap. xlviii.-xlix.
[2] *Eccl. Hist.* ii., xvi.
[3] Du Cange, p. 63.   He quotes the fifth-century author Idatius.
[4] Ed. Bonn, i., p. 523, and i., p. 530.

the doors of the church different curtains (*amphithuriai*) of gold ; and for the outside gateways (*puleones*) many others with gold threads." According to the late Anonymous author (see page 129), "in the reign of Theodosius the Great (†395) and in the patriarchate of Nectarius (381–398), seventy-four years after the church was built, the roof of the church was destroyed by fire ;" he probably really meant the fire of 404 in Arcadius' reign. At that time S. John Chrysostom, incurring the dislike of the Empress Eudoxia, was banished. He was brought back at the end of two days, once more preached in S. Sophia, and was exiled again, with disastrous results, for his partisans set fire to the church and destroyed it. "This happened on the 20th of June, in the consulship of Honorius and Aristaenetus" (404).[1]

The fire was by some thought to be of supernatural origin. Palladius, the bishop's biographer, writes, "Then a flame seemed to burst from the centre of the throne in which he used to sit, and climbed up by the chains [of lamps] to the roof . . . and crept like a wriggling snake upon the back of the houses of the church." There was also burnt the Senate, "lying many paces to the south opposite the church ; and the fire spared only the little house, in which the sacred vessels were kept."

The church was again injured by fire, restored by Theodosius II., and rededicated in 415.[2] Fresh relics were required for this rededication.[3] One fact of importance in regard to this church is related by Sozomenus of the Empress Pulcheria. "She dedicated an altar in the church of Constantinople, a most wonderful work of gold and precious stones, on behalf of her virginity and her brothers' empire. And she wrote this on the face of the table so that it might be clear to all."[4]

From this time until the outbreak known as the Nika sedition, in January 532, the church is not said to have been further altered. According to Cedrenus, the records and charters perished with the church.

[1] Socrates, *Hist. Eccl.* vi., 18.
[2] Du Cange, § 3.
[3] *Pasch. Chron.* ed. Bonn, i., p. 572.   [4] *Eccl. Hist.* ix., 1.

There cannot be a doubt that the present S. Sophia occupies the site of the first church. A church once made holy by dedication and the reception of relics could not be transported. Indeed it is possible that it may occupy the site of one of the Greek temples, for there was a constant tendency to this supersession on one sacred site; and the present church stands on the very crest of the old Acropolis. If there were any sufficient reason to identify the site with that of the altar of Pallas, the dedication of the church itself would evidently be one of the many instances of a transference of title from the old worship. The Parthenon—where Hellenic rites survived to the sixth century—became a church in this way dedicated to the Holy Wisdom.[1] The axis of the church seems to point somewhere between 30° and 35° south of east, where there is a considerable sea prospect and a low horizon. This direction, either by accident or intention, must agree very closely with sunrise at the winter solstice:[2] the latitude of the church being 41° 0' 26". The plan will show that the ancient Hippodrome, and probably the other buildings, were set out in relation to this axis.

In comparing the early Basilicas of Constantinian date, both those that exist and those of which we have descriptions, we find that they generally, if not invariably, had their doors of entrance at the *east* end, and their apses towards the west, exactly the opposite of the more recent custom. Rohault De Fleury says this was usual in the East till the fifth century, and the custom continued much later in Rome. Kraus, in the best study of the subject,[3] writes : " S. Agatha at Ravenna must be mentioned as the first which had its altar at the east end : it was built in 417, and in this century the practice became general."

Socrates († 440) says of the church of Antioch that "the altar stood not at the east but at the *west*," but he speaks of

[1] See Tozer's note, Finlay, vol. i., 45.
[2] Justinian's church was opened at Christmas.
[3] Art. "Orientirung" in *Real Encyklopädie der Christlichen Alterthümer*, 1886, based on Mothes' schedule in *Die Basilikenformen*, 1865. We hope to show on another occasion that the present church at Bethlehem which points to the east was entirely rebuilt by Justinian. There is no proof that S. George Salonica is older than fifth cent.

this as contrary to the usual custom at the time he wrote.
This church was founded by Constantine and finished by his
son. The Church of the Apostles at Constantinople, built
by Constantine to contain the relics of S. Luke, seems also to
have been entered at the east, for S. John Chrysostom [1] speaks
of the emperor being buried "in the part in front of the
doors," and an anonymous author, who wrote about the
imperial sepulchres, says that Constantine's sarcophagus was
"in front towards the east."[2]

We shall thus be following the reasonable suggestion of
comparative archæology in saying that the first church of S.
Sophia almost certainly had its entrance doors at the east—
the sanctuary end of the present church.

The church was probably only of medium size ; the
length of the present church is about 250 feet, its vastness
being in its width. The *Paschal Chronicle* speaks of "its
stupendous and marvellous columns all being ἐκ τετραέντου " ;
but owing to a variant reading it is difficult to determine
whether it means that the pillars were square, or were set in
a square, or formed four bays. Glycas and Codinus, who
wrote a thousand years after the foundation of the church,
say that it was basilican (*dromika*), and had a wooden roof
(*xulotroullos*), and the latter says that the church of
Theodosius had cylindrical vaults. As it is evident from
the rapid destruction by fire that the roofs of the early
churches were of wood, they were probably Basilicas. Only
a few minor particulars, such as the existence of an atrium,
and the right of sanctuary in the bema (*thusiasterion*), can
be gathered from the homilies of S. Chrysostom. Socrates
tells us that this patriarch was wont to preach "in the ambo
for the sake of being better heard." [3] From Palladius we
learn that there was a baptistery (in which the Sixth Council
of Constantinople, A.D. 394,[4] appears to have met) attached
to the church, and it was here Chrysostom took leave of the
deaconesses at his banishment, as described in a passage diffi-

---

[1] *Homilies* xxvi. and lx.
[2] *De Sepulcris Imperatorum*, Migne S. G., vol. 157, p. 726.
[3] Migne, p. 674.
[4] Bingham, *Antiquities of the Christian Church*, vol. iii., p. 120.

cult to interpret. " He went out of the baptistery on the east side, for there was no western (exit). The mule which he usually rode was made to stand westwards before the gate to the church, where is the porch, so that he might escape the people who were expecting him." The passage from the same author about the waters of the font being stained with blood does not, as is sometimes supposed, necessarily refer to S. Sophia.

In applying the plan of a church of mean size so that the doors should face eastwards, we are at once struck by finding that the western hemicycle of the present church would lie about the apse ; and we cannot but suggest that in this we may have the very *raison d'être* of the remarkable plan of the present church, which it would seem might be properly classed with those churches which have apses at both ends, like the early basilica at Orleansville near Tunis ; [1] the MS. plan of S. Gall is the best known example ; our own early church at Canterbury was another instance, the result of adding to a church with a western apse ; France furnishes Besançon and Nevers, and Germany numerous examples.

It is indeed possible that some parts of the old structure may have given practical and positive reasons contributing to this result, and a thorough examination of the cisterns beneath the present floor of S. Sophia may yet yield full evidence of the first basilica ; or if these vaults were entirely built for Justinian's church, their material would almost certainly be derived from the earlier building.

We suggest that the circular brick building lying at the north-east angle of the present church belonged to the pre-Justinian church, and formed its baptistery. It is about forty-five feet exterior diameter, and the plan as given by Salzenberg shows great resemblance to other circular structures of the Constantinian age; such as S. Constantia in Rome, the "tomb of Helen" at Rome, and the round tomb buildings which adjoined S. Peter's as shown in the plan of Ciampini.[2]

---

[1] *Revue Archéologique*, vol. iv., p. 659, and Kugler, *Geschichte der Baukunst*, vol. i., p. 372.

[2] For similar early circular baptisteries see Martigny, *Dict. Christ. Antiq.*

The entrance doorway of this building was to the *east*.

As to its use. In the contemporary account of Justinian's church, the poet Paulus, describing the north aisle, says, "On the north is a door admitting the people to the founts that purify the stains of mortal life and heal every scar." He does not mention the present south-west building, nor has he any other reference to a font. We suppose therefore that this isolated building on the north-east escaped the Nika fire, and served as the baptistery of the new church, until the square building, on the side of the church towards the Augusteum, which is spoken of in the *Ceremonies* as the "Great Baptistery by the Horologium," was erected for or diverted to this purpose.

We very probably have some relics of the earlier buildings in certain capitals which Salzenberg found in the church:[1] the inscribed bricks,[2] and a Byzantine Corinthian capital now lying in the courtyard, may likewise have belonged to it. The fine bronze doors to south porch are evidently earlier than the present church, and so probably are the slabs of which the screen on south side of first floor is partly made up.

[1] See Salz., plate xx., figs. 4, 5.   [2] *Ibid.* p. 19.

CHAPTER II

JUSTINIAN'S CHURCH

The New Church.—The pre-Justinian church was burnt on the 15th January, 532 [1]—the first day of the sedition— and the work of reconstruction was begun on the 23rd of the following month.[2]

Theophanes [3] says the period employed in the construction was five years eleven months and ten days; the statements therefore of Codinus and Glycas, that it took seventeen years to build, are completely at variance with this more credible author.

The solemn dedication took place, as Marcellinus Comes describes,[4] on 26th December, 537, Indiction 15, in the eleventh year of Justinian's reign.

A description of this dedication ceremony is given by Theophanes.[5] "The procession started from the church of Anastasia, Menas the patriarch sitting in the royal chariot, and the king walking with the people."

In the thirty-second year of Justinian's reign an earthquake destroyed a great portion of the newly erected church.[6]

Now Procopius, whose contemporary history of the

---

[1] *Chron. Pasch.* ed. Bonn, p. 622.

[2] Zonaras also gives the true date; according to the Byzantine era the year of the world 6040. In Cedrenus it appears as 6008, a copyist's error in writing η' for μ'.

[3] Ed. Bonn, p. 338.

[4] Migne, *S.L.* vol. li., p. 943.

[5] Ed. Bonn, p. 378.

[6] *Theo.* p. 359.

edifices built by Justinian was, according to Krumbacher,[1] finished and published in the year 558 or the spring of 559 at latest, makes no mention of this earthquake of 558, though he describes in full how, during the building of the church, which was completed in 537, the piers of the eastern arch threatened to give way before it was finished. We may therefore conclude that he describes Justinian's church in its first state.

The translation from Procopius here given is based on that of Mr. Aubrey Stewart, published by the Palestine Pilgrims' Text Society, which has been compared with the original. We give in Fig. 3 a plan of the church as built by Justinian, so far as the evidence will allow of an approximately certain restoration.

As the several different curved portions of the plan are difficult to distinguish, we propose so far as possible to reserve certain words for separate parts. The small eastern semicircle and its vault will be called apse and apsoid respectively. Hemicycle and semidome will refer to the great semicircle at the east or west and its vault. The pairs of curved spaces forming the lateral recesses in the hemicycles we propose to name exedras and their half-domes conchs.

Procopius.—" The lowest dregs of the people in Byzantium once assailed the Emperor Justinian in the rebellion called Nika, which I have clearly described in my *History of the Wars*. To prove that it was not merely against the emperor but no less against God that they took up arms, they ventured to burn the church of the Christians which the people of Byzantium call Sophia, a name most worthy of God. God permitted them to effect this crime, knowing how great the beauty of this church would be when restored. Thus the church was entirely reduced to ashes ; but the Emperor Justinian not long afterwards adorned the new one in such a fashion, that if any one had asked the Christians in former times, if they wished their church to be destroyed and thus restored, showing them the appearance of the

---

[1] *Geschichte der Byzantinischer Litteratur,* 1893, p. 42. Ramsay says it could not have been completed until 560. See *Historical Geography of Asia Minor,* p. 205.

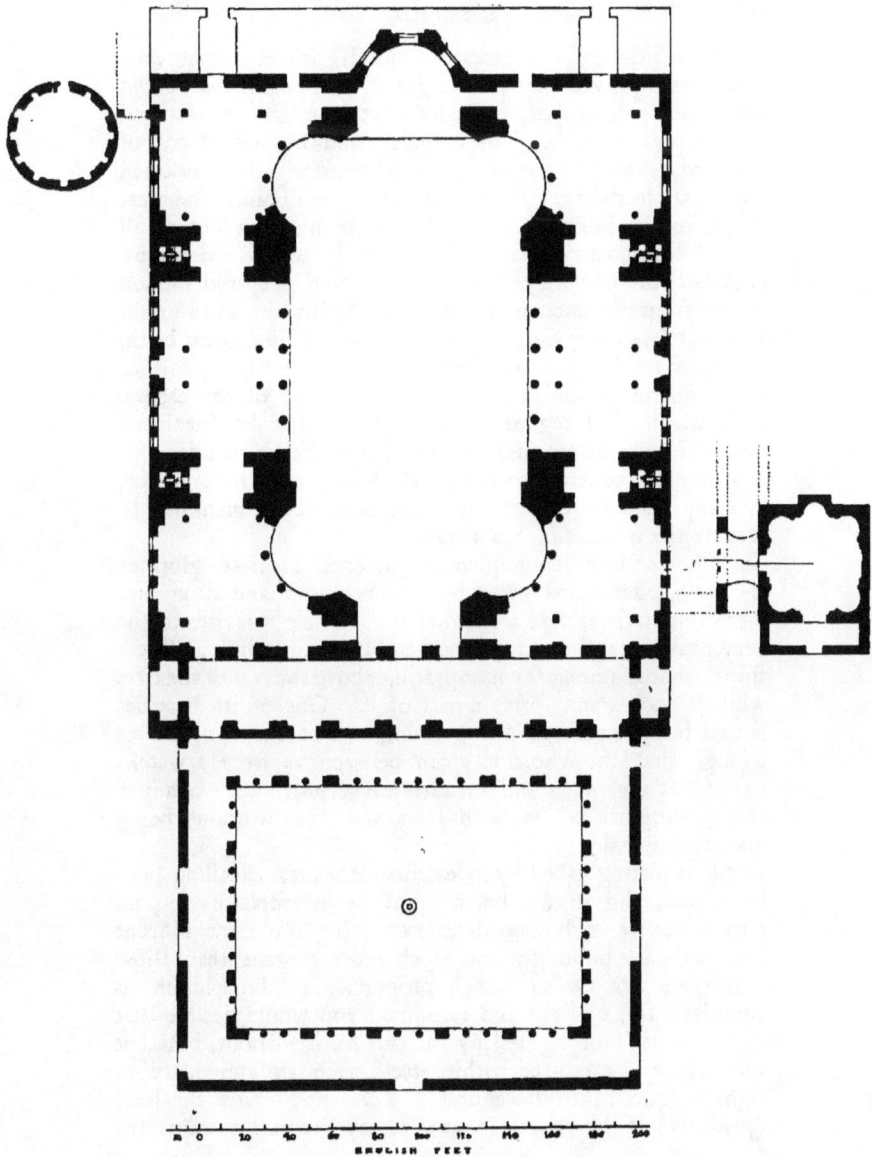

FIG. 3.—Plan of S. Sophia as built by Justinian.

ENGLISH FEET

church which we now see, I think it probable that they would have prayed that they might so soon as possible behold their church destroyed, in order that it might be changed into its present form. The emperor, thinking not of cost of any kind, pressed on the work, and collected together workmen (*technitai*) from every land. Anthemius of Tralles, the most skilled in the builder's art, not only of his own but of all former times, carried forward the king's zealous intentions, organised the labours of the workmen, and prepared models of the future construction. Associated with him was another architect (*mechanopoios*) named Isidorus, a Milesian by birth, a man of intelligence, and worthy to carry out the plans of the Emperor Justinian. It is indeed a proof of the esteem with which God regarded the emperor, that he furnished him with men who would be so useful in effecting his designs, and we are compelled to admire the wisdom of the emperor, in being able to choose the most suitable of mankind to execute the noblest of his works.

"The church consequently presents a most glorious spectacle, extraordinary to those who behold it, and altogether incredible to those who are told of it. In height it rises to the very heavens, and overtops the neighbouring buildings like a ship anchored among them, appearing above the rest of the city, while it adorns and forms a part of it. One of its beauties is that being a part of and growing out of the city, it rises so high that the whole city can be seen as from a watch-tower. The length and breadth are so judiciously arranged that it appears to be both long and wide without being disproportioned.

"It is distinguished by indescribable beauty, excelling both in its size, and in the harmony of its measures, having no part excessive and none deficient ; being more magnificent than ordinary buildings, and much more elegant than those which are not of so just a proportion. The church is singularly full of light and sunshine ; you would declare that the place is not lighted by the sun from without, but that the rays are produced within itself, such an abundance of light is poured into this church. *The Apse.*—Now the head (*prosopon*) of the church (that is to say the part towards the rising sun, where the sacred mysteries are performed in honour of God) is built as follows. The building rises from the ground not in a straight line, but setting back somewhat obliquely, it retreats in the middle into a rounded form which those who are learned in these matters call semicylindrical, rising perpendicularly. *Apsoid and Semidome.*— The upper part of this work ends in the fourth part of a sphere, and above it another crescent-shaped (*menoeides*) structure is raised upon the adjacent parts of the building, admirable for its beauty, but causing terror by the apparent weakness of its construction ; for it appears not to rest upon a secure foundation, but to hang dangerously over the heads of those below, although it is really supported with especial firmness and safety. *Exedras.*—On each side of these parts are columns standing upon the floor, which are not placed in a straight line, but arranged with an inward curve of semicircular shape, one beyond another like the dancers in a chorus. These columns support above them a crescent-shaped structure. Opposite the east wall is built another wall, containing the entrances, and upon either side of it also stand columns, with stone-work above them, in a half-circle exactly like those previously described. *Great Piers and Arches.*—In the midst of the church are four masses of stone called piers (*pessoi*), two on the north, and two on the south sides, opposite and alike, having four columns in the space between each pair. These piers are formed of large stones fitted together, the stones being carefully selected, and cleverly jointed into one another by the masons,[1] and reaching to a great height. Looking at them, you would compare them to perpendicular cliffs. Upon them, four arches (*apsides*)[2] arise over a quadrilateral space. The extremities of these arches join one another in pairs, their ends resting upon the piers, while the other parts of them rise to a great height, suspended in the air. Two of these arches, that is those towards the rising and the setting of the sun, are constructed over the empty air, but the others have under them some stone-work, and small columns. *Dome*

---

[1] λιθολόγος—really one who picks out and lays stones.
[2] ἀψίς, "a binding together," used for either an arch or a semidome.

and Pendentives.—Now above these arches is raised a circular
building of a curved form through which the light of day first
shines; for the building, which I imagine overtops the
whole country, has small openings left on purpose, so that
the places where these intervals occur may serve for the
light to come through.   Thus far I imagine the building
is not incapable of being described, even by a weak and
feeble tongue.   As the arches are arranged in a quadrangular
figure, the stone-work between them takes the shape of a
triangle, the lower angle of each triangle, being compressed
where the arches unite, is slender, while the upper part becomes
wider as it rises in the space between them, and ends against the
circle which rests upon them, forming there its remaining
angles.   A spherical-shaped dome (*tholos*) standing upon this
circle makes it exceedingly beautiful; from the lightness
of the building, it does not appear to rest upon a solid
foundation, but to cover the place beneath as though it
were suspended from heaven by the fabled golden chain.
All these parts surprisingly joined to one another in the air,
suspended one from another, and resting only on that which
is next to them, form the work into one admirably harmonious
whole, which spectators do not dwell upon for long in the
mass, as each individual part attracts the eye to itself.   The
sight causes men constantly to change their point of view,
and the spectator can nowhere point to any part which he
admires more than the rest.   Seeing the art which appears
everywhere, men contract their eyebrows as they look at each
part, and are unable to comprehend such workmanship, but
always depart thence, stupefied, through their incapacity.
So much for this.

   " The Emperor Justinian and the architects Anthemius and
Isidorus used many devices to construct so lofty a church with
security.   One of these I will now explain, by which a man
may form some opinion of the strength of the whole work;
as for the others I am not able to discover them all, and find
it impossible to describe them in words.   It is as follows:
The piers, of which I just now spoke, are not constructed in
the same manner as the rest of the building; but in this
fashion; they consist of quadrangular courses of stone, rough

by nature, and made smooth by art ; of these stones, those which make the projecting angles of the pier are cut angularly (*engonios*), while those which go in the middle parts of the sides are cut square (*tetragonos*).

"They are fastened together not with lime (*titanos*), called 'unslaked' (*asbestos*), not with asphaltum, the boast of Semiramis at Babylon, nor anything of the kind, but with lead, which, poured into the interstices, has sunk into the joints of the stones, and binds them together ; this is how they are built.

"Let us now proceed to describe the remaining parts of the church. The entire ceiling is covered with pure gold, which adds to its glory, though the reflections of the gold upon the marble surpass it in beauty. There are two aisles one above another on each side, which do not in any way lessen the size of the church, but add to its width. In length they reach quite to the ends of the building, but in height they fall short of it ; these also have domed ceilings adorned with gold. Of these two porticoes one [ground floor] is set apart for male and the other [upper floor] for female worshippers ; there is no variety in them, nor do they differ in any respect from one another, but their very equality and similarity add to the beauty of the church. Who could describe these gynaeceum galleries, or the numerous porticoes (*stoai*) and cloistered courts (*peristuloi aulai*) with which the church is surrounded ? Who could tell of the beauty of the columns and marbles with which the church is adorned ? One would think that one had come upon a meadow full of flowers in bloom ! Who would not admire the purple tints of some, and the green of others, the glowing red and the glittering white, and those too, which nature, painter-like, has marked with the strongest contrasts of colour? Whoever enters there to worship perceives at once that it is not by any human strength or skill, but by the favour of God, that this work has been perfected ; the mind rises sublime to commune with God, feeling that He cannot be far off, but must especially love to dwell in the place which He has chosen ; and this is felt not only when a man sees it for the first time, but it always makes the same impression upon him, as though he

had never beheld it before. No one ever became weary of
this spectacle, but those who are in the church delight in what
they see, and, when they leave, magnify it in their talk.
Moreover it is impossible accurately to describe the gold,
and silver, and gems, presented by the Emperor Justinian ;
but by the description of one part, I leave the rest to be
inferred.—That part of the church which is especially sacred,
and where the priests alone are allowed to enter, which is
called the Sanctuary (*thusiasterion*), contains forty thousand
pounds' weight of silver.

"The above is an account, written in the most abridged and
cursory manner, describing in the fewest possible words the
most admirable structure of the church at Constantinople,
which is called the Great Church, built by the Emperor
Justinian, who did not merely supply the funds for it, but
assisted at its building by the labour and powers of his mind,
as I will now explain. Of the two arches (*apsides*), which
I lately mentioned—the architects (*mechanopoioi*) call them
loroi [1]—that one which stands towards the east had been built
up on each side, but had not altogether been completed in
the middle, where it was still imperfect·; when the piers
(*pessoi*) upon which the building rested, unable to support
the weight which was put upon them, somehow all at once
split open, and seemed as though before long they would fall
to pieces. Upon this Anthemius and Isidorus, terrified at
what had taken place, referred the matter to the emperor,
losing all confidence in their own skill. He at once, I know
not by what impulse, but probably inspired by Heaven, for he
is not an architect, ordered them to complete this arch ; for
it, said he, resting upon itself, will no longer need the piers
(*pessoi*) below.[2] Now if this story were unsupported by
witnesses, I am well assured that it would seem to be written
in order to flatter, and would be quite incredible ; but as
there are many witnesses now alive of what then took place
I shall not hesitate to finish it. The workmen performed his
bidding, the arch was safely suspended, and proved by ex-

---

[1] λωρός, "a thong" or a belt.
[2] The author seems here to mistake the piers for the temporary support
of the arch while it was being built.

periment the truth of his conception. So much then for this part of the building ; now with regard to the other arches, those looking to the south and to the north, the following incidents took place. When the arches called *loroi* were raised aloft during the building of the church everything below them laboured under their weight, and the columns which are placed there shed little scales, as though they had been planed.

" Alarmed at this, the architects (*mechanikoi*) again referred the matter to the emperor, who devised the following scheme. He ordered the upper part of the work that was giving way to be taken down where it touched the arches for the present, and to be replaced afterwards when the damp had thoroughly left the fabric. This was done, and the building has stood safely ever since, so that the structure, as it were, bears witness to the emperor's skill."

Fall of Dome and Restoration.—On the 7th of May, 558, the eastern part of the dome, "built by Isaurian workmen, with the apse, was thrown down by an earthquake, destroying in its fall the holy table, the ciborium, and the ambo."[1] Reference is made to this in the opening lines of the Silentiary's poem (see Chapter III.). According to Theophanes "the architects attributed its fall to the fact that to save expense the piers had been made too full of openings. The emperor restored the piers and raised the dome twenty feet." The church was again consecrated in the fifth year after the catastrophe by Eutychius in the thirty-sixth year of Justinian, on the 24th of December.[2] Theophanes[3] describes the emperor and patriarch as riding together to the church in a chariot, and bearing the gospel with them, "while the people chanted the ' Lift up your gates.' "

The church, after its repair, is described by three contemporary authors—Paul the Silentiary, Agathias, and Evagrius. The poem of the first of these is given in the next chapter.

---

[1] Theophanes, *Chronographia*, ed. Bonn, vol. i., p. 359.
[2] *Chron. Pasch.* ed. Bonn, and Zonaras.
[3] *Chron.* ed. Bonn, p. 369.

Agathias.—Agathias, surnamed the scholar, was born in
536 at Myrina in Asia Minor,[1] studied at Alexandria, and
came in 554 to Constantinople, where he became known as
a historian and a poet, and died in 582.

Justinian, he says, restored several buildings after the earthquake, his especial care however was the great church of
S. Sophia.[2] "Now the former church having been burnt
by the angry mob, Justinian built it up again from the
foundations as big and more beautiful and wonderful, and
this most beautiful design was adorned with much precious
metal.   He built it in a round form with burnt brick and
lime, it was bound together here and there with iron, but
they avoided the use of wood, so that it should no more be
easily burnt.   Now Anthemius was the man who devised and
worked at every part.

"And as by the earthquake the middle portion of the roof
and the higher parts had been destroyed, the king made it
stronger, and raised it to a greater height.   Anthemius was
then dead, but the young man Isidorus and the other craftsmen, turning over in their minds the previous design, and
comparing what had fallen with what remained, estimated
where the error lay, and of what kind it was.   They determined to leave the eastern and western arches (*apsides*) as
they were.   But of the northern and southern (arches) they
brought towards the inside, that portion of the building
which was on the curve.[3]   And they made these arches wider
so as to be more in harmony with the others, thus making
the equilateral symmetry more perfect.   In this way they
were able to cover the measurelessness of the empty space,
and to steal off some of its extent to form an oblong design.
And again they wrought that which rose up over it in the
middle, whether orb (*kuklos*), or hemisphere, or whatever
other name it may be called.   And this also became more
straightforward and of a better curve, in every part agreeing
with the line ; and at the same time not so wide but higher,
so that it did not frighten the spectators as formerly, but was
set much stronger and safer."

[1] Krumbacher, p. 49.   [2] Agathias, lib. v. ed. Bonn, p. 296.
[3] τὴν ἐπὶ τοῦ κυρτώματος οἰκοδόμιαν.

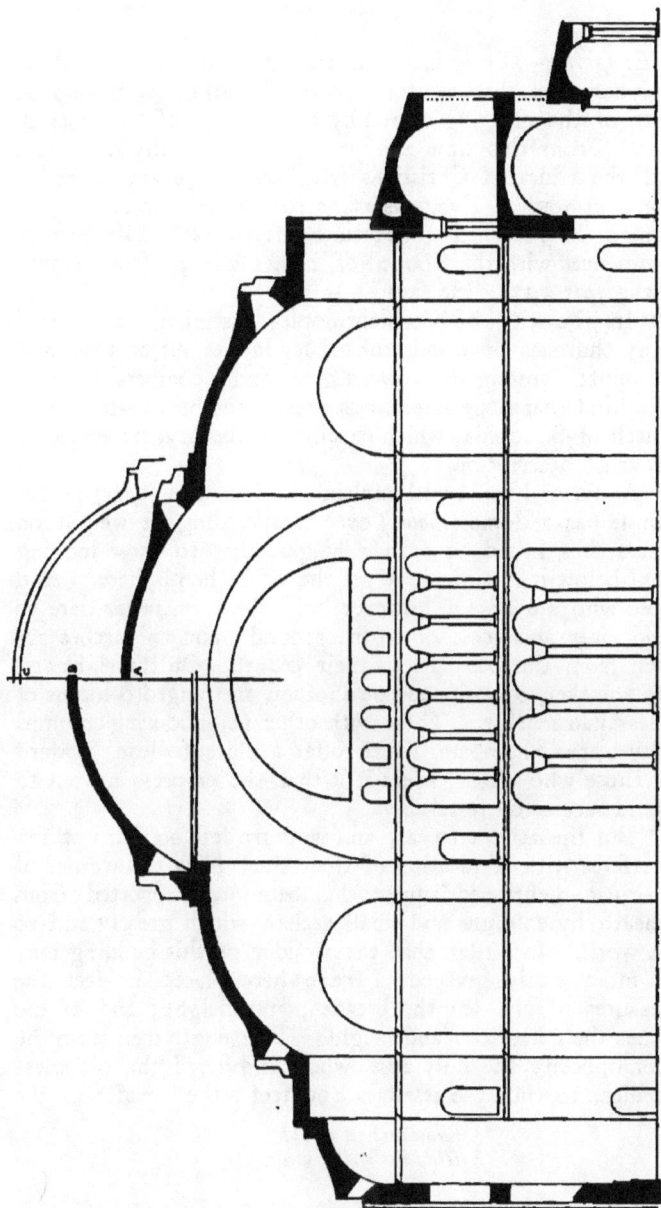

Fig. 4.—Longitudinal Section, having regard to Dome as first built.

Evagrius.—This historian was born in 536 A.D.[1] at Epiphania on the Orontes. In his *Ecclesiastical History* we learn of the suffering caused by the invasion of Chosroes in 540. From this time all Syria was continually·disturbed, and the educated Christians fell back more and more on Constantinople. Evagrius came to Constantinople in 589, though he returned to Antioch afterwards. His history commences with the Council of Ephesus in 431 and extends to the year 593. He says[2] :—

" In the city of Constantinople Justinian constructed many churches of wonderful beauty in honour of God, and the saints among them was a great and incomparable work of a kind that none like it was ever remembered—the great church of S. Sophia; which excelling in beauty, far surpasses power of description.

"As far as I can I will explain it. The nave (*naos*) of the temple has a dome (*tholos*) over it spreading its weight on four arches, raised to such a height, that to those looking from below it is difficult to see the whole hemisphere. And those who are above, however bold they are, never dare to bend over and look on to the ground : and the arches are open from the base up to their crown. On the right and left however, opposite to one another, are ranged columns of Thessalian marble. These with other neighbouring columns carry upper chambers, which offer a place to lean forward for those who wish. Here it is that the empress is wont to attend service on festal days.

"But the arches to east and west are left so that nothing interferes with admiration of their size. Now the arcades of the just mentioned upper chambers are supported from beneath by columns and small arches, which greatly add to the work. In order that the wonder of this building may be more easily grasped, I have here placed in feet the measures of the length, breadth, and height ; and of the arches their diameter and height. The length then from the door opposite the holy apse, where is offered the bloodless sacrifice, to the apse itself is 190 feet ; the breadth of the

[1] Krumbacher, p. 53.
[2] *Hist. Eccles.* iv., chap. 31.

nave from north to south is 115. The height from the
centre of the dome to the ground is 180 feet. And of the
arches, the width of each in feet is [no number given].
And the length from east to west is 200 feet. The width of
the opening is 75 feet.[1] There are also to the west two fine
porticoes, and everywhere open courts of wonderful beauty."

Paul the Silentiary.—As this author's really detailed
account of the church is of considerable length, we have
reserved it for the next chapter, although it was written before the descriptions just given by Agathias and Evagrius.
For the little that is known of the author we are almost
entirely indebted to his friend Agathias, who says : " If any
one living perchance far from this city, wishes to know and
see everything as if present and looking on, let him read
what Paulus, son of Cyrus, son of Florus, has written in
hexameter verse ; he is chief of the Royal Silentiaries, and
sprung from a noble race ; inheriting ancestral wealth, yet
zealously brought up in the study of letters, by which he
was the more glorious and famous. He wrote a number of
other poems worthy of memory and praise, but it seems to
me that that which he wrote on the Great Church is completed with the most skill and labour, even as its subject is
more worthy than any other. For you will find in his poem
the arrangement of the form, and the nature of the stones
explained ; the beauty and purpose of the curtains ; the
lengths and heights, what is curved and what straight, what
projects and what is suspended. You will learn, too, how
with silver and gold the more sacred part, intended for the
divine mysteries, was adorned ; as well as whatever ornament
great or small is there, which those who frequent the church
may see."

The Silentiaries, of whom Paulus was one, were court
officials. Their office was an exalted one, as they ranked
with the senators, and were employed on all kinds of service,
not unfrequently becoming the historians of the emperor.
Paulus belonged to the cultivated and literary circle, who
during Justinian's reign interested themselves in literature,

---

[1] The dimensions appear so inaccurate that we do not attempt to
explain them.

and to him are attributed more than eighty poems in the
Anthology.[1]

The description or rather explanation of S. Sophia was
most probably written and recited as an Opening Ode at the
Encaenia of December 24th, 563. Körtum (in Salzenberg) conjectures that the poem was recited in "a hall of
the Imperial Palace," but Du Cange is probably more
correct in assigning only the first eighty lines to the Palace.
The succeeding lines he says " were addressed to the clergy in
the Patriarch's Palace," but we believe, from the antithesis
between the Palace of the Emperor and the House of God,
that the address to the patriarch was spoken within the
walls of the church itself, and that the whole poem, which is
divided into three parts, was written to be recited in connection with the opening ceremony mentioned above.

It shows us how much architecture was esteemed by
Justinian, that the historian of his wars wrote also a history
of his buildings ; and the court poet was employed to celebrate the greatest of them in verse. On many accounts
the poem is the best ancient architectural description
extant. It is exact in accuracy, most orderly in its sequence
when read with a knowledge of the building, and must have
been written within its walls. A close and careful study
written when architectural ideas were in the ascendant—the
chief subject of thought in times of peace—it is no futile
attempt to explain a work of genius in terms of mechanics
and foot-rule measurements, after the manner of an architectural lecture, but it translates the ideas of the artist into
the words of the poet. The conceit of Homeric metre
and phrasing is almost a charm at this distance of time,
the poet's enthusiasm being quite sufficient to carry off the
affectation of attempting an architectural epic. It is not
however in its form but in its stimulus to imagination that
we see its chief value.

[1] Salz. *Alt. Baud.*

CHAPTER III

THE first eighty lines of the Prelude are an eulogy on the emperor. The succeeding lines were addressed to the clergy. "We come to you, sirs, from the home of the emperor, to the home of the Almighty Emperor, the Deviser of the Universe, by whose grace victory cleaves to our lord. The august head of our state lent a kindly ear to our words, as he sat in the hall ; now we see the chief of the sacred priests. May he too favour us, and may none of those who listen carp at our words."

The poem itself, in long Homeric hexameters, begins by describing the general peace throughout the Roman world at the time of the restoration of S. Sophia   Dr. Körtum notes the following references to events only then recently passed. The rule of the Vandals in Africa had been destroyed by Belisarius (534), and a later insurrection quelled (545) ; the reign of the Ostrogoths in the West had come to an end (554), and peace had just been concluded with the Persians (561). There is also an allusion to the conspiracy of this same year, when an attempt was made on the emperor's life.

The poet then, describing the ruin caused by the earthquake (558) at S. Sophia, tells us that "the very foundations of the dome failed, and thick clouds of dust darkened the midday sun. Yet the whole church did not fall, but only the top of the eastern vault, and a portion of the dome above. Part lay on the ground, part open to the light of day, hung suspended in the air." "But the emperor soon began to build again, the Genius of New Rome by his side."

When the emperor went to the ruins of the church he praised the skilful craft of Anthemius ; " he it was who laid the first foundations of the church, one skilled to draw a circle or set out a plan.[1] And he gave to the walls strength to resist the pushing arches, which were like active demons. This time it was not merely the crown of the arch that gave way [see above, p. 28], for the very piers were shaken to their foundations."

The poet now describes the building : "Whoever raises his eyes to the beauteous firmament of the roof, scarce dares to gaze on its rounded expanse sprinkled with the stars of heaven, but turns to the fresh green marble below, seeming as it were to see flower-bordered streams of Thessaly, and budding corn, and woods thick with trees ; leaping flocks too and twining olive-trees, and the vine with green tendrils, or the deep blue peace of summer sea, broken by the plashing oars of spray-girt ship. Whoever puts foot within the sacred fane, would live there for ever, and his eyes well with tears of joy. Thus by Divine counsel, while angels watched, was the temple built again.

"At last the holy morn had come, and the great door of the new-built temple groaned on its opening hinges, inviting emperor and people to enter ; and when the inner part was seen sorrow fled from the hearts of all, as the sun lit the glories of the temple. 'Twas for the emperor to lead the way for his people, and on the morrow to celebrate the birth of Christ. And when the first gleam of light rosy-armed driving away the dark shadows, leapt from arch to arch, then all the princes and people with one voice hymned their songs of prayer and praise ; and as they came to the sacred courts, it seemed to them as if the mighty arches were set in heaven.

Apse and Exedras.—" Towards the East unfold triple spaces of semicircular form ; and above, on an upright band of wall, soars aloft the fourth part of a sphere. Even so, high

[1] καὶ κέντρον ἑλεῖν καὶ σχῆμα χαράξαι.

over its back and triple crest, shimmer the tail feathers of a peacock, with their countless eyes. These crowning parts men learned in the builder's art call conchs ; and certain it is they call them so from a shell of the sea, or 'tis a craftsman's name.

Apse.—" The middle apse holds the stalls (*thokoi*) and steps (*bathra*) ranged circle-wise. Some on the level of the ground are massed close together round the centre ; and as they rise higher, with the spaces between them, they widen out little by little, until they come to the stalls of silver. Thus with increasing circles they ever wheel round a fixed circle in the pavement.

Bema.—" Now the apse is separated [from the nave] by a space between vertical walls built on strong foundations, with an arch [1] above, not a portion of a sphere, but in the form of a cylinder cleft in twain.

Exedras.—" And westwards again are two conchs on columns, one on either side ; projecting as if stretching out bent arms to embrace the people singing in the church. They are borne by columns of porphyry, bright of bloom ranged in semicircular line, and with capitals (*karenoi*) of gold, carrying the weight of the arches (*kukloi*) above. These columns were once brought from the cliffs of Thebes, which stand, like greaved warriors, by the banks of Nile. Thus, on two columns, on either side, rise the lower parts of either exedra (*apsis*). And for the support of each, the skilled workman has bent from below three small semi-circular arches (*apsides*) ; and, beneath their springing, the tops (*kareata*) of the columns are bound with well-wrought bronze, overlaid with gold, which drives away all fear. Now above the porphyry columns stand others from Thessaly, splendid flowers of fresh green. Here are the fair upper galleries for the women. These too have arches, as may be seen from below, though they show six Thessalian columns and not two. And one wonders at the power of him, who bravely set six columns over two, and has not trembled to fix their bases over empty air.[2]

---

[1] ἄντυξ, the circular rim of a shield. Used here for the bema-arch.
[2] Column does not stand directly over column.

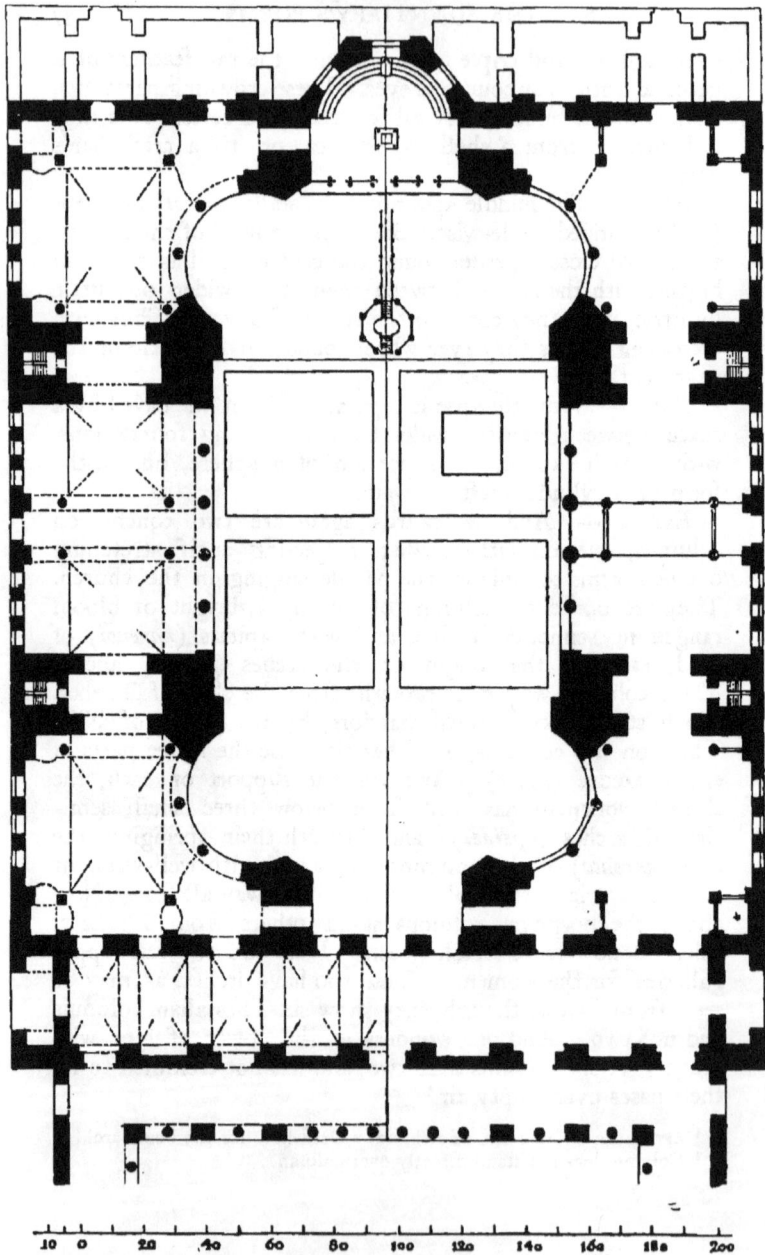

ENGLISH FEET

FIG. 5 —Ground Plan.

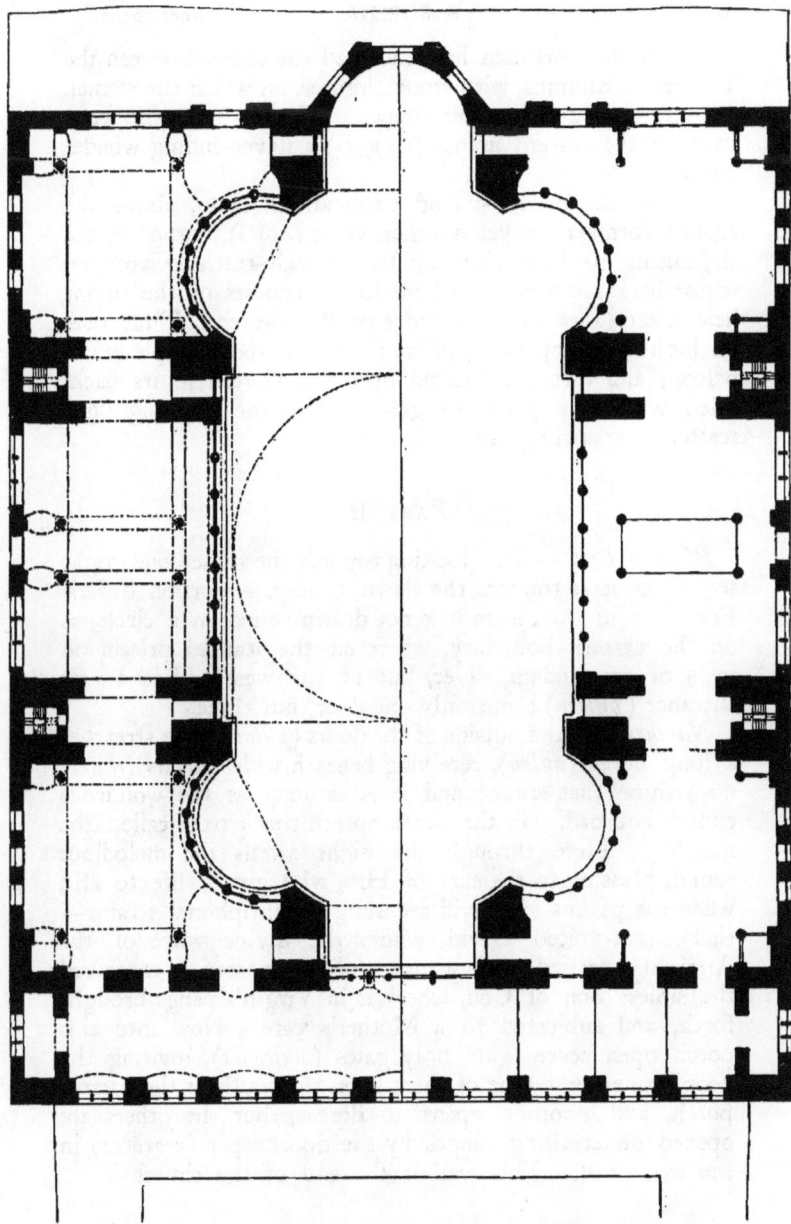

Fig. 6.—Plan of Gynaeceum Galleries. The left-hand side of each plan shows the vaults, and the right-hand side the iron ties and wood struts at springing of vaults.

"Now the workman has fenced all the spaces between the Thessalian columns, with stone closures, on which the women can lean and support their elbows. Thus as you raise your gaze to the eastern arches (*antuges*) a never-ending wonder appears.

Eastern Semidome.—"And upon all of them, above the curved forms rises yet another vault (*apsis*), borne on the air, raising its head aloft up to the wide-reaching arch, on whose back are firmly fixed the lowest courses of the divine head-piece (*koros*) of the centre of the church. Thus rises on high the deep-bosomed vault, borne above triple voids below ; and through fivefold openings, pierced in its back, filled with thin plates of glass, comes the morning light scattering sparkling rays.

PART II

Western End.—"And looking towards the sunset, one might see the same as towards the dawn, though a portion differs. For there in the centre it is not drawn round in a circle, as on the eastern boundary, where sit the learned priests on seats of resplendent silver, but at the west end is a vast entrance (*puleon*) ; not only one door, but three.

Narthex.—"And outside of the doors (*pulai*) there stretches a long porch (*aulon*), receiving beneath wide portals (*thuretroi*) those that enter ; and it is as long as the wondrous church is broad. In the Greek speech this part is called the narthex. Here through the night swells the melodious sound, pleasing to the ears of Him who giveth life to all ; when the psalms of David are sung in antiphonal strains— that sweet-voiced David, whom the divine voice of the Almighty praised, and whose glorious posterity conceived the sinless Son of God, who was in Virgin's pangs brought forth, and subjected to a Mother's care. Now into this porch open seven wide holy gates (*puleones*), inviting the people to enter. One of them is on the south of the narrow porch, and another opens to Boreas, but the others are opened on creaking hinges by the doorkeeper (*neokoros*) in the west wall. This wall is the end of the church.

"Whither am I carried? What breeze has driven, like a
ship at sea, my errant speech? The very centre of the
famous church is all forgotten ; return, my muse, to see
the wonders scarcely to be believed when seen or heard.

The Four Piers.—"Alongside of the eastern and western
curves (*kukloi*)—the half-circles with their pairs of columns
from Thebes—stand four strong well-built piers (*toichoi*),
naked to look on in front, but on their sides and backs they
have supporting arches, and the four rest on strong foundations of hard stones. In the joints the workman has mixed
and poured the dust of fireburnt stone, binding all together
with the builder's art.

"Above them spring measureless curved arches like the
many-coloured bow of Iris : one opens towards the home of
Zephyr, another to Boreas, another to Notus, and yet another
to the fiery Eurus. And every arch (*antux*) has its foot at
either end fixed unshaken, and joined to the neighbouring
curves. But as each rises slowly in the air in bending line,
it separates from the other to which first it was joined.

The Pendentives.—"Now the part between these same
arches (*apsides*) is filled with wondrous skill. For where,
as needs must be, the arches bend away from one another,
and would have shown empty air, a curved wall, like a
triangle, grows over, touching the rim of the arches on either
side. And the four triangles, creeping over, spread out, until
they become united above the crown of each arch. The
middle portion of the arches, as much as forms the curved rim,
the builder's skill has formed with thin bricks (*plinthoi*), and
has thus made fast the topmost curves of the house of stone.

"Now in the joints they have put sheets of soft
lead, lest the stones, as they lie on one another, adding
weight to weight, should have their backs broken. Thus
with the lead inserted, the pressure is softened, and the stone
foundation is gently burdened.

Cornice of Dome.—"A rim (*antux*) curving round, is firmly
fixed on the backs (of the arches), where rests the base of the
hemisphere [1] ; this is the circle of the lowest course which

---

[1] σφαίρης ἡμιτόμοιο, the ἡμισφαίριον of Agathias and Evagrius. This
word is used by Eusebius for the dome of the Holy Sepulchre.

they have set as a crown on the backs of the arches (*apsides*). And just under the projecting firmament (*kosmos*), the hanging stones form a narrow curved path, on which the man who cares for the sacred lights can walk fearlessly, and trim each in turn.

The Dome.—" And above all rises into the immeasurable air the great helmet [of the dome], which, bending over, like the radiant heavens, embraces the church.   And at the highest part, at the crown, was depicted [1] the cross, the protector of the city.   And wondrous it is to see how the dome gradually rises, wide below, and growing less as it reaches higher.   It does not however spring upwards to a sharp point, but is like the firmament which rests on air, though the dome is fixed on the strong backs of the arches."

(Here is a lacuna in the Greek text ; two broken lines, 94, 95, speak of "window openings made in the apses, through which streams the splendour of the golden morning light.")

" With dauntless pen I will describe what plan the emperor devised for the broad church, and how, with builder's skill, both the curves of the arches and the vault of the wide-extended house were formed with thin bricks (*plinthoi*), and raised on firm foundations.   Thus the skilful master-man, well versed in every craft, formed a ceiling to the lofty nave.   Yet he did not send to the hills of Phœnician Lebanon, nor to search the dark woods of the Alpine crags, nor where some Assyrian or Celtic woodman goads on the oxen in dense forests, nor did he think to use fir (*peuke*) or pine (*elate*) to roof the house.   From neither the glades of Daphne [2] by Orontes, nor from the wooded crags of Patara [3] came cypress wood, to form a covering for the mighty temple.   For our noble king, since nature could produce no timber great enough, had it covered with stones (*lithoi*) laid in a round form.   Thus on the four arches (*apsides*) rose,

---

[1] ἔγραφε leaves no doubt that a mosaic cross on the interior is intended, and not, as Salzenberg suggests, a cross on the outside.   The full expression for representations in mosaic was καταγράφειν ψηφῖδι : as in Joannes Lydus († 550), *De Magistratibus* ii. 20, in his description of the palace built by the Praetorian Prefect.

[2] Near Antioch.   [3] A town of Lycia.

like a beauteous helmet, the deep-bosomed swelling roof
(*kaluptra*) : and it seems that the eye, as it wanders round,
gazes on the circling heavens. And beneath the two great
arches (*apsides*), to the east and to the west, you must know
that it is all open, and extended in the air.

" But towards the murmuring south wind and the cold dry
north, a wall, mighty in strength, rises to the under side of
the rounded arch (*antux*). Now this wall is made bright
with eight windows, and rests below on great props of
marble. For beneath it six columns, like the fresh green of
the emerald, in union support untired the weight of wall.
And these again are borne on strong columns fixed immovable
on the ground, glittering jewels of Thessalian marble, with
capitals above them like locks of golden hair. These separate
the middle portion of the glorious nave from the neighbouring aisle (*aithousa*) that stretches alongside. Never were
such columns, blooming with a many-hued brightness,[1] hewn
from the craggy hills of sea-washed Molossis.

North Aisle, Centre Division.—" And in the aisle itself, in
the middle space Anthemius of many crafts, and with him
Isiodorus the wise,—for both of them, acting under the
will of the king, built the mighty church—have placed two
pairs of columns, and in measure they are less than those
others near them, but they are as bright with fresh green
bloom, and they came from the same quarry.

" Yet their bases are not placed in a row, one after the
other, but they stand on the pavement two facing two
opposite ; and above their capitals on fourfold arches (*seireai*)
rises the underside of the women's galleries. And close
by these columns on the north side is a door, admitting the
people to the founts that purify the stains of mortal life,
and heal every deadly scar.

" Thus on four columns of beautiful Thessalian stone, in
order, placed here and there, towards the twilight and to the
dawn, along the length of the aisle (*aithousa*) there curves a
weight of bending vaults (*kulindroi*) extending to the walls,
which are pierced with openings ; on the northern side they

[1] ἄνθος, a bud, sprout or flower ; hence brightness and bloom
generally.

lean on the spaces that join the twin windows,[1] but on the south, instead of windows are empty spaces like a colonnade.

North Aisle, East and West Divisions.—" And again towards the east and west stand two columns from Thessaly, with lofty crests, and twin piers (*stemones*) from famous Proconnesus, fixed close by the doors. Towards the east there is but one door, though on the side of the cold north they walk through twain.

South Aisle.—" On the south you will see a long aisle as on the north, yet made bigger. For a part is separated off from the nave by a wall, and here the emperor takes his accustomed seat on the solemn festivals, and listens to the reading of the sacred books.

Gynaecea.—" And whoever mounts will find on both sides of the church the aisles for women similar to those below, and there is yet another, though not like those on either side, above the narthex.

Atrium.—" Now on the western side of this divine church you will see a great open court (*aule*) surrounded by four cloisters. One of these joins on to the narthex, but the others spread round the sides, where stand their several paths. In the very centre of the wide garth stands a spacious phiale, cleft from the Iassian peaks ; and from it bubbling water gushes forth and throws a stream into the air, leaping up from the pressure of the brazen pipe—a stream that purges away all suffering, when the people, in the month of the golden vestments [2] at the mystic feast of Christ, draw the unsullied waters in vessels by night. And the water shows the power of God ; for never will you find decay on its surface, even if it remains in its vessel, and away from the fountain for more than a year.[3]

" Everywhere the walls glitter with wondrous designs, the stone for which came from the quarries of seagirt Procon-

---

[1] θύρετρος is elsewhere a door. But "twin doors" has no meaning here. See plan.

[2] January ; the consuls then entered on their year of office, and wore chitons of gold thread. See Du Cange, *S. Sophia*, § 22.

[3] This custom at Antioch is mentioned as early as the time of S. John Chrysostom in a sermon on the Baptism of Christ.

nesus. The marbles are cut and joined like painted patterns, and in stones formed into squares or eight-sided figures the veins meet to form devices; and the stones show also the forms of living creatures.

"And on either side along the flanks and outskirts (*antuges*) of the beautiful church, you would see open courts (*aulai*). These were all planned about the building with cunning skill, that it might be bathed all round by the bright light of day.

The Marbles.—"Yet who, even in the measures of Homer, shall sing the marble pastures gathered on the lofty walls and spreading pavement of the mighty church? These the iron with its metal tooth has gnawed—the fresh green from Carystus, and many-coloured marble from the Phrygian range, in which a rosy blush mingles with white, or it shines bright with flowers of deep red and silver. There is a wealth of porphyry too, powdered with bright stars, that has once laden the river boat on the broad Nile. You would see an emerald green from Sparta, and the glittering marble with wavy veins, which the tool has worked in the deep bosom of the Iassian hills, showing slanting streaks blood-red and livid white. From the Lydian creek came the bright stone mingled with streaks of red. Stone too there is that the Lybian sun, warming with his golden light, has nurtured in the deep-bosomed clefts of the hills of the Moors, of crocus colour glittering like gold ; and the product of the Celtic crags, a wealth of crystals, like milk poured here and there on a flesh of glittering black. There is the precious onyx, as if gold were shining through it: and the marble that the land of Atrax yields, not from some upland glen, but from the level plains ; in parts fresh green as the sea or emerald stone, or again like blue cornflowers in grass, with here and there a drift of fallen snow,—a sweet mingled contrast on the dark shining surface.

Sectile and carved Spandrils.—"Before I come to the glitter of the mosaic,[1] I must describe how the mason (*laotoros*), weaving together with skill thin slabs of marble, has figured on the flat surface of the walls intertwining curves

---

[1] ψηφῖδες—pebbles. The usual word for mosaic tesserae.

laden with plenteous fruit, and baskets, and flowers, and birds
sitting on the twigs. And the curved pattern of a twining
vine with shoots like golden ringlets, weaves a winding
chain of clusters; little by little does it put forth shoots,
until it overshadows all the stone near with ripples like
beauteous tresses. Such ornament as this surrounds the
church.

The Capitals.—"And the lofty crest of every column,
beneath the marble abacus (*peze*), is covered with many a
supple curve of waving acanthus—a wandering chain of
barbed points all golden, full of grace. Thus the marble in
bulging forms crowns the deep red columns, as wool the
distaff; the stone glittering with a beauty that charms the
heart.

The Floor.—"And gladly have the hills of Proconnesus
bent their backs to necessity, and strewed the floor with
marble. In parts too shimmers the polish of the Bosporus
stone, with white streaks on black.

The Mosaic.—"Now the vaulting is formed of many a
little square (*psephos*) of gold cemented together. And
the golden stream of glittering rays pours down and strikes
the eyes of men, so that they can scarcely bear to look.
One might say that one gazed upon the midday sun in
spring, what time he gilds each mountain height.

Iconostasis.—"Our emperor has levied from the whole
earth, and brought together the wealth of the barbarians of
the west ; for as he did not deem stone a fitting adornment
for the divine, eternal temple, on which [New] Rome has
centred the expectancy of joy; he has not spared enrich-
ments of silver, and so the ridge of Pangaeus[1] and
the height of Sunium[2] have opened all their silver veins,
and many treasure-houses of our subject kings have yielded
their stores.

"For as much of the great church by the eastern arch as
was set apart for the bloodless sacrifices, no ivory, no stone,
nor bronze distinguishes, but it is all fenced with the silver
metal. Not only upon the walls, which separate the holy

[1] In Macedonia. The mines are mentioned by Herodotus.
[2] The promontory on the south of Attica. The mines were at Laurium.

priests from the crowd of singers,[1] has he placed mere plates
of silver, but he has covered all the columns themselves
with the silver metal, even six sets of twain ; and the
rays of light glitter far and wide.   Upon them the tool
has formed dazzling circles, beautifully wrought in skilled
symmetry by the craftsman's hand, in the centre of which is
carved the symbol of the Immaculate God, who took upon
Himself the form of man.   In parts stand up an army of
winged angels in pairs, with bent necks and downcast mien
(for they could not gaze upon the glory of the Godhead,
though hidden in the form of man to clear man's flesh from
sin).   And elsewhere the tool has fashioned the heralds of
the way of God, even those by whose words were noised
abroad, before He took flesh upon Him, the divine tidings
of the Anointed One.   Nor had the craftsman forgotten
the forms of those others, whose childhood was with the
fishing-basket and the net ; but who left the mean labours
of life and unholy cares to bear witness at the bidding of a
heavenly king, fishing even for men, and forsaking the skill
of casting nets to weave the beauteous seine of eternal life.
In other parts art has limned (*kategraphe*) the Mother of
Christ, the vessel of eternal Light, whose womb brought
Him forth in holy travail.

"But on the middle panels of the sacred screen, which
forms the barrier for the priests, the carver's art has cut one
letter that means many words, for it combines the name of
our king and queen.   And he has also wrought a form like
a shield with a boss, showing the cross in the middle parts.
And through the triple doors the screen opens to the
priests.   For on each side the skilful hand of the workman
has made small doors.

The Ciborium.—"And above the all-holy table of gold
rises in the air a tower (*purgos*) indescribable, reared on
fourfold arches of silver.   And it is borne aloft on silver
columns, on whose tops every arch rests its silver feet.
And above the arches rises a figure like a cone, yet it is not
complete.   For at the bottom its edge (*antux*) does not
turn round in the circular form, but has an eight-sided base,

---

[1] πολυγλώσσοιο ὁμίλου, the choir.

and from a broad plan it gradually diminishes to a sharp point, having eight sides of silver. And at the juncture of each to other is, as it were, a long backbone (*rachis*) which seems to join with the triangular faces of the eight-sided form, and rises to a single crest, where is artfully wrought the form of a cup. And the edges of the cup bend over and assume the form of leaves, and in the midst of it has been placed a shining silver globe, and the cross surmounts it all. May it be an omen of peace! But above the arches many a curve of acanthus twines round the lower part of the cone, and the plant shows sharp projections which rise up from the groundwork like the fruit of a fragrant pear, glittering with light.

" Now where the fitted edges join the flat base are fixed and set bowls of silver. And in each cup stands as it were a candle, though it is a glittering symbol not made of wax, and beauty flashes from them and not light. For they are made round of silver, brightly polished. Thus the candle flashes a silver ray not the light of fire.

The Altar.—" And on columns of gold is raised the all gold slab [1] of the holy table, standing on gold foundations, and bright with the glitter of different stones.

" Whither am I carried? whither tends my unbridled speech? Let my voice be silent, and not lay bare what is not meet for the eyes of the people to see.

Altar Curtains.—" But, ye priests, as the sacred laws command you, spread out the curtain dipped in the red dye of the Sidonian shell and cover the sacred table. Unfold the veils (*kaluptrai*) hanging on the four sides of silver, and show to the countless crowd a multitude of beautiful designs in gold of skilful handiwork. On one side is cunningly wrought the form of Christ. And this was not worked by skilful hands plying the needle on the stuff, but by the web, the produce of the worm [2] from distant lands, changing its coloured threads of many shades. A garment shimmering with gold, like the rays of rosy-fingered dawn, flashes down to the divine knees, and a chiton, deep red from the Tyrian

---

[1] νῶτον, a back, and hence, any wide, flat surface.
[2] μύρμηξ, the ant; here the silkworm.

shell dye, covers the right shoulder beneath its well-woven web. The veiling upper robe has slipped away, and pulled up across the side it only covers the left shoulder, while the forearm and the hand are bare. He seems to point the fingers of the right hand, as if preaching the words of Life, and in the left hand He holds the book of the divine message, —the book that tells what the Messiah accomplished when his foot was on the earth. And the whole robe shines with gold ; for on it a thin gold thread is led through the web, as if a fair chain was laid on the cloth in a groove or channel and bound with silken thread by sharp needles. And on either side stand the two messengers of God—Paul, full of divine wisdom, and also the mighty doorkeeper of the Gates of Heaven, binding with both heavenly and earthly chains. One holds the book pregnant with sacred words, and the other the form of a cross on a staff of gold. And both the cunning web has clothed in robes of silver white, and over their sacred heads rises upward a temple of gold, with triple apses fixed on four columns of gold.

" Now on the extreme borders of the curtain shot with gold, unspeakable art has figured the works of mercy of our city's kings ; here one sees hospitals for the sick, there sacred fanes, while on either side are displayed the miracles of Christ ; such is the grace and beauty of the work.

" But on the other curtains you see the kings of the earth on one side with their hands joined to those of the Virgin, on the other side with those of Christ, and all is cunningly wrought by the threads of the woof with the sheen of a golden warp. Thus is everything adorned with splendour. Thus may you see all that fills the eyes with wonder.

The Lighting.—" No words can describe the light at night-time ; one might say in truth that some midnight sun illumined the glories of the temple. For the wise fore-thought of our king has had stretched from the projecting rim (antux) of stone, on whose back is firmly planted the temple's air-borne dome, long twisted chains (seirai) of beaten brass, linked in alternating curves with many windings. And these chains, bending down from every part in a long course, come together as they fall towards the ground. But

E

before they reach the pavement, their path from above is
checked, and they finish in unison on a circle.

" And beneath each chain he has caused to be fitted silver
discs, hanging circle-wise in the air, round the space in the
centre of the church.   Thus these discs, pendent from their
lofty courses, form a coronet above the heads of men.   They
have been pierced too by the weapon of the skilful workman,
in order that they may receive shafts [1] of fire-wrought glass,
and hold light on high for men at night.

"And not from discs alone does the light shine at night,
but in the circles close by a disc you would see the symbol
of the mighty cross, pierced with many holes, and in its
pierced back shines a vessel of light.   Thus hangs the
circling chorus of bright lights.   Verily you might say that
you gazed on the bright constellation of the Heavenly
Crown by the Great Bear, and the neighbouring Dragon.

"Thus through the temple wanders the evening light,
brightly shining.   In the middle of a larger circle you
would find a crown with lightbearing rim ; and above in
the centre another noble disc spread its light in the air, so
that night is compelled to flee.

" Near the aisles too, alongside the columns, they have hung
in order single lamps (*lampter*) apart one from another ; and
through the whole length of the far-stretching nave is their
path.   Beneath each they have placed a silver vessel, like a
balance pan, and in the centre of this rests a cup of well-
burning oil.

" There is not however one equal level for all the lamps,
for you may see some high, some low, in comely curves of
light ; and from twisted chains they sweetly flash in their
aerial courses, even as shines twin-pointed Hyas fixed in the
forehead of Taurus.

"One might also see ships of silver, bearing a flashing
freight of flame, and plying their lofty courses in the liquid
air instead of the sea, fearing no gale from south-west, nor
from Boötes, sinking late to rest.   And above the wide floor
you would see shapely beams (with lamps), running between

[1] οὐρίαχος.   Used in Homer of the butt end of a spear ; hence long
narrow glass lamps.   See our Fig. 17.

two-horned supports of iron, by whose light the orders
of priests, bound by the rubrics, perform their duties.

"Some there are along the floor, where the columns have
their bases, and above again others pass, by far-reaching
courses, along the crowning work of the walls.   Neither is
the base of the deep-bosomed dome left without light, for
along the projecting stone of the curved cornice the skilful
workman suspends single lamps to bronze stakes.   As when
some handmaid binds round the neck of a royal virgin a
graceful chain shining with the glitter of fiery gold ; even
so has our emperor fixed round all the cornice lights in
circle-wise, companions everywhere to those below.

"There is also on the silver columns [of the Iconostasis],
above their capitals, a narrow way of access for the lamplighter, glittering with bright clusters ; these one might
compare to the mountain-nourished pine, or cypress with
fresh branches.   From a point ever-widening circles spread
down until the last is reached, even that which curves round
the base ; instead of a root, bowls of silver are placed
beneath the trees, with their flaming flowers.   And in the
centre of this beauteous wood, the form of the divine cross,
pierced with the prints of the nails, shines with light for
mortal eyes.

"A thousand others within the temple show their gleaming
light, hanging aloft by chains of many windings.   Some are
placed in the aisles, others in the centre or to east and west, or
on the crowning walls, shedding the brightness of flame.   Thus
the night seems to flout the light of day, and be itself as
rosy as the dawn.   And whoever gazes on the lighted trees,
with their crown of circles, feels his heart warmed with joy ;
and looking on a boat[1] swathed with fire, or some single
lamp, or the symbol of the Divine Christ, all care vanishes
from the mind.   So with wayfarers through a cloudless night,
as they see the stars rising from point to point ; one watches
sweet Hesperus, another's attention is fixed on Taurus, and a
third contemplates Boötes, or Orion and the cold Charles'
Wain; the whole heaven, scattered with glittering stars, opens
before them, while the night seems to smile on their way.

[1] ἐπακτρίς, a small row-boat.

E 2

" Thus through the spaces of the great church come rays of
light, expelling clouds of care, and filling the mind with joy.
The sacred light cheers all: even the sailor guiding his bark
on the waves, leaving behind him the unfriendly billows of
the raging Pontus, and winding a sinuous course amidst
creeks and rocks, with heart fearful at the dangers of his
nightly wanderings—perchance he has left the Ægean and
guides his ship against adverse currents in the Hellespont,
awaiting with taut forestay the onslaught of a storm from
Africa—does not guide his laden vessel by the light of
Cynosure, or the circling Bear, but by the divine light of
the church itself. Yet not only does it guide the merchant
at night, like the rays from the Pharos on the coast of Africa,
but it also shows the way to the living God."

CHAPTER IV

THE AMBO

THE third part of the description of the Silentiary is devoted to the ambo, the chief feature in Justinian's reinstatement of the interior. It stood far out from the bema, on the central axis of the church. Germanus, Patriarch of Constantinople from 715-740 A.D., and Simeon of Thessalonica both speak of this as the right position for ambones; "the most holy bema should be towards the east, with the ambo in front of it, if there is room." [1] The two flights of steps, by which the ambo—the name of which is derived from the Greek for ascending—was reached, were on the east and west sides. In the ambo the Gospel was read, and here was recited a prayer [2] at the conclusion of the liturgy, which seems to have been a compendium of those previously uttered in the sanctuary ; the priest left the bema, ascended the ambo on the east side, and prayed with his face towards the west. Important offices in coronations were also performed here.

Paulus' description of the ambo opens with a preface of thirty iambic lines in praise of the emperor, who has added the "one thing needful to our all-glorious church." The importance of this work is made an excuse for interrupting the "usual pursuits of his hearers even for a third time." Twenty hexameter lines are devoted to an invocation to the apostles and saints, and then follows the description of the ambo.

[1] See Du Cange, S. Sophia, § 70.
[2] Called ὀπισθάμβωνος εὐχή, the " back " of the ambo.

" Now in the central space of the wide temple, yet tending rather towards the east, rises a tower (*purgos*), fair to look upon, set apart for the reading of the sacred books. Upright it stands on steps, reached by two flights, one of which stretches towards the west, but the other towards the dawn. So are they opposite to one another, and both lead to a space formed like a circle. Now one stone curves round to form this circular space, though it is not altogether equal to a complete curve (*tornos*), but it agrees with it except where the edge of the stone is lengthened ; for towards east and west a flight of steps is drawn out like a neck, projecting from the circled stone.

"And up to the height of a man's girdle our godlike king has formed, with the help of silver, beauteous walls curving like crescents. He has not bent silver right round the stone, but a silver plaque (*plax*) is spread out in the centre, to adorn the circling wall. Thus has the skilful workman spread out two sure crescents and opened on either side a flight of steps.

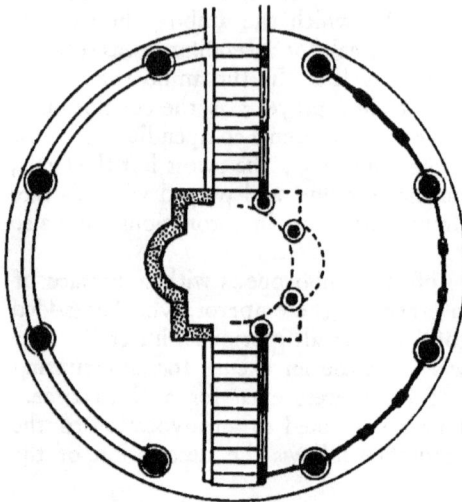

FIG. 7.—Plan of the Ambo both above and below.

" Nor does fear seize those descending the sacred steps, because the sides are unfenced ; for hedge walls of glittering marble have been reared there ; and they are high above the steps for the hand of a man to hold as he mounts, grasping them to ease his way ; so on each side they grow upwards in a rising line, and stop at length with the steps which are

between them.   Thus good use is made of the stone ; for
they have quarried savage hill, and steep promontory, to have
a far-stretching safeguard to the long flight.   And the whole
is cunningly wrought with skilful workmanship, and glitters
with ever-changing brightness.   In parts it seems that whirl-
pools eddy over the surface, intertwining circles winding
under the wandering curves of other circles.   In parts is seen
a rosy bloom, mingled with wan paleness, or fair gleams of
light, as from bright spearheads ; in other places shines a
softer glory, like the radiance of boxwood, or the delightsome
bees-wax, which mortal men ofttimes lay on the unsullied
cliffs, and turn over beneath the rays of the sun, while it
changes to a silver white ; yet not completely altering its
substance, it still shows veins of gold.   Even so the deep-
stained ivory of many a year's growth expands its gleaming
flesh on the curved breast.   At times it seems to have a pale
green hue.   Yet the craftsman has not left it pallid and un-
adorned, for he has fixed it in fair and cunningly wrought
designs on the stone.   Thus over all in many a curve its
beauty is displayed.   In parts the broad surface is tinged
with the choicest tint of the pale crocus, or appears almost
without colour, like light creeping round the pointed horns
of the new-born moon.

   " Now near a rocky hill stands the sacred city—Hierapolis
—which gives its name to a well-known marble ; and of this
is made all the fair floor of the place where they read the
divine wisdom of the holy books ; and it is fitted by the
craftsmen's skill on eight cunningly wrought columns.   Two
of these are towards the north, two towards the southern
wind, two towards the east, and two towards the home of
evening.   Thus is the floor raised up.   And beneath there
is as it were another space, where the priests continue their
sacred song.   The stone is a covering to those below, but
above it is like a spreading plain, untouched by the feet of
mortals.   And the underside the mason (*laotomos*) has cut
out and hollowed, so that, by the craftsmen's skill, it rises
from the capitals, curving over like the hollow shell-back of
the tortoise, or some oxhide shield held up over the helmet,
when the warrior leaps in the mazes of the Pyrrhic dance.

" Now the rugged surface (*metopon*) of the stone they have girdled everywhere with the silver metal ; and there the skilled workman, cutting, with the point of his iron, twining foliage and lovely flowers, has inlaid the beauteous leaves of ivy, with its clusters and budding shoots.

" But with all its steps and floor and the columns as well, the artificers have formed for it a fixed foundation, and raised a base (*krepis*), the height of a man's foot, above the floor of the church ; and in order that they might widen the foundation of the space they have placed on either side, round the belly (*gaster*) in the middle, half-circles in stone, and they have surrounded the space with separate columns arranged in semicircles. Thus the whole belly is widened by means of four rich columns on either side, to north, and to south ; and the cave space (*speos*), like a house, is surrounded on all sides by a fence of circling stone.

" Some of the fair columns that the masons have set up are from the Phrygian land, towards the Mygdonian heights, hewn with strong axes : and looking on these flowers of stone, one would say that white lilies mingled with rose cups, or the soft petals of the shortlived anemone. Here is abundance of red and a mere tinge of white, there thin sinews mix with the veins which dye the columns deep red, as with drops from the Laconian shell.

" First then at the bottom they have placed the fairly wrought plinth (*krepis*) supporting all, made beautiful with twisting curves ; and above it they have set stone bases, firmly fixed, cut from the rich quarries of the Bosporus. Quite white, they glitter, and in branching veins a deep blue line wanders in the shining flesh. And the bases on the eight sides the mason has adorned with moulded bronze rings fixed circlewise round each base, as round a neck. And through the space of the whole church shines the glory of each column fixed on its polished base, like a white cloud wrought into patterns by the ruddy rays of the rising sun.

" Thus are ranged in half-circles the company of four, and this half with the other four they have connected by a fair chiton of stone, even round the well-formed hollow (*antron*) ; for the three spaces between the four columns have been

closed by the skilful mason with fencestones of marble from
Hierapolis, firmly fixed on the plinth (*krepis*). And it is
meet that this crown of stone on the fair floor of the sacred
fane should be called of 'the Holy City' (*Hierapolis*). In
the boundary is placed a door, slightly curved, through which
enters the priest, to the floor of the hollow cavern (*antron*).

"Now you must know that the curve (*spelunx*), with
columns, and plinth (*krepis*), and fence wall, is alike on either
side, towards Garamas on the south and towards Arimaspus
[to the north]. But the doors the workmen have not fixed
in like places, but one is westwards and the other eastwards—
the western one inclines towards the north, but the southern
gate is towards the east. Moreover the fence-walls do not
stand the same height as the columns, but they rise above the
beauteous pavement, as much as to hide a man in the hollow
space (*antron*). But the eight columns with fair carved
capitals come out above the fence wall, and stand round it on
the base with equal spaces between them, even on the stone
plinth. The capitals shine with gold, like high peaks which
the golden-rayed sun strikes with its arrows.

"And all the capitals on high are crowned above in circled
order by an embracing rim of beams (*douratea antux*), which
binds the columns together in one curve, though at the same
time each column is separate from its fellow. And fixed
upon the rim you might see trees, with clusters as of fire,—
the glitter of silver boughs shining afar. Nor does each
sapling wander at will, but it is restrained in a cone-like form
of many edges, from a wide circle ever lessening to a point
at the top. Now the fair girdle (*zoster*) that forms the rim
is all crowned with golden ivy-leaves, and coloured with
the sapphire dust. But towards the home of Zephyr, and
also towards the fiery-winged Eurus, there are fixed upon the
rim (*antux*) two crosses of silver, with a curved spike (*hêlos*)
above each, bending like a shepherd's crook, flashing a thousand lights to the eyes.

"In this manner is the shining ambo made ; thus have they
called it 'the place ascended' (*ambatos*), by holy paths, and
here the people direct their eyes, as they gaze on the divine
gospel.

" And it is to good purpose that they have placed the cut stones in steps, on whose white surface one might descry thin veins of deep red like the dye of the sea-shell. For the un-polished stones the mason has hewn into a long flight (*rachis*) of steps, a strong support for the feet of men, lest any one slipping from above and falling should descend all unsteady to the floor ; thus in order and in continuous line one stone, as it rises above another, recedes from it, even as much as a man ascending plants one step in turn in front of another.

" And as an island rises amidst the swelling billows, bright with patterns of cornfields, and vineyards, and blossoming meadows, and wooded heights, while sailors, as they steer by it, are gladdened, and the troubles and anxieties of the sea are beguiled ; so in the middle space of the boundless temple rises upright the tower-like ambo of stone, with its marble pastures like meadows, cunningly wrought with the beauty of the craftsman's art. Yet though it stands in the middle, it is not quite cut off, like an island girdled by the sea, but is rather like some wave-washed land, extended by a narrow isthmus through the gray billows into the middle of the sea, and were it not for this binding chain, it would be cut off and seen as a true island ; but though it projects into the ocean, it is still joined to the mainland coast by the isthmus, as by a cable.

" Such is the ambo ; for a long path starts from the last step of its eastern flight, and stretches out until it comes to the space by the twin silver doors, even striking with its lengthy plinth the fence wall of the sacred rites ; and the path is warded on both sides by walls. Now for these fence walls they have not placed lofty slabs, but they are as high up as the navel of a man standing by them ; and here the priest, as he holds the golden gospel, passes along, and the surging crowd strive to touch the sacred book with their lips and hands, while moving waves of people break around.

" Thus is this path prolonged like an isthmus, wave-washed on either side, and it leads the priest as he descends from the distant ambo with its lofty cliffs, to the shrine of the holy table. And the whole path on both sides is fenced with the fresh green stone of Thessaly ; and the abundant rich

meadows of the stones bring the delight of beauty to the
eyes. Now at both ends of each slab from Thessaly stand
posts of equal height, not like a cylinder in form : one
skilled in figures would say that the posts were not equal-
sided, but have the shape of a lengthened cube. And the
masons (*laotoroi*) have made the joints of the Molossian slabs,
by wedging one stone into another ; it is from the Phrygian
land that the stone-cutter (*laotupos*) has had these posts
quarried. And resting the wandering glance there one might
see snake-like coils twining over the fair marble, winding in
beauteous paths ; there white and fiery red are set alongside
of one another and a flesh colour between both, the lines
bending in alternating coils, as they roll round in their
courses. First on one side, then on another, are seen the
forms of the moon and stars.

"And on the uppermost rim of the fence wall they have
fitted another long stretching stone, quarried from the same
foreland crag, so that the Thessalian slab is fixed below on
the firm foundations of the plinth, and is bound above by
another band of marble ; and the edges of the Thessalian
slabs are joined together as in a chain by the square
columns, which are set upright and firm on the foundation.

"And as when one winds the gold twisted thread in and
out over the many-coloured surface of a Tyrian robe, and
adds a fitting pattern round the bottom edges, or in the fair
centre of the robe, or about the sleeve-holes for the arms
while the fresh green web of the cloak shines like a
meadow in spring,—the glory of the golden warp adding
beauty to beauty, and decking it as if with flowers ; even so
the cunning workman has cast on the fresh green stones of
the sacred rock the glitter of golden rays, giving a brighter
beauty to them.

"But at the eastern end of the passage, by the holy fence
walls of the altar, they have cut off the isthmus, so as to form
a speedier path for those who pass from side to side.

"Such works as these has our emperor, bestowing splendid
gifts, built for God the King. For to the great bounties of
his peaceful reign he has added this much-praised temple, so

that with divine foresight he might prepare a gift for the
Creator of the world, Christ, King of All. Be thou, O glory
of the eternal Trinity, thrice favourable to this city of Rome,
to our citizens, our emperor, and our much-loved temple."

In following this description we see that it begins on
the raised floor of the ambo which was rounded on two
sides, the others being open to the steps at the east and west.
The breast wall on each side was largely covered with applied
silver wrought into patterns ; and the rest, together with
the parapet slabs to the steps, were inlaid in ivory, probably
carved like the contemporary bishop's throne at Ravenna.
The body of the ambo inlaid thus with ivory and silver was
upheld on eight columns, the underside of the floor stone
being hollowed into a flat dome like the fluted soffite of the
still older ambo at S. Apollinare at Ravenna. On either
side, around the ambo, was a semicircle of large columns of
rosy-veined Synnada marble on white bases with bronze
annulets and gilt capitals ; between the columns breast-
high slabs of Hierapolis marble inclosed a space. The
circle of columns stood on a raised step, and above they were
bound together by a carved beam, the pattern being gilt
with the interspaces painted in ultramarine. On this to east
and west stood silver crosses ; their upper limbs "bent like
shepherds' crooks" doubtless formed the XP monogram.
Silver candelabra, cones of diminishing circles, stood round
about on the top of the beam. From the eastern steps a
passage way ran back to the step of the iconostasis,
inclosed on both sides by marble slabs grooved into posts,
bearing a top rail. This closure of Verde antique slabs was
inlaid in white and red patterns and gold mosaic.

In this description two separate parts appear, the ambo
proper reached by the narrow inclosed way and ascended by
steps ; and the space entered by two doors screened off about
it by the circle of large columns and closure slabs, "where
the priests continue their sacred song." So in Constantine
Porphyrogenitus' *Book of the Ceremonies* [1] we read of the
"psaltae" placed in the ambo singing, "Christ is risen."

[1] Ed. Bonn, p. 74. See also our page 79.

We know little of the later history of the ambo. The Anonymous Author, who probably wrote not earlier than the twelfth century, comparing the mythical splendour of an earlier ambo destroyed by a fall of the dome to another which he attributes to Justinian's nephew, Justin, says they made the latter of marble, with columns covered with silver, and with silver screens going round the solea. It had no dome. Immediately after he compares the pavement which he says was destroyed at the same time with one that *now is*. So that we may assume that he wrote of an ambo then existing, and that therefore in this instance he may be trusted.[1] The work attributed to Justin by the Anonymous is really the restoration under Justinian ; he seems to have confused the nephew of the architect who was then employed with the nephew of the emperor. Rohault De Fleury,[2] who accepts this story, suggests that a canopied ambo which appears in the *Menologium* of Basil (976–1025) figures one in S. Sophia which may have replaced the former ambo after the fall of the dome in 975. Robert de Clari (1200) merely says, " The place from which they read the Gospel is so rich and noble, that we do not know how to describe the making of it." [3] The ambo of that time was destroyed by the Crusaders (1203).[4] Clavijo, the Spanish ambassador, who saw S. Sophia two hundred years later, has left this description of the covered ambo then existing. " On the floor in the centre of the area is a pulpit placed on four columns of jasper ; and the sides of it are overlaid with panels of jasper of many colours, and this pulpit is surmounted by a cover, which stands on eight very large jasper columns ; and here they preach and read the Gospel on feast days."

Coronations.—We shall now quote two descriptions of the ceremonies associated with the ambo at coronations. These are of the age of the Palaeologi, and the first is especially

[1] See Nicetas also on our p. 75.
[2] *La Messe.*, Art. "Ambon," vol. iii., p. 9.
[3] Hopf, *Chroniques Gréco-Romanes*, p. 96.
[4] See our p. 75.

interesting as describing the *Megale Eisodos* and the Celebration.

"And about the second hour of the same day the prince who is to be anointed is set upon a shield ;[1] the reigning emperor, who may be his father, and the patriarch take hold of the front part of the shield, which is also held by the officials of rank and the nobility. They then raise it, and show the new emperor to the assembled populace. After he has been greeted with acclamation, they attend him into the church, where the rest of the ceremony must be completed. Now a little edifice of wood has previously been prepared for this very purpose, into which they lead the new emperor, and put on him the purple and the diadem, which have been blest by the bishops. And round his head it is customary to put only a chaplet. After this the service of the Mass (*mustagogia*) proceeds. And near the erection just mentioned a set of movable steps, also of wood, are prepared, and these they cover with purple silk. And upon it are placed golden thrones, according to the number of the princes, not like other thrones, but raised on four or five steps ; here the princes take their seats. The princesses also ascend with them, and sit on the thrones, wearing their crowns, but she that is about to be crowned wears a chaplet. Now before the hymn *Trisagion* is sung, the patriarch comes out of the bema and ascends the ambo, and with him are the rulers of the church, all wearing their sacred robes. He then dismisses them, and summons the princes, and they immediately arise from their thrones and come to the ambo, while profound silence is kept by the whole congregation. Then the patriarch goes through the prayers appointed for the anointing, some silently by himself, others out loud, praying for the blessing of God on him who is about to be anointed. After this the new emperor removes from his head whatever he is wearing, and then it is right for all, as many as are present, to stand with bared heads. Then the patriarch with the holy oil anoints the head of the emperor with the form of the cross, saying with a loud voice 'Holy' ; and as soon as they hear it those standing on the ambo pronounce it three times, and

[1] Cantacuzenus, *Hist.* lib. i., chap. 41, ed. Bonn, p. 196.

after them all the people. After this the crown is brought by deacons from the bema where they keep it (now it is not above the Holy Table as some say), and taken to the ambo. If any previously crowned emperor be there, he and the patriarch take the crown together, and place it on the head of the prince, the patriarch saying ' Holy' in a loud voice. Those in the ambo repeat it three times, and the people, as after the anointing. Then the patriarch repeats some more prayers, and the prince descends from the ambo, not on the side by which he ascended, but on the side which is turned towards the solea. If he is unmarried he then ascends the steps and reseats himself upon his throne, but if he has a wife then she also must be crowned. She is then led, as she rises from the throne, by two kinswomen one on either side, or if she has no relatives, eunuchs lead her down from the steps, and stand with her before the solea. Then the emperor descends from the ambo, and takes the crown held ready by the kinswomen or eunuchs, and places it upon the head of his wife, and she kneels before her husband, swearing fealty to him. And the patriarch, standing by the solea, offers up a prayer for the emperor and empress, and all their people. Thus the emperor crowns his own wife. And then both ascend the steps, and sit upon their thrones, and the rest of the mysteries are proceeded with. But at the singing of the *Trisagion*, or at the reading from the apostolic writings, or the Gospels, they stand up.

" And on both sides of the nave, on wooden steps made for this purpose, are those called protopsaltae, and domestici, and others of ecclesiastical rank who know how to sing, and who are called because of this *kraktai* ; [1] all these sing anthems especially made for the occasion. But when the part of the mysteries which is called *The Great Entrance* [2] is beginning, the chief of the deacons comes and summons the emperor, and he comes with them into the prothesis, where

[1] A shortened form of κεκράκται.

[2] ἡ μεγάλη εἴσοδος, when the Bread and Wine are brought from the table of the prothesis and placed upon the Holy Table, while the Cherubic Hymn is sung in honour of "the King of all, invisibly attended by the spears of the Angelic Hosts." See Dr. Freshfield's article in the *Archaeologia*, vol. xliv., p. 386 ; he translates a parallel account from Codinus.

are set out the Holy Elements, and, standing outside the prothesis, a golden mantle is put upon him over the diadem and the purple ; and in the right hand he holds the cross, which he usually carries when he wears his crown, but in the left he carries the rod, which he who is called *deputatus* usually carries. With these in both hands the emperor leads the sacred entrance, and on both sides of him march the Varangi with their axes, and the sons of the nobility armed and unarmed, about a hundred in all, follow ; and immediately behind him come the deacons in order, and the priests, carrying the vessels for the service—and other most holy things. And after going round the nave, as is their wont, when they come into the solea, all the others stand outside, but the emperor alone enters the solea and finds the patriarch standing at the sacred screen, and after bowing to one another the patriarch goes inside, but the emperor remains without, and then the deacon who followed immediately after the emperor, holding in his right hand a censer, and in his left what is called the *maphorion* of the patriarch, approaches and censes the emperor. The emperor bows his head, while the deacon with a loud voice calls out, ' May the Lord be mindful of the power of thy kingdom in His universal kingdom, now and always and for ever and ever, Amen.' And in order the rest of the deacons and the priests approach and say the same. And when this is finished the emperor bows to the patriarch, takes off the mandya, which is taken away by the refendarius. The emperor again ascends the tribune and sits down on the throne, but he stands during the creed, the Lord's Prayer, and the elevation of our Lord's body. And after the eleva-tion, if he is not prepared for the Communion he remains seated till the end of the service. But if he is prepared, the deacons again come and summon him. And with them he enters into the bema and, having been given a censer, he censes the Holy Table, looking first of all to the east, then north, west, and south, and having again censed towards the east, he censes the patriarch also. The patriarch bows to him and takes the censer, and censes the emperor in return. After this the emperor removes the crown, and gives it into the hands of the deacons. Then the patriarch puts into his hand a portion of our Lord's body, and after that he drinks of the life-giving blood, not from a spoon like the rest of the people, but from the cup itself like the priests. Then the emperor replaces the crown, and comes out of the bema,. and after the congregation has shared in the Communion, and he has been blessed by the patriarch, and the priests, and has kissed their right hands, they lead him to the part called catechumena to receive the acclamations of the people. When this is finished, he comes down again, and he and the empress mount on horseback, and ride back to the palace to partake of a banquet." [1]

Codinus Curopalata [2] has also a description, almost in the same words, but with some additions. The future emperor is " led to the triclinium called Thomaites, which looks on to the Augusteum, where are standing the populace with the army. But before the emperor shows himself, what are called epicombia are thrown to the people by one of the senators, whom the emperor has selected. These epicombia are made as follows. They cut pieces of cloth, and in each piece they bind up three gold and as many silver numismata and three obols, and then throw them to the people, and they scatter as many thousands of these as the emperor shall arrange. Now it is customary to throw these epicombia in the proaulion of the great church, that is in the part called Augusteum ;—he who scatters them standing above the steps of the Augusteum." Inside the church a wooden tribunal had been prepared in the gynaeceum, and at the end of the ceremony " the young emperor with his wife the empress, and the emperor, his father, and his mother, ascend. But the golden velothyra hide the tribunal, so that they shall not be seen. Then the psaltae sing 'Lift up,' and immediately the velothyra are raised, and the princes in the gynaeceum are greeted with acclamations by the people."

---

[1] A Russian pilgrim describing the coronation of Manuel in the fourteenth century says, " The imperial procession advanced so slowly that it took three hours to walk from the royal door to the thrones." Soc. de l'Orient Latin, séries géog. vol. v., p. 143.
[2] De Officiis Palatii, chap. xvii., ed. Bonn, p. 87.

CHAPTER V

Main Divisions.—Du Cange, in the commentary to his edition of the Silentiary's Poem, was the first to make a serious attempt to elucidate the interior arrangements of S. Sophia. This appeared with the poem in the folio of 1670,[1] but a revised edition was incorporated in his *Historia Byzantina*, 1680.[2]

In the first his knowledge of the actual state of the church seems to have been limited to the description of Gyllius unassisted by any plan. Drawings of S. Sophia were desiderata at that time, and Grelot tells us how he was induced to attempt to make them by a knowledge that others who had been commissioned by the King of France had failed. Before the publication of his revised edition of 1680 Du Cange had obtained a plan. This appeared in the same year as Grelot's work, and divergences seem to show that the plans were, in great measure at least, independent of one another. The main text of his commentary however remained the same, and the alterations, although crucial, were mostly made by the omission of a few lines here and there without any attention being specially called to the fact.

This has been the cause of much confusion, as it has unfortunately happened that the first edition has been

---

[1] In *Nicephori Bryennii. . . . Pauli Silentiarii comment.*
[2] *Hist. Byz. duplici commentario illustrata.*

reproduced without remark in the series of Byzantine texts published at Bonn and in Migne's *Patrologiae Cursus Completus*. In this Du Cange placed the iconostasis " under the great eastern arch which supports the dome," and thus included the whole eastern hemicycle in the bema. He devoted the whole central square under the dome to the " priests and singers," separating it from the western hemicycle by " marble columns," which were obtained by a curious misreading of Gyllius' description of the verde antique columns in the western opening on the *first* floor. In the centre between these " marble columns " he placed the " Beautiful " or " Royal Gate," and the western hemicycle outside this was alone allotted to the people. In the corrected edition of 1680 the bema is confined to the eastern extension, the eastern hemicycle became the solea, and the central area and western hemicycle are given to the people.

There is actually very little diversity of opinion in regard to the main divisions of the church between Du Cange, Neale,[1] and Salzenberg, but Rohault de Fleury has been misled into making an engraving of the iconostasis, stretching across the whole hundred feet of the hemicycle.

Bema.—A church, as Simeon of Thessalonica writes, is properly "divided into three parts, the pronaos, the naos, and the bema." The bema (see Plan, Fig. 5) is the raised part within the screen or iconostasis included by the apse. This was the place set apart for the priests, who are hence sometimes called " they of the bema." [2] Decrees were passed from time to time to enhance its sacred character ; as that no member of the laity should pass beyond the screen, except with the consent of a bishop. Even the emperor was only allowed there during a few portions of the liturgy.

The bema of S. Sophia was indifferently called the *adyta, hierateion, thusiasterion*. The history of Michael Attaliotas also speaks of it as the " second skene, that is, the Holy of Holies." [3] The apse proper is by Paulus mentioned apart from the space contained by the straight

[1] Introduction to the *History of the Eastern Church*.
[2] Du Cange, *S. Sophia*, § 49.   [3] Ed. Bonn, p. 259.

walls, and it is possible that this is the *kuklios* (cyclius) of
Porphyrogenitus. From the poet we gather that the priests'
stalls against the wall were plated with silver. The upper
part of the curved wall is incrusted with precious marble of
sombre golden tones, beneath which the surface has been
disturbed and is now covered by plain gray slabs. When
we recall the immense quantity of silver that Procopius
says was used in the sanctuary, and remember that the
iconostasis and the altar-ciborium were of silver and the
Holy Table of gold, it seems likely that the plating of the
silver stalls covered the whole of this narrow strip, which
would not be more than six or eight feet above the top seat,
the level of which we suppose is marked by the projection
of the lower part of the wall. In the small oratory of the
Saviour built by Basil in the palace "the whole pavement
was of massive silver wrought by the hammer and enriched
by niello, and the walls to the right and left were covered
with great plates of silver damascened in gold and glistening
with precious stones and pearls."[1]   To this space we should
refer the four panels with images in the wall mentioned in
the *Novgorod Chronicle*,[2] which we suppose were of embossed
silver or enamel. The most eastward point of the apse was
occupied by the patriarch's throne.[3]   A bishop's chair with
a canopy preserved in the cathedral church of S. George at
Constantinople, said to have belonged to S. Sophia, is in any
case quite late. It is of wood, ornamented with inlaid work
representing the two-headed eagle, which was not adopted
earlier than the tenth century.

In Fig. 8 we give an outline of a miniature in the *Menologium* (Jan. 16) of the adoration of S. Peter's chains, which
were kept in the chapel of S. Peter attached to the great
church. We have here a bema fully represented with the
altar, ciborium, and apsidal stalls for the clergy. We can
hardly suppose that these latter could have belonged to a
small dependent chapel, and hence the miniature in the
symbolic way of these old drawings is probably intended as a
view of the great apse.

[1] Cons. Porphyr. in Labarte, *Pal. Impérial*, p. 92.
[2] See our p. 75.   [3] See Anon. p. 138 below.

Altar.—The central object of the bema was the altar, which stood beneath the cylindrical vault, on the under side of which the two great watching angels are represented in the mosaic. Paulus says, " On columns of gold is raised the all golden slab of the Holy Table ; it stands too on a base of gold, and from it gleams the brightness of precious stones." The doubtful Anonymous says that it was "supported on four columns, overlaid with gold," and again that

FIG. 8.—View of Bema from the *Menologium.*

"it was set up on solid columns of gold, studded with precious stones ; " and that beneath the altar was a " sea " (*thalassa*) ornamented with gold and precious stones.[1] This seems to refer to the " base of gold " beneath the columns.

According to Labarte, the description by the Anonymous (see p. 138) shows that the altar itself was decorated with

[1] The *Euchologium*, ed. 1647, p. 499, speaks of taking the garments of those about to become conventuals and placing them on or in the "little sea" (*thalassidion*) of the Holy Table. Here Goarus interprets it as "the hollow recess of the Holy Table," which seems to have been beneath the table, and used for washing the vessels, like the piscina in the later Latin church.

the bright diversity of enamel. This he seems to prove by passages in Suidas [1] and Cedrenus. The last-named writes : " It is formed of gold, of silver, of every kind of stone and metal and wood, and everything which earth, sea, or the whole universe contains. Of all these he (Justinian) collected the most valuable, with some small amount of commoner ones. He then melted those that would melt, added those that were dry, and poured them into a mould till it was filled. He wrote upon it, ' We (Justinian and Theodora) thy servants, O Christ, bring thee of thine own, praying that thou wilt graciously accept it, O Son and Word of God made flesh and crucified for us. Strengthen us in the true faith, increase and guard this state, which thou hast intrusted to us, through the mediation of Mary, the holy Virgin, the Mother of God.' "

However doubtful these late Greek writers are as authorities for Justinian's time, enamel was used in later days in the most extravagant manner, and we cannot doubt that at the time when the Crusaders took the church the altar was of enamel.[2] Robert de Clari,[3] writing at this time, says, " the chief altar of the church (S. Sophia) is so rich that one cannot value it ; for the slab which forms the altar is of gold and of precious cut stones (*esquartelées*) and pearls (*molucs*) all thrown together." Nicetas is even clearer ; describing the capture of Constantinople and the sack of the church, he says : " The Holy Table, made of all kinds of precious materials, cemented together by fire, and formed into a many-coloured harmony so as to be the wonder of all nations, was broken in pieces and distributed by the soldiers."[4]

It is very probable that some of the enamels added to the

[1] " ἔλεκτρον or ἀλλότυπον united with glass and fine stones ; such is the material of which the Holy Table of S. Sophia is made." *Glossary of Suidas* quoted by Labarte in *Recherches sur la Peinture en Email*, p. 89.

[2] Porphyrogenitus describes the table in the chapel built by Basil the Macedonian as "a mixture of all precious materials placed in order and bound together by fire into a many-coloured mass of surpassing beauty, which is the wonder of all nations." We also read of "Holy Tables of silver, having gold and precious stones and pearls poured over them, forming a compact union together."

[3] Hopf, *Chroniques Gréco-Romanes*.

[4] Nic. *Chron. Hist.*, ed. Bonn, p. 758.

Pala d'Oro at Venice after the sack of Constantinople came from the sanctuary of S. Sophia, possibly from its altar. Sylvester Sguropulus [1] who accompanied John Palaeologus to Venice in 1438, describes the Pala d'Oro as " an icon which is formed out of many, and we heard that some of these were taken from the Church of S. Sophia." It may be only a coincidence that one of the panels of the Pala contains the figure of Solomon with the Greek inscription, " Wisdom hath builded her house," that being the usual legend for Solomon.

The altar would have been covered, like the altars shown in the mosaics at Ravenna, and the illustrations of the *Menologium*,[2] by a cloth reaching on all sides to the floor. These cloths bear very simple devices—in the centre a plain cross, circle, or star, and at the four corners *gammidae* ⌐⌐ which in the code of symbolism probably expressed the four corners of that world, for which the daily sacrifice was offered.

Others however were more richly embroidered. In the *Liber Pontificalis* of Agnellus [3] it is said that Maximian, the Archbishop of Ravenna in Justinian's time, ordered a most precious altar-cloth (*endothis*) of byssus, on which was embroidered the whole history of the Saviour. " It is not possible to imagine the human figures, or the beasts and birds which are made on it." The figure of the archbishop was represented with the inscription, " Praise the Lord with me, for he hath raised me from the dust." The Continuator of Theophanes also speaks of an altar-cloth on which " the birth of the Lord was represented." [4]

The general Greek name for altar-cloth was *endute*. Those at S. Sophia are thus spoken of by the Anonymous, and we read that Michael Palaeologus sent to the Pope " an *endute* of the Great Church, of rose red, with gold and pearls worked on it."[5]

---

[1] *Vera Historia Unionis*, Hague, 1660.
[2] A MS. Greek service-book made for Basil II. (976-1025) now in the Vatican Library. A folio was printed from it at Urbino in 1727.
[3] Migne, S. L. vol. 106, p. 610.   [4] Migne, S. L. vol. 106, p. 603.
[5] Pachymeres, *de Mich. Pal.* ed. Bonn, vol. ii., p. 385.

Ciborium.—The altar stood under a canopy of silver
called a *kiborion*, as is fully described by Paulus. According to the Anonymous it was patterned with niello or
damascening (see p. ´ 138). Such ciboria are frequently
spoken of in the *Lives of the Popes*.[1] Thus Gregory I.
made for S. Peter's a " ciborium with four columns of pure
silver," and Leo III. " made for the basilica of S. Paul
a ciborium with large and beautiful columns of the purest
silver." The ciborium of S. Demetrius at Salonica, a fifth-
century work described in the *Acta Sanctorum*, was also of
silver. It supported at the top " a solid sphere of silver,
with wonderful lily-leaves curved round it, and a cross
above."[2]

An illustration[3] in an eighth-century Gospel preserved at
Venice represents a ciborium, like that at S. Sophia. We see
four arches on four columns, and from the flat top above
rises an octagonal cone. At the four corners stand bowls,
and in each bowl is a candle or a representation of one, as
the Silentiary describes. Pope Leo III. placed " above the
altar of S. Peter four large cups of the purest silver, every
one having in its centre a candle of silver-gilt."[4]

The ciborium at S. Sophia described by Paulus may have
lasted till 1203 ; Robert de Clari, writing at this time, says :
" Around the altar there are columns of silver, which carry
a canopy (*abitacle*) over the altar, made like a tower (*clokier*),
which is all of massive silver, and so rich that one cannot
estimate its value."

Crowns, &c.—From the first a crown and dove of gold
would have been suspended from the centre of the canopy ;
such doves are spoken of as being in use in Constantinople
during the Council of 536.[5] Theophanes says : " On Easter
Day Sophia, the widow of Justin II., and Constantia, the wife
of Maurice, gave the Emperor Maurice a crown of exceeding
value. When the emperor saw it, he took it to S. Sophia,
and hung it above the Holy Table by triple chains of gold and

[1] Du Cange, *S. Sophia*, § 57.   [2] Texier, *Arch. Byz.*, p. 134.
[3] De Fleury, *La Messe*, vol. ii. and plate cii.
[4] Du Cange, § 58.
[5] Bingham, *Antiq. Christ. Church*, vol. iii., p. 123, note.

precious stones."[1] This, Nicephorus Callistus says, was preserved there till the taking of the city by the Latins.[2] According to Buzantios, the emperor Leo IV. and his wife Irene also suspended crowns here. Nicetas speaks of the "crown of the great Constantine, which hung above the Holy Table ; " and again of one " John, surnamed Crassus, who rushed into S. Sophia and placed on his head a small crown, one of those which hang round the Holy Table; "[3] and it appears from the account of the Russian pilgrim Anthony, given in the next chapter, that just before the Crusade there were thirty crowns suspended from the ciborium—a beautiful symbolism.

The splendid hanging crowns at Monza and in the Cluny Museum show us that these votive crowns were broad circlets of gold incrusted with large uncut rubies and emeralds with borders of pearls, and strings of jewels, and other pendants hanging from the rim. A small enamelled crown for suspension above an altar which is amongst the Constantinople treasures at S. Mark's is inscribed ΛΕΟΝ ΔΕСΠ(ΟΤΗС) ; this, according to Labarte, must be Leo VI., who died in 911.[4]

Altar-veils.—Round the four sides of the ciborium were suspended the curtains described in such detail by Paulus. They were all the more wonderful at this time as being silk-woven and not embroidered.[5] The gold thread however seems to have been " laid " on. By the later Greeks those curtains were named tetrabela. They were often of deep red embroidered with gold, and were usually hung on rods going from capital to capital of the ciborium, as some of the illustrations in the *Menologium* show, though others seem to have been suspended from the curves of the arches.

The Iconostasis.—For a description of the screen in front of the bema, with its columns, beam, panels, and doors plated with silver, we refer to the Silentiary. A screen of this kind, from the sacred paintings with which it is adorned, is now called the iconostasis, but by the Byzantine writers it is

[1] Ed. Bonn, vol. i., p. 433.   [2] Migne, *S. G. Tom.* 147, p. 414.
[3] Ed. Bonn., pp. 450 and 697.
[4] Figured in Ongania's *Il Tesoro di San Marco.*
[5] Bayet, *L'Art Byzantin.*

usually named *herkos*, *druphrakta*, *kinklidai*, or *kankelloi*.
Such screens were generally of bronze or marble. The
Church of S. John the Evangelist, built by Galla Placidia at
Ravenna, had a screen of silver. At the Church of the
Apostles at Constantinople, built by Constantine, the iconostasis was gilded bronze. The screen of S. Peter's in Rome
was formed by the twelve beautiful antique columns which
figure in Raphael's tapestry, standing in two rows.[1] Eusebius
connects twelve columns which stood about the tomb in the
Sepulchre church with the number of the apostles, and it is
possible, as De Fleury suggests, that in the six pairs of pillars
forming the iconostasis at S. Sophia a reference may be seen
to the dismissal of the apostles two by two. From the
narrowness of the bema it seems certain that the coupling
of the pillars was transversely to the screen as shown on our
plan, Fig. 5. Thus they easily supported the passage way,
where stood a great gemmed cross and a row of branched
silver candelabra. This was the " narrow way for the lamplighter above the silver columns " described by the Silentiary.

The decoration of the silver plating of the breastwork
and the beam by figures of apostles, prophets, and angels,
and with circles bearing crosses and monograms, may have
been formed in *repoussé*, like a beautiful gilt panel with a
figure of the Virgin and Greek inscription now at Kensington
Museum, which formed a part of the decoration of the
screen at Torcello, but we think it more probable that it
was damascened with gold like the silver work in Basil's
chapel.

The iconostasis probably reached up to the base of the
porphyry strip which forms the border of the marble plating
of the bema; if so it was about twenty feet high; it had
three doors—" The Holy Doors "—that in the centre being
the largest.

The " gold and silver columns in the middle of the temple "
seen by Benjamin of Tudela, 1173, must refer to the iconostasis.

When the Crusaders practically sacked the church, the
iconostasis, ciborium, and altar were broken up and distri-

[1] De Fleury, *La Messe*.

buted. Nicetas says, "The furniture of surpassing beauty, the silver, which went round the screen of the bema, the ambo, the doors, and many ornaments, in which gold was used, were carried away." The *Novgorod Chronicle*[1] gives a fuller account of the eventful morning when the doors were broken through and S. Sophia was invaded. "They broke down the podium of the priests, ornamented with silver, the twelve silver columns, the four panels in the wall, decorated with images, and the Holy Table. They also destroyed the screen walls of the altar placed between the columns, and twelve crosses which stood above the altar ; amongst these were crosses of metal, like trees, higher than a man. All these things were made of silver.

"They carried off also the wonderful table, with the gems and a great pearl ; so great a crime did they commit in ignorance. Moreover they snatched away forty cups standing on the altar, and silver candelabra, whose number was so great that it is not possible to enumerate them, as well as the silver vessels which the Greeks use, more especially on feast days.

"They stole a Gospel, that was used for the services, and sacred crosses and single images and the covering which was above the altar, and forty censers made of pure gold : they laid hands on all gold and silver and on priceless vessels in the cupboards, walls, and other places, in such quantity that they cannot be numbered."

Grelot says that before the Turks altered the church the iconostasis had figures of the Virgin and S. John Baptist between the central and side-doors and the Twelve Apostles over.[2]

Prothesis and Diakonikon.—Two chapels that in Byzantine churches almost invariably occur right and left of the bema with which they communicate directly are usually called the prothesis and diakonikon ; they were sacristies, used respectively for the preparation of the mass and as a treasury or vestry. Du Cange in both editions placed them in the two exedras of the eastern hemicycle, and in this he is followed by Salzenberg. The impossibility of this arrangement is shown by Neale, who suggests that two chambers on either side of

---

[1] Hopf, *Chroniques Gréco-Romanes.*　　　　　[2] Compare our p. 126.

76	S. SOPHIA

the bema which Du Cange thought were only supplementary
were the sacristies in question. The chapels at the east end
of S. Sophia have now been built up, but the doors that led
into them still exist. We are not however certain that these
chapels were built with the church. Paulus does not mention
them, and there do not appear to have been chapels in this
position at S. Sergius. In regard to the use of the prothesis
and diakonikon, Dr. Freshfield [1] considers that the procession
with the bread and wine called the *Megale Eisodos*, described
in our last chapter, only became a part of the ritual in the
reign of the successor of Justinian, to whose time the Cherubic
Hymn sung during the ceremony is referred. The earlier
liturgies, he says, contain no directions for this ceremony, but
merely speak of the deacon as moving the elements from the
prothesis table to the altar, and he concludes that the two
side-chapels found in so many churches belong to a time
subsequent to Justin II. Two narrow passages however,
right and left of the bema, at S. Sophia, S. Sergius, S. Irene,
and S. Vitale seem to show that they were intended for access
to lateral portions used in connection with the bema, even if
these parts were merely screened from the aisles, and a comparison of many early churches in Syria and Asia Minor
proves that such chapels were in frequent use if not essential
long before Justinian built his church.[2] See our figures 31
and 32, and compare Cattaneo, page 60.

The prothesis and diakonikon of S. Sophia are very in-
frequently mentioned by those names. In the catalogue of
the Constantinopolitan patriarchs we read of " relics being
kept in the diaconicum." [3] The diakonikon is also named
where Codinus speaks of the emperor as " hearing the prayers
of S. Basil near the diakonikon," and the prothesis is mentioned in the passage on p. 63. Certain divisions of the
church at the east end are however frequently mentioned by

[1] *Archaeologia*, vol. xxxiv.
[2] Paulinus, describing the church at Nola, writes : " Cum duabus
dextra laevaque conchulis intra spatiosum sui ambitum apsis sinuata
laxetur, una earum immolanti hostias jubilationis antistiti patet, altera
post sacerdotem capaci sinu receptat orantes." Migne, *S.L.*, vol. 61,
p. 337.
[3] Suicerus, *Thesaurus Ecclesiasticus verb. Diaconicum.*

Porphyrogenitus, the Anonymous, and the Russian pilgrims. Thus we have the skeuophylakium (treasury of vessels) and other chapels referred to. The skeuophylakium of the Anonymous seems to be the same as the " lesser sanctuary " of Anthony, by which stood the cross which gave the exact height of Christ. This lesser sanctuary, or skeuophylakium, is probably the diakonikon—" the oratory in front of the metatorion "—where the relics of the Passion were kept.[1] Again we read : " Then by the right-hand side of the bema, they enter the oratory where stands the silver crucifix . . . . after worshipping they ascend by the cochlea [spiral stair, we suppose at south-east angle where minaret now is] which is by the part called the Holy Well, to the eastern part of the right-hand catechumena." Again, " Then by the right-hand side of the bema, they enter the oratory where stands the silver crucifix." [2]

The Holy Well and Metatorion.—The Holy Well, so frequently mentioned in the *Ceremonies*, seems to have been not merely an object but a division of the church. Labarte makes it a chamber external to the church on the south side, but the Anonymous shows that it was to the east, by speaking of " that part of the temple in which was the Holy Well, the bema, and the ambo." The author of an account of " the miracle in the Holy Well of the Great Church " speaks of a picture of Christ as being by the eastern gate, " where is the holy mouth of the well of Samaria." [3]

The Russian pilgrims generally speak of the Samaritan well, from which flowed water from the Jordan, as "in the sanctuary : " the Anonymous Russian says "in the chapel to the right." At this time it was probably in one of the eastern chapels, which may have been identical with the prothesis or diakonikon. Some passages of the *Ceremonies* seem to imply that in the tenth century the Holy Well was without the building ; thus we hear of the "embolos [portico] of the Holy Well : " and again, "from the Holy Well, they enter by the door leading to the church ; " [4] possibly it was moved later, but probably one of the eastern

[1] See p. 96.   [2] *Cer.* pp. 636 and 565.   [3] Du Cange, § 76.
[4] *Cer.* p. 27.   A Holy Well is frequently found in the Prothesis.

attached chapels will fulfil the conditions.   In our Fig. 5 we
have followed Du Cange's ground-plan in the distribution of
these eastern chapels.   It is possible that the round north-
east building was used as a great sacristy as Salzenberg suggests; Grelot calls it so on his plan, and T. Smith says this
was a tradition.   The Anonymous definitely distinguishes the
Skeuophylakium, the Holy Well, and the Chapel of S. Peter.

The Metatorion, frequently spoken of together with the
Holy Well, Labarte and Paspates place on the south side,
external to the church.   We think it was probably the name
of portions of the side-aisles screened off by curtains.
This would agree with Unger,[1] who thinks that the word
means a "quarter of the church" (*metatio*), and that Du
Cange was mistaken in deriving it from *mutatorium*.   In the
Ceremonies,—"The princes go out of the right side of the
bema and enter the metatorion."   Again, the patriarch
stands within the iconostasis "on the right-hand side of
the bema, towards the metatorion."   From the metatorion
a small door led to the Holy Well.   Again, "they leave
the bema by the right-hand side through the small holy
door (in iconostasis) and proceed to the porphyry columns
(of exedra), and by the staircase of the metatorion they
enter the catechumena."[2]   Again, "the emperor takes off
his crown in the metatorion within the Beautiful Gate," and
"within the veil, hanging in the metatorion at the back of
the narthex door."   Metatoria in the catechumena of S.
Sophia and of S. Sergius are also referred to.[3]

Solea.—The later writers often mention the solea of
S. Sophia.   Thus Cantacuzenus speaks of the emperor
passing through the solea up to the "Holy Doors."[4]   It
was immediately outside the iconostasis, and must have
closely agreed with the choir of the singers in a Western
church.   Paulus does not use the word, but he describes the
singers as occupying the space in front of the Holy Doors,
and embraced by the exedras.   The ambo, with its long

---

[1] *Quellen für Byzantischer Kunstgeschichte.*
[2] *Cer.* pp. 17 and 167.   [3] *Cer.* pp. 157 and 160.
[4] See account of Coronation in previous chapter and of Adoration
of Cross below,

passage of approach from the step of the Holy Doors, divided this space in two, so it is clear that the singers stood on either side of the ambo. The portion round about the ambo screened by the circle of columns was reserved for the leaders of the choir, the Protopsaltae.[1] We cannot infer from the Silentiary that there was any other screen to the Solea, and no stalls for the singers are mentioned.

It is possible that in the tenth century, when the *Book of the Ceremonies* was written, the ambo had been modified at least in regard to the approach from the bema, and that a considerable space was interposed between it and the Holy Doors, in front of which there was at this time a porphyry omphalion stone (see our page 96). Paspates [2] says this is still quite intact, somewhat oval in shape, seven feet across, and adorned with a mosaic of marbles. It seems probable from the Anonymous that in these later days the solea was inclosed by a screen which he says was of silver.[3]

Paulus describes a part on the south side as being inclosed for the emperor, and in Porphyrogenitus we read that the emperor had his seat "near the Holy Doors on the right-hand side." It is probable that opposite the emperor's throne there was another bishop's chair, for that in the bema might only be occupied by the bishop in his own diocese. Grelot indeed reports that the emperor's and bishop's thrones were opposite one another.

Nave.—We now come to the central division of the church, the naos or nave, the square space beneath the dome contained between the four main piers : its centre was called *omphalos, mesomphalos,* or *mesonaos.*

The pavement, according to the poet Paul, was covered with white Proconnesian marble and darker Bosporus stone. In the opening lines of the description before given he seems to compare the veined marble to flowing streams, or foam-flecked sea, and the ambo is likened to an island rising from the sea. According to Glycas and Codinus the first pavement was

---

[1] On Mount Athos ; "the Kanonarches, or master of the choir, prompts the cantors, who sing without books." A. Riley's *Mount Athos.*
[2] *The Great Palace,* p. 96.
[3] Compare S. Germanus ; *La Messe,* iii., p. 91.

of various hues like the ocean. The Anonymous, in comparing a pavement which he says was laid down afterwards with this supposed earlier one, says that "messengers were sent to Proconnesus, and marble of a green colour was worked there, as is seen now like rivers flowing into the sea." Codinus says, "four rivers of leek-green marble were like the four streams which flow from Paradise to the sea." *As is seen now* certainly seems to bring something definite before our eyes, and so far as the pavement can be seen through the narrow chinks of the matting there is much to confirm this part of the Anonymous. Grelot tells us that the pavement is laid in compartments. It is of whitish gray Proconnesian marble, laid in slabs about 4 × 10 feet, with here and there strips of verde antique about 2 feet wide, which suggest the quartering of the floor by a great cross. Moreover the square of rich Alexandrine work still existing, and figured by Salzenberg, lies on a diagonal, and would thus exactly occupy one of four square spaces left in the angles (see Fig. 5). Now in the palace the floor of the bed-chamber of Basil had four rivers or streams of Thessalian-green marble which seemed to flow away from the centre, and the quarters were filled with mosaics of large eagles.[1] It may also be noticed that four rivers are depicted as flowing away from the cross on the central bronze door of narthex. Many parallel examples of pavements, still existing, confirm the Anonymous in this respect. The mosaic floors of Italy furnish many instances where the four rivers of Eden are represented in the several angles as human forms pouring from urns, waters which are inscribed with the names Gihon, Tigris, Euphrates, and Pison. The design of the pavement of the Baptistery at Florence has been much disturbed, but it seems to have represented flowing streams, which led from the font in the middle to the doors like four paths. It has been pointed out that the carpet of Chosroes, which is described as having represented a garden with flowing streams, was a traditional pattern of which an example showing four streams quartering the field

---

[1] *Theoph. Contin.*, ed. Bonn, p. 333.

is in the possession of Mr. Colvin.[1]   We understand that a similar carpet is now in New York.

We give here a representation of a square of pavement at the centre of the Western Gynaecéum ; it is of Proconnesian slabs with border, and a disc of verde antico.

Font.—A fine marble font formerly in the precincts of the Mosque Zeinab Sultana at the west of S. Sophia, and now in the Imperial Museum, is the one referred to by

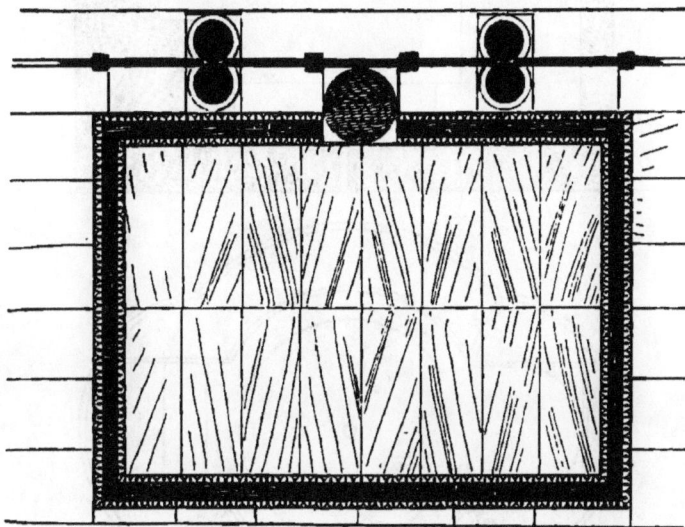

FIG. 9.—Marble Pavement at centre of West Gallery.

Paspates as being probably the font of S. John Baptist (the Baptistery).   He writes that there were only two remaining in Constantinople, the other being a smaller font in the precincts of the Mosque Kotza Mustapha Pasha.[2]   The font in the museum which we illustrate is 8 feet 2½ inches long, 6 feet 1½ inches wide, and 4 feet 6 inches high, wrought out of one fine block of Proconnesian marble.   The outside is carefully finished, which shows that it stood above the floor. The inside is formed into steps, and about the rim are

[1] Mr. Conway in *Art Journal*, 1891.   [2] *Great Palace*, pp. 120, 129.

several roughly sunk crosses, which we suggest were filled
by inlaid votive crosses of metal.   Similar fonts are shown
in the mosaics at S. Mark's and other places.   Texier found
one in the marble quarries of Synnada with steps inside, and

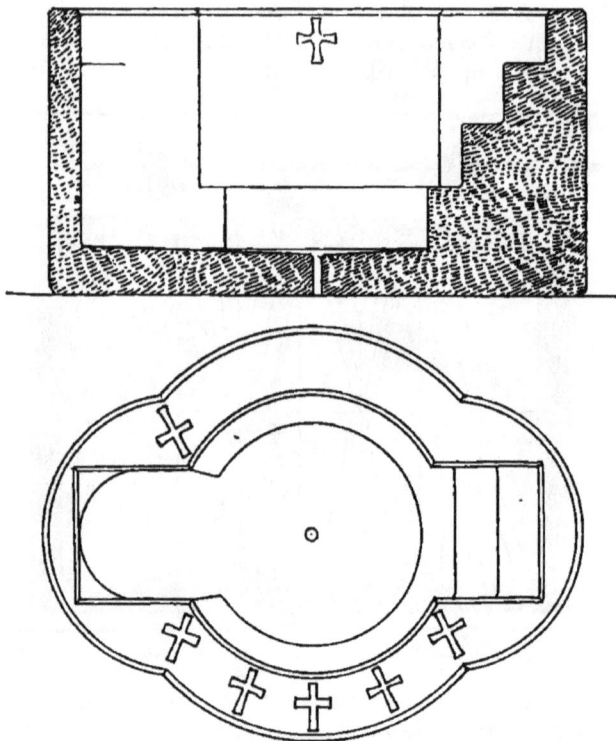

FIG. 10.—Font from Constantinople.

others are found in Palestine, one of which, illustrated in
the *Memoirs* of the Exploration Fund,[1] closely resembles
this at Constantinople, which we may therefore look on as a
typical Byzantine font.

[1] Vol. iii., p. 321.

Consecration or other Crosses.—On the great verde antico columns of the north side of the nave, about six feet above the floor, appear sunk crosses about six inches high; on the south side shallow sunk panels occupy similar positions, formed we may suppose by the Turks for the purpose of destroying the crosses. Similar sunk crosses occur on some of the marble columns in the gallery at S. Sergius and at Bethlehem; at Sinai the nave columns bear inlaid bronze crosses. From the character of those at S. Sophia we should suppose that they were also formerly filled by inlaid metal; their similarity in size and the regularity with which they are placed seem to show that they are of the nature of consecration crosses rather than being merely votive, or rather that they were made by the builders, just as a farmer crosses his bags of wheat. In most of the cisterns of Constantinople one column at least bears a large fairly wrought cross.

Miraculous Marbles and Mosaics.—Clavijo describes a large white slab in the right of the gallery naturally figuring "the Virgin with Christ in her most holy arms:" beneath this was an altar in a little chapel where they said mass. These marbles, in which accidental resemblances to figures might be traced, were evidently much valued. Felix Fabri describes a slab at the Holy Sepulchre in which S. Jerome and his lion appeared. "This picture was not produced by art, but by simple polishing alone."

The column of S. Gregory Thaumaturgus, mentioned by Anthony of Novgorod as by the entrance and "covered with bronze plates," may possibly be the celebrated "sweating column," which is the first square pillar in the north aisle. At about five feet from the floor it is cased with bronze, in which a hole is left over the cavities in the pillar which are supposed to exude the dampness. The indents are smooth, and look like natural cavities discovered in the marble when it was wrought. Canon Curtis, who was kind enough to examine the pillar for us, says it was perfectly dry, and the attendants assured him that water never oozed out of the cavities, although " a few drops of water might be easily kept in each of them." Sweating columns are well known in the legends of the middle ages. Benjamin of Tudela speaks of

two in Rome which sweated on the anniversary of the fall of
Jerusalem, and Mandeville mentions four pillars in the Holy
Sepulchre "that always drop water, and some men say that
they weep for our Lord's death." Stephen of Novgorod
speaks of a mosaic of Christ in S. Sophia from which holy
water flowed from the wounds of the feet.

Water Vessels.—At the west end of the church in the
right and left exedras stand two large white Proconnesian
marble urns about seven feet high, of beautiful gourd-like
forms. They rise from the centre of polygonal basins, and
water is drawn from them through bronze taps. It has
been said that they were brought from Pergamus or
Marmora by Sultan Murad III.[1] The carving of the turban-
like tops is certainly Turkish, but the vessels seem to be of
Byzantine form, and we are disposed to agree with Grelot,
who saw them in their present position before 1680. He
says they were kept full of water "to cool the Moham-
medans overheated by their devout gesticulations." "If
they are not very ancient, they stand in the place of others,
which contained holy water for the Christians who entered
the church." He associates with these the palindrome inscription given by Gruter (see our page 191), which he says
was written on these, or similar, vessels in gold letters.[2]

Now a beautiful cantharus in the Church of S. Peter
and S. Andrew, on the island of Murano,[3] which is almost
identical with those of S. Sophia, is stated to have been
brought back thence with the Venetian booty, and bears a
Byzantine inscription :—

ΑΝΤΛΗCΑΤΑΙ · ΥΔѠΡ · ΜΕΤΑ · ΕΥΦΡΟCΥΝΗC · ΟΤΙ · ΦѠΝΗ.

K̄Υ · ΕΠΙ · ΤѠΝ · ΥΔΑΤѠΝ ·

("Draw the water with gladness, for the voice of the

[1] Fossati : also Paspates' *Byzantinae Meletai*, p. 343.

[2] *Relation d'un Voyage de Constantinople*, p. 160. This idea he may
have obtained from Rosweyd's note to Paulinus (1569), saying fountains in
front of churches were succeeded by lustral vases placed at the vestibule
of the temple. "The rim of such a one seems to be figured in Gruter,
p. 1046, with an inscription which was selected from the Anthology,
as is shown by Rigaltius. This line was [also] written on the sepulchre
of St. Diomede."

[3] Paciaurdi 1758, *De sacris Balneis*, tab. vi.

Lord is upon the waters ") ; together with a monogram
which reads NIKOMEΔOY. Beneath the monogram appears
a stopping where evidently a tap was fixed, in exactly the
position of those to the urns in S. Sophia. The first half
of the latter inscription is on a small vessel of lead found
at Tunis, which, from the character of the decoration, cannot
be later than the fourth or fifth century. The first mention
of the vessels in S. Sophia which we have been able to find
is by an English traveller, Fynes Moryson (1595), who
says, " I did see two nuts of marble of huge bigness and
great beauty."

We give in Fig. 11 the vessel in the south exedra at
S. Sophia, together with that of Murano, and for further
comparison some beautiful vessels from a relief of Justinian's
time on the ivory throne at Ravenna. We have omitted
the Turkish top of the former. Canon Curtis, who has
specially examined them, writes to us that between the top
and body of each vessel is a copper band which conceals the
joint, if there is a joint.

Images and Tombs.—Very few fragments of Christian
sculpture remain in Constantinople. The Silentiary does
not mention any sculpture at S. Sophia. Probably the
feeling which was mature in Leo the Isaurian was always
latent ; Oriental Christians sharing in the dislike with
which Jew and Moslem regarded statues. Canon Curtis
writes : " On the northern side of the sweating column I
used to see parts of a bas-relief representing, as I thought,
a procession, but it was almost concealed by the metal
plates, and now it is entirely hidden." The wealth of the
church in icons at a late period may be gathered from
incidental references. Not until a late time do we hear
of any tombs in the church. S. Chrysostom and most of
the other patriarchs were buried in the Church of the
Holy Apostles.

Pachymeres mentions "the stele of the three Germani
(Patriarchs of Constantinople) near the porphyry columns
on the west." Nicephorus Gregoras [1] also writes that the

---

[1] Ed. Bonn, vol. i., p. 262.

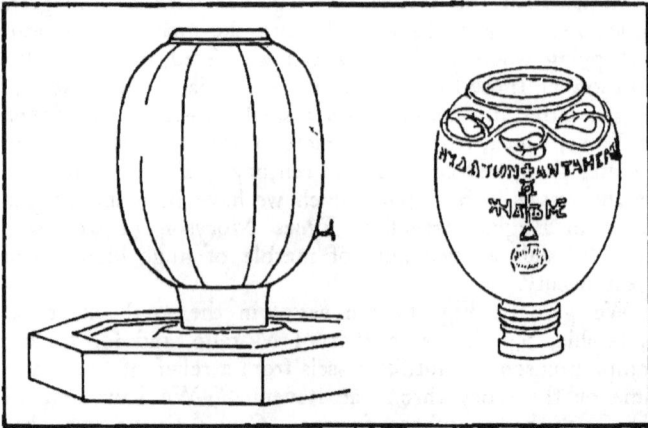

FIG. 11.—Water Vessels from S. Sophia and Murano.

remains of the patriarch Arsenius were buried in the great Church of S. Sophia.

Hangings.—The descriptions on several occasions mention veils and hangings by the names of *vela* and *velothyra*. With mosaics and miniatures to help us it is possible to judge of the lavish way in which these hangings were used.

The mosaics at Ravenna show veils hanging at the door of the church through which Theodora is about to enter, and the large elevation of the Palace of Theodoric, likewise in mosaic, shows hangings in all the arches of the portico. Such textiles suspended at entrance doorways are often mentioned by contemporary authors.[1]   At S. Sophia the doors entering the narthex, and those between it and the church, all have bronze hooks, to which such "door veils" were suspended ; and embroidered Turkish hangings, which roll up from the bottom by means of cords and pulleys, are still hung to them. In the Byzantine mosaics the hangings are often shown raised by being gathered into a loose knot, or by being drawn to the sides and passed once round the pillars between which they hang.

[1] E. Muntz, *Tapisserie.*

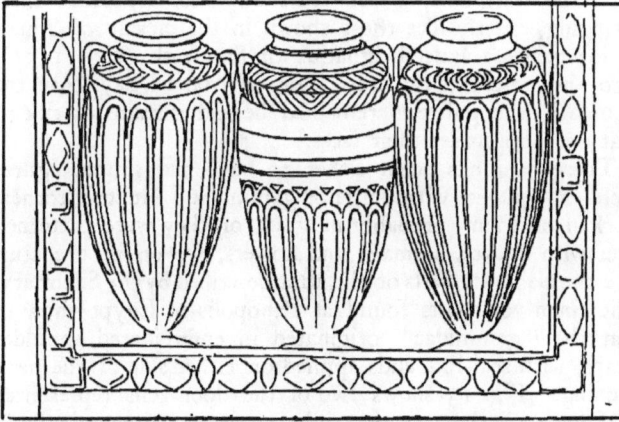

FIG. 12.—Vessels of Sixth Century : from Ivory Throne, Ravenna.

The account of the coronation ceremony describes how the royal persons were seated in the gynaeceum, screened by "golden velothyra," so that they should not be seen until the psaltae sang the "Lift up," when immediately the velothyra were raised. Of these hangings in the interior we have a picture in the account given in the continuation of Theophanes of an ambassador, Iber Curopalates, who visited Constantinople in 923, and "was taken to the church of S. Sophia, that he should inspect its beauty and size and precious ornaments. Now the walls were all draped with cloth of gold before they led him in, and he, struck with the great size of the church and its wealth of adornment, exclaimed, 'Truly this is the house of God,' and returned home." [1] The *Ceremonies* mention gold hangings in Catechumena above Royal Door.[2] Nicetas tells us how the Crusaders "spared neither the house of God nor His ministers, but stripped the great church of all its fine ornaments and hangings, made of the richest brocades of inestimable value."

We have no doubt that S. Sophia was frequently adorned inside by the arcades of both tiers having hangings suspended

[1] Ed. Bonn, p. 402 and p. 894. [2] *Cer.* I., p. 591.

from the iron bars, which cross all these arches at their
springing, exactly like those shown in the mosaic of Theodoric's palace. Indeed Ignatius of Smolensk (*circ.* 1395),
who was present at the coronation of Manuel, says that the
women in the galleries remained behind curtains of silk so
that none might see their faces.[1]

These hangings seem either to have had simple figures
such as squares with large "gammidae" at the corners
worked on them, probably in gold, or they were patterned
over with figures, animals, and flowers, woven in the stuff
like the elaborate veils of the altar described by the Silentiary.
The linen vestments found at Panopolis in Egypt show us
that the "gammidae" originated in embroidered shoulder
straps, with seal-like ends applied on either side of the neck
opening. Fig. 13 shows two of the door veils represented
at Ravenna ; that on the right is from the mosaic in S.
Apollinare Nuovo showing the palace. The gammidae are
here exactly of the form found on the early Coptic linen
vestments, and it cannot be doubted that they were "applied"
in a similar way. The pattern on the left is the door-hang-
ing from the mosaic of S. Vitale ; the plain squares are of
gold. The designs on the robes in this mosaic are interesting. Justinian's chlamys is covered with birds in circles, the
border of Theodora's robe displays the three Magi making
their offerings ; one of her attendants has a robe powdered
with swimming ducks and a mantle with four petalled red
roses on a gold ground, and another robe has five pointed
leaves scattered over its field. Many examples of the figured
silks are preserved in museums. There is at South Kensington Museum a piece of pictured silk of this kind,
probably of Justinian's time, which is covered with circles,
in each of which is figured a man and a lion. More
than a century before the time of Justinian, Asterius,
Bishop of Amasius, had made these elaborately figured
stuffs a subject of satire : "When men so draped appear
in the streets the passers-by regard them like painted walls.
Their clothes are pictures which little children trace out
with their fingers. There are lions, panthers, and bears,

---

[1] *Soc. Orient. Latin, séries Géographique*, vol. v. 1889, p. 143.

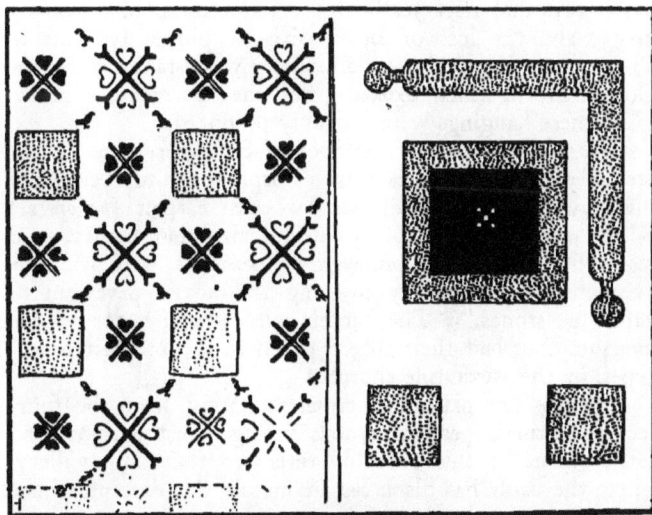

FIG. 13.—Door Veils of the Sixth Century : Ravenna Mosaics.

also rocks, woods, and hunters. The most devout carry Christ, His disciples, and His miracles. Here we may see the marriage in Galilee and the pots of wine ; there is the paralytic carrying his bed, the penitent woman at the feet of Jesus, or Lazarus come again to life." [1]

' Later the patterns became more heraldic and larger in scale, figuring for the most part great displayed eagles, and griffons, or lions affronted. A piece of a textile of this kind in the museum at Düsseldorf, of which there is a full-size copy at South Kensington, bears golden lions about two feet six inches long, and the names of Constantine VIII. and Basil on a pallid purple ground. Frauberger [2] compares this with another signed example of the same age and similar design preserved at Siegburg, and a third at Autun, " all of which were intended for church hangings." The same

[1] See E. Muntz, *Tapisserie*, and M. F. Michel, *Recherches sur* . . . . *des étoffes de Soie.*

[2] *Jahrbuch des Vereins von alterthumsfreunden in Rheinlande*, 1892, p. 224.

writer says that after Justinian's introduction of silk weaving
in 552 and the loss of Bosra with its purple-dye vats to
Chosroes, an imperial textile industry was established by the
Golden Horn, which existed until the fourteenth century.
Here these hangings were probably produced.

Carpets.—Portions of the floor of S. Sophia were almost
certainly strewn with carpets. Porphyrogenitus relates of
the New Church of Basil that "woollen carpets (*nakopetai*)
called prayer carpets, of wonderful size and beauty, and
resembling the bright plumage of peacocks, were laid one
over another, completely covering the mosaic pavement of
valuable stones." The carpets and prayer-rugs of the
mosques thus had their direct parallels, if not their proto-
types, in the Byzantine churches.

Synods.—The patriarchal registers, dating from the fourteenth century, speak of synods sitting "in the right-hand
catechumena"; this probably refers to the south gallery,
where the vault has displayed in mosaic the descent of the
Holy Ghost on the Apostles.

Across this gallery there is at present a screen, which
possibly, as Paspates suggests, shut off the part used by the
Synods. (See dotted line on Fig. 6.) The screen is made
up of two marble slabs, each sculptured into the form of
panelled double doors, with architraves and carved panels.
Above the opening left between these is a coloured marble
slab. At the top is a carved wood beam, which, being exactly
like the permanent vault ties, is evidently of Justinian's age;
but the whole is certainly not an original assemblage of
the parts. Each slab, which imitates a pair of wood doors,
has a representation of a bronze ring handle and a lock-plate
on one half, and a hasp on the other, all exactly copied in
sculptured marble. We believe that these imitation doors
are earlier than the church; the idea was common in late
classic times. De Vogüé and Dr. Merrill[1] found several
tomb doors, similarly panelled, studded with imitation nails,
and having elaborate knockers, all carved in stone. An
example in marble now in the museum at Leeds closely
resembles the S. Sophia slabs.

[1] *Across the Jordan.*

Clergy and Ritual.—In the time of Justinian the total number of clergy was 525, but at the time of Heraclius this had been increased to 600.[1] They were thus divided:—

Presbyters . .	80	Readers . . .	160
Deacons . . .	150	Singers . . .	25
Deaconesses . .	40	Doorkeepers .	75
Subdeacons . .	70		
		Total .	600

The subdeacons, according to the forty-third canon of the Council of Laodicea, stood by the doors. Porphyrogenitus [2] speaks of the emperor "passing through the narthex of the gynaeceum, where the deaconesses have their usual place." The same author also mentions [3] "hypurgi of the narthex, readers for alternate weeks, ostiarii of the Holy Well, a domesticus of the subdeacons, and deputati of S. Sophia." A series of seals of the officers of S. Sophia is given by Schlumberger; [4] the seals are those of the klerikos, diakonos, manglabites, ekdikos, deuteroboetes, protospatharios, and the chartophulax. An anonymous author [5] gives a list of the officers of the "holy and great" church which is too long to be given in full, but we may note some of the duties mentioned.

The Oeconomus held "one of the flabella, and stood at the right hand of the altar, when the patriarch was officiating ;" while "the sacellarius, holding a napkin, stood on the left." The skeuophylax stood in front of the skeuophylakium, so as to be ready to hand any vessel that might be wanted. The chartophulax stood near the "holy doors," and pronounced the words of the service, "Approach, ye priests." The castensius holds the censer, and draws the curtain at the *Trisagion.* The refendarius and deputati carried the orders of the patriarch to the princes and nobles,

[1] See Paspates and Salz. [2] Ed. Bonn, vol. i., p. 182. [3] Vol. i., p. 801.
[4] *Sigillographie de' l'Empire Byzantin.* The seal of the church itself represents Justinian and the Virgin or Theodora supporting the building. Cp. Lenormant, *Revue Numismatique,* 1864, p. 268, pl. xii.
[5] *Explicatio Officiorum sanctae ac magnae Ecclesiae, Auctore incerto a Bernardo Medonio edita,* 1655. A Tupikon or Ritual Book of S. Sophia has been recently found at Patmos : *Byz. Zeit.,* 1893.

and summoned them to his presence. When the patriarch was officiating, the protopapas took precedence of all the other priests, and even gave the communion to the patriarch. The protopsaltes " stood in the middle of the church between the right and left choirs," and led the singing. On one occasion the number of priests was so great " that the church of S. Sophia, though it is the greatest of all on the earth, seemed then too small." [1]

Up to the eleventh century, services were only performed in S. Sophia on Sundays and Saints' days. In the middle of the eleventh century, Monomachus arranged that the service should be every day, and for this extra salaries were given.[2]

Some idea of the ritual of the services may be gathered from the offices in the *Euchologium*, edited by Goar, the Cherubic and other hymns, together with the *Ceremonies* of Porphyrogenitus. An account given by Anthony of Novgorod is quoted in the next chapter. Bertrandon Brocquière writes : " I was curious to witness the manner of the Greeks performing divine service, and went to S. Sophia on a day when the patriarch officiated. The emperor was present accompanied by his wife, his mother, and his brother, the despot of the Morea. A Mystery was represented, the subject of which was the three youths whom Nebuchadnezzar had ordered to be thrown into the fiery furnace."

Having in our last chapter quoted the description of the procession and celebration of the Mass, we now give the accounts of the Adoration of the Cross given by Arculf[3] in the seventh century, and by Porphyrogenitus in the tenth ; together with the directions for the emperor's procession to the great church.

The Adoration of the Cross.—" In the northern part of the interior of the house (S. Sophia) is shown a very large and beautiful aumbry, where is kept a wooden chest, in which is shut up that wooden cross of salvation on which our Saviour hung for the salvation of the world. This notable chest, as the sainted Arculf relates, is raised with its treasure of such preciousness upon a golden altar, on three consecutive days

[1] *Cantacuzenus*, Bonn, ii., p. 15. [2] *Cedrenus*, vol ii., p. 609.
[3] Pal. Pil. Text. Soc.

after the lapse of a year. This altar also is in the same round church, being two cubits long, and one broad. On three consecutive days only throughout the year is the Lord's cross raised and placed on the altar, that is on the day of the supper of the Lord, when the emperor and the armies enter the church, and, approaching the altar, after that sacred chest has been opened, kiss the Cross of Salvation. First of all the emperor of the world kisses it with bent face, then going up one after another in the order of rank or age all kiss the cross with honour. Then on the next day, that is on the sixth day of the week before Easter, the queen, the matrons, and all the women of the people approach it in the above-mentioned order, and all kiss it with reverence. On the third day, that is on the Paschal Sabbath, the bishop, and all the clergy after him, approach in order with fear and trembling and all honour, kissing the Cross of Victory which is placed in its chest. When these sacred and joyful kissings of the sacred cross are finished, that venerable chest is closed, and with its honoured treasure it is borne back to its aumbry. But this should also be carefully noted, that there are not two but three short pieces of wood in the cross, that is the cross beam and the long one which is cut and divided into two equal parts; while from these threefold venerated beams when the chest is opened, there arises an odour of a wonderful fragrance,[1] as if all sorts of flowers had been collected in it, wonderfully full of sweetness, satiating and gladdening all in the open space before the inner walls of the church, who stand still as they enter at that moment ; for from the knots of those threefold beams a sweet-smelling liquid distils, like pressed-out oil, which causes all men of whatever race, who have assembled and entered the church, to perceive the above-mentioned fragrance of so great sweetness. This liquid is such that if even a little drop of it be laid on the sick, they easily recover their health, whatever be the trouble or disease they have been afflicted with."

The passage from the *Book of the Ceremonies*[2] describing

---

[1] In the *Ceremonies*, book ii., we read that the three crosses kept in the palace were anointed by the protopapas with balsam, before being shown. Ed. Bonn, p. 549.　　　　　　　　　[2] Ed. Bonn, p. 125.

the Exaltation of the cross on September 14th begins with
the emperor " passing through the palace Manaura, and the
upper corridors, ascending by the wooden staircase, and entering the *catechumena* [1] of the great church." After he has
reached the catechumena and " lighted candles, and prayed,
he takes his seat in the part on the right-hand side." " The
emperor then summons the patriarch, who remains for a short
time with the emperor, and then goes out, and comes to the
small secretum, where is kept the Holy Wood, and receives
the emperor there. And as the congregation begin the
' Glory to God in the Highest,' the emperor enters, and kisses
the Sacred Wood, and comes out into the great secretum.
Then the emperor, following the Cross, descends by the great
winding staircase, keeping to the left, and passes through the
Didaskalion,[2] where the paschalia are inscribed, and having
gone down the steps, he enters through the great gate of
the narthex, and reaches the royal doors and stands there."
The emperor and patriarch now pass through the middle of
the nave, and on the right of the ambo into the solea ; here
the emperor stands before the Holy Doors, and gives the
candle he is carrying to the praepositus. He then enters the
bema, and having kissed the Sacred Wood, and turning round,
he comes out again, and passes through the solea, then mounts
the third or fourth step of the ambo and stands there, holding the candle. The patriarch then comes out of the bema
and mounts the ambo with the Sacred Wood, and the emperor
gives his candle to the praepositus, and remains there until
the Wood has been elevated in the four quarters of the ambo.
The emperor and patriarch then descend from the ambo and
enter the bema, and the Wood being placed before them
the emperor prays and kisses it, and coming out through
the side of the bema he is conducted by the patriarch

[1] κατηχούμενα, a " place for instruction," used both of upper and lower
aisles.

[2] The college with a provost (*didaskalos*) and twelve fellows was between
S. Sophia and the Chalkoprateia (see Bury, ii., p. 433), and therefore
according to Mordtmann north of S. Sophia. Descending steps are only
found in the north porch, and this is conclusive against Labarte and
Paspates, who saw in the Didaskalion a mere passage attached to the south
side of the church. Paschalia are the tables of Easter.

to the Holy Well, and having kissed it, he continues to the palace."

It would almost appear that whereas in the time of Arculph (*circa* 680) the Cross was kept in one of the north-eastern chambers by the bema, in the time of Porphyrogenitus (tenth century) it was preserved, during certain periods, in a secretum accessible from the gynaeceum. Possibly the small upper chapel on the south side with mosaic ceiling, and the additions over the south porch, both built about the tenth century, may be the chambers in question. At the end of the ceremony the Cross was left in the bema, and it may be that only on the occasion of the Festival of the Cross was it taken up to the gallery, preparatory to a procession through all parts of the church.

Procession to the Church.—The following is an account ot a pageant, which is the first in the *Book of Ceremonies*—the order of the royal procession to the Great Church. On the day preceding the feast, notice was given so that the way might be adorned with flowers. The emperor and princes carried gifts, and processional candles, and the Cross of St. Constantine.[1] Priests were sent to receive him with the Cross of the Lord, which was taken from the church by the Sacristan (*skeuophulax*).

In proceeding to the church there were six "receptions." Three were in various parts of the palace, "and the princes come to the gate (Chalké), and the fourth reception takes place outside the barrier of Chalké; the fifth reception takes place in front of the Great Gate which leads into the Augusteum; and the sixth reception is at the Horologium of S. Sophia."[2]

"And from thence the princes enter through the Beautiful Gate, and have their crowns removed by the praepositi within the curtain that hangs in the chamber, that is to say, the propylaeum of the narthex. And the patriarch receives them at the door of the narthex with the usual ceremony. . . . . The lords remove their crowns, kiss the holy Gospel

---

[1] At this time more than one "life-giving cross" was kept at the palace and occasionally taken to S. Sophia. *Cerem.* 549.

[2] Ed. Bonn, p. 14.

carried by the archdeacon, greet the patriarch, and proceed
up to the royal doors.   Bearing the candles and bowing
thrice, the entrance is made after a prayer by the patriarch ;
then those carrying the sceptres and vessels stand right and
left of the church ; but those bearing the banners and the
books stand on either side in the solea ; and the Cross of St.
Constantine is placed on the right side of the bema.   And
when the lords come to the Holy Doors and to the porphyry
omphalion, the patriarch alone enters within the screen, by
the holy door on the left.   The princes, after bowing thrice,
enter with the candles, following the patriarch, and coming
to the holy table they kiss the holy cloth, and they place
as is usual on the holy table the two white veils, and kiss the
holy chalices, and the two discs and the holy corporal cloth,
which are handed to them by the patriarch.   And then by
the right-hand side of the bema the princes enter with the
patriarch the *Kuklis*, where is placed the Holy Crucifix of
gold, and again they bow with the candles three times
praising God ; and the patriarch gives the censer to the
emperor and he censes the crucifix : then they kiss the
patriarch, and take leave of him and enter the oratory,
which is in front of the metatorion, and there, bowing
three times and praising God, they kiss the Holy Cross
as well as all the Instruments of our Lord's Passion, and
then enter the metatorion."

CHAPTER VI

§ I.—RELICS.

The True Cross.—There would seem to be little doubt that a discovery was made about 326 of what was supposed to be the true Cross. S. Cyril of Jerusalem, writing some twenty-five years later, says that portions of the Cross were spread all over the world. We have seen (p. 14) that early historians relate that a portion of this precious relic was sent to Constantinople by Helena. The principal part however remained at Jerusalem until it was taken by Chosroes. It is described by some of the pilgrims to the holy city as being encased in silver. Brought back from Persia by Heraclius in 628 together with the spear and sponge, it rested for a brief interval in S. Sophia, where it was "uplifted"; but it was again returned to Jerusalem until 636,[1] when under the fear of the coming troubles the larger portion at least was removed. Rohault de Fleury, who devoted a folio volume to the Instruments of the Passion, quotes a letter from Anseau, a priest of the Holy Sepulchre in the twelfth century, which was sent to Paris with a portion of the Cross. According to this account the Holy Wood was divided into nineteen small Crosses, of which Constantinople possessed three besides the "Cross of the Emperor," and Jerusalem retained four. We have positive evidence that in the century before Heraclius Constantinople was a centre where portions of the Cross were to be obtained : thus

[1] Drapeyron, *L'Empereur Heraclius,* 279.

H

Radegunde, wife of Clothaire, received a fragment from
Justin II. and Sophia in 569.[1]   At this time, according to
John of Ephesus, there was "a day of the adoration of the
Holy Cross of our Saviour ; on this festival the Cross is
brought out and set up in the Great Church, and the senate
and all the people of the city assemble to worship it." [2]
Probably the Exaltation was celebrated concurrently at
Jerusalem and at Constantinople.

When we more definitely hear of the True Cross at S.
Sophia, it is evident, from the frequent occasions in which it
is transported to different parts of the church, and to the
palace, that it was quite small, a relic in fact.

Arculf (circa 680), as we have seen, describes it as kept in
a chest, on a golden altar, which was only two cubits long
by one broad.   He says : "it should be specially noticed
that there are not two but three short pieces of wood in the
cross ; that is, the cross beam, and the long one divided into
two equal parts."

Now in the *Menologium* of Basil we have a representation
of the Exaltation of the Cross, which the patriarch is up-
lifting in an ambo.   It is represented as a double cross made
up of three pieces, not of two.   A miniature of the finding
of the Cross in the National Library of Paris shows the
same form.   Didron remarks that the cross with double
branches probably originated in Greece, "for it is constantly
seen in Attica, in the Morea, and on Mount Athos."   This
form appears frequently on the later coins of Constantinople,
and we find that most of the relics of the True Cross which
still exist on Mount Athos and other places are made up
with double arms.   A reliquary for the fragment, said to be
that which was sent to Radegunde, was preserved in the
monastery of S. Cross at Poitiers in the last century.   The
field was of *cloisonné* enamel, blue with here and there a
red flower.   A drawing of this relic, of which we give an
outline,[3] shows that this fragment of the True Cross was
made up in the double-armed form, which was repeated in

---

[1] Fortunatus celebrated its acceptance by a hymn.
[2] *J. of Ephesus*, ed. R. P. Smith, 140.
[3] Figured in Molinier's *L'Emaillerie*, Paris, 1891.

the relic at the Ste. Chapelle.[1] Two such relics now at Venice are doubly interesting, for besides a cross of this form two supporting figures are represented which are inscribed Constantine and Helena.[2] Now Cedrenus and other late writers say that in the Kamara of the Milion were the figures of Constantine and his mother, with the cross between them. The same composition appears in the mosaics at the monastery of S. Luke. The two Venice relics bear the names of the Empresses Maria (1180) and Irene (1350).

FIG. 14.—Showing form of True Cross at S. Sophia.

Fig. 14 represents the Poitiers reliquary; the True Cross as shown in the *Menologium*; and a cross from a late coin. We cannot doubt that the Cross at Constantinople was of this form. Was it the result of the conjunction of three pieces as mentioned by Arculph, or did the upper arm from the first represent the label?

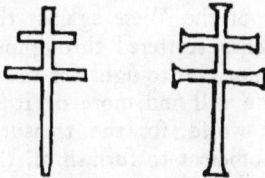

With the Cross were associated the other Instruments of the Passion—the Crown of Thorns, the Sponge and Spear, and slabs from the Tomb.

The catalogue of relics by Nicholas Thingeyrensis (1200) says, " In S. Sophia is the Cross of the Lord which Helena the Queen brought ; " [3] but at that time the greater part of the Cross and other relics of the Passion seem to have been transferred to the chapel in the palace of Boucoleon, where they were seen by Robert de Clari (1200). The

[1] Figured in Schlumberger's *Nicephorus Phocas*.
[2] See Ongania, *Il Tesoro*, Fig. 33 and p. 102.
[3] Riant, *Ex. Sac. C.P.*, vol. ii., p. 213.

anniversary of the day on which they were moved from
S. Sophia, August 14th, was kept as a holiday. According
to Paspates all the relics of the Passion were removed in
1234. Baldwin II. took the Crown of Thorns which was
acquired by S. Louis. It is evident, however, from the
later Pilgrims quoted below, and from Mandeville, that a
part of the Passion relics remained or that others were
acquired.

Other Treasure and Relics.—"Not only kings and
patriarchs, but also private individuals and monks brought
to Constantinople relics of the apostles and martyrs, ancient
ikons, and all kinds of sacred objects connected with the
saints of the church. Anything of value in the whole land
of Palestine was for the most part moved to Constantinople, and such was the reverence for relics that no church,
monastery, nor oratory was built without them."[1] So early
as 415, when S. Sophia was rededicated, it was necessary to
have fresh relics (see page 16).

A description of the relics and the treasure of Constantinople is given in the letter supposed to have been written in
1095 by Alexius Comnenus to Robert, Count of Flanders,
in which he craves the assistance of the West against the
Turks. After enumerating the relics scattered throughout
the city, he continues, "If you do not care to fight for these,
and gold will tempt you more, you will find more of it at
Constantinople than in the whole world, for the treasures
of its basilicas alone would be sufficient to furnish all the
churches of Christendom, and all their treasures cannot
together amount to those of S. Sophia, whose riches have
never been equalled even in the temple of Solomon."

The dispersion of the relics and treasures of S. Sophia
and the other churches at Constantinople has been exhaus-
tively treated by Count Riant.[2] The description by
Anthony, Archbishop of Novgorod, who visited S. Sophia
in 1200, three years before the capture by the Crusaders,

---

[1] Paspates, *Byzantinae Meletae,* p. 285.
[2] *Des Dépouilles Religieuses enlevées à Constantinople au xiii siècle par les
Latins,* 1875, and the fuller work, *Exuviae Sacrae Constantinopolitanae,*
1877.

furnishes the best account of the accumulated riches of the great church. We give this in full from the French version contained in *Itinéraires Russes en Orient*.[1]

"I, Antonius, Archbishop of Novgorod, an unworthy and humble sinner, by the grace of God and by the help of S. Sophia, who is the Wisdom and the Eternal Word, reached in safety the imperial city, and entered the great Catholic and Apostolic Church. We first worshipped S. Sophia, kissing the two slabs of the Lord's sepulchre. Furthermore we saw the seals, and the figure of the Mother of God, nursing Christ. This image a Jew at Jerusalem pierced in the neck with a knife, and blood flowed forth. The blood of the image, all dried up, we saw in the smaller sanctuary.

"In the sanctuary of S. Sophia is the blood of the holy martyr Pantaleon with milk,[2] placed in a reliquary like a little branch or bough, yet without their having mixed. Besides that there is his head, and the head of the Apostle Quadratus, and many relics of other saints : the heads of Hermolaus and Stratonicus ; the arm of Germanus, which is laid on those who are to be ordained patriarchs ; the image of the Virgin which Germanus sent in a boat to Rome by sea ; and the small marble table on which Christ celebrated His Supper with the disciples, as well as His swaddling clothes and the golden vessels, which the Magi brought with their offerings.

"There is a large gold 'disc' for the mass, given to the patriarch by Olga, a Russian princess, when she came to the imperial city to be baptized.[3] In this disc there is a precious stone which displays the image of Christ, and the seal-impressions from this are used as charms ; but on the upper side the disc is adorned with pearls.

"In the sanctuary is likewise preserved the real chariot of Constantine and Helena, made of silver ; there are gold plates, enriched with pearls and little jewels, and numerous others of silver, which are used for the services on

---

[1] *Soc. Orient Latin. Séries Géog.*, vol. v.

[2] Alluded to on a single page of MS. in the British Museum (*Cott. Claud.* iv.)

[3] In the reign of Constantine Porphyrogenitus, see *Ceremonies*, vol. ii., ch. xv.

Sundays and feast days : there is water also in the sanctuary
coming out of a well by pipes.

"Outside the smaller sanctuary[1] is erected the 'Crux
Mensuralis,' which shows the height of Christ when on
earth ; and behind that cross is buried Anna, who gave her
house to S. Sophia, where now is the smaller sanctuary, and
she is buried near. And near this same smaller sanctuary
are the figures of the holy women and of the Virgin Mother
holding Christ, and shedding tears which fall on the eyes of
Christ. They give of the water of the sanctuary for the
blessing of the world.

"In the same part is the chapel of S. Peter the Apostle,
where S. Theophania is buried. She was the guardian of
the keys of S. Sophia, which people used to kiss. There is
also suspended the carpet of S. Nicholas. The iron chains
of S. Peter are kept there in a gold chest ; during the feast
of 'S. Peter's Chains' the emperor, the patriarch, and all the
congregation kiss them [see Fig. 8]. Near by, in another
chapel, is also shown the crystal of the ancient ambo,
destroyed when the dome fell.

"By the side of [the images of] the holy women is the
tomb of the son of S. Athenogenius. . . . . There are no
other tombs in S. Sophia except that, and a lamp hangs
in front of it, which once fell, full of oil, without being
broken. The place is inclosed by a wood screen, and the
people are not allowed to enter.

"When one turns towards the gate one sees at the side the
column of S. Gregory the Miracle-Worker, all covered with
bronze plates. S. Gregory appeared near this column, and
the people kiss it, and rub their breasts and shoulders against
it to be cured of their pains ; there is also the image of S.
Gregory. On his feast day the patriarch brings his relics to
this column. And there placed above a platform is a great
figure of the Saviour in mosaic ; it lacks the little finger of
the right hand. When it was finished, the artist looked at
it and said, 'Lord, I have made thee as if alive.' Then a
voice coming from the picture said, 'When hast thou seen

[1] The French translation has *Diakonikon:* Riant, in *Exuv. Sacrae,*
C.P. says "smaller sanctuary : " the Anon. says *skeuophylakium.*

me ? ' The artist was struck dumb and died, and the finger was not finished, but was made in silver-gilt.

" Above the gate is depicted on a large panel the Emperor Leo the Wise, and in front of it is a precious stone, which illuminates S. Sophia at night-time. This same Emperor Leo took a certain writing from Babylon, which was found in the tomb of the prophet Daniel. It was copied, and on it were written the names of the Greek emperors. At the royal gate is a bronze romanistum [1] or bolt by which the door is closed. Men and women are brought to it, and if they have drunk serpent poison or any other poison, they cannot remove the bolt from the mouth, until all the evil of the disease has trickled away with the saliva.

" By the great altar on the left is the place where an angel of the Lord appeared to the boy who was guarding the workmen's tools, and said, ' I will not leave this spot as long as S. Sophia shall remain.' Three figures are shown in this place, for the angels are painted there ; and a multitude of people come there to pray to God. Not far from there is the place where they boil the holy oil, burning underneath it old ikons, whose features one can no longer trace. With this oil they anoint children at baptism. Above the sanctuary there rises in the air a great hollow vault covered with gold. In the sanctuary are eighty candelabra of silver for use on feast days, which occupy the first place, besides numberless silver candelabra with many golden apples.

" Above the great altar in the middle is hung the crown of the Emperor Constantine, set with precious stones and pearls. Below it is a golden cross, which overhangs a golden dove. The crowns of the other emperors are hung round the ciborium, which is entirely made of silver and gold. Thus the altar pillars and the sanctuary and the bema are built of gold and silver, ingeniously made, and very costly. From the same ciborium hang thirty smaller crowns, as a remembrance to Christians of the pieces of money of Judas. To the ciborium were attached curtains,

[1] This must be the same as Robert de Clari's "buhotiaous" fastened to the ring of the great door of S. Sophia.

which were formerly drawn by the bishops during the services. We asked why they did so, and they answered so that the priests should not see the women and the people, but should serve the supreme God with a pure heart and soul. Later the heretics,[1] when nobody could see them as they were behind the curtains, took the body and blood of Christ, and spat them out, and trampled on them. The Spirit warned the fathers of this heresy, and the fathers fixed the curtains to the columns of the ciborium, and set an archdeacon near the patriarch, metropolitan, or bishop, so that they should worship God holily without heresy. . . . When Jerusalem was taken by Titus many sacred vessels and curtains were brought to [New] Rome with the royal treasures and given to the church of S. Sophia. In S. Sophia also are preserved the tables of the Law, as well as the Ark and manna. The subdeacons, when they sing ' Alleluia' in the ambo, hold in their hands tablets like those of Moses. During the procession of the Holy Sacrament the eunuchs commence to sing, and then the subdeacons, and then a monk chants alone. Then many priests and deacons carry the Holy Sacrament in procession ; at this time all the people not only below, but also in the galleries, weep in great humility. What then ought to be the fear and humility of the bishops, the priests, and the deacons in this holy service ?

" How magnificent are the gold and silver chalices, garnished with precious stones and pearls ! When the splendid chest, called Jerusalem, is brought out with the flabella, there rises amongst the people a great groaning and weeping. . . . . But here is a wonderful miracle, which we saw in S. Sophia. Behind the altar of the larger sanctuary is a gold cross, higher than two men, set with precious stones and pearls. There hangs before it another gold cross a cubit and a half long, with three gold lamps, which hang from as many gold arms (the fourth is now lost). These lamps, the arms or branches, and the cross, were made by the great Emperor Justinian who built S.

---

[1] *I.e.*, the iconoclasts, of whom a number of stories are told by the Russian pilgrims.

Sophia. By virtue of the Holy Spirit the small cross with the lamps ascended above the big cross, and again slowly came down again without going out. This miracle took place after matins, before the commencement of the mass : the priests who were in the sanctuary saw it, and all the people in the church who saw it cried with fear and joy, ' God in His mercy has visited us.' . . . This great and wonderful miracle was wrought by God in the year 6708 [A.M.] on Sunday, May 21st, being the Commemoration of S. Constantine and his mother Helena, during the reign of the Emperor Alexius and the patriarchate of John. It was on the feast of the 318 fathers. Iverdiatinus Ostromitza was then living at Constantinople ; he was an ambassador from the great Roman duke. Nedanus, Domagirus, Demetrius, and Novgaro were also there.

" At S. Sophia on the right near the sanctuary is a piece of red marble, on which they place a golden throne ; on this throne the emperor is crowned. This place was surrounded by bronze closures to prevent people walking on it ; but the people kiss it. At this place the Holy Virgin prayed to her Son, our Lord, on behalf of all Christians ; a priest who was guarding the church at night saw her. On the same side is also the grand icon of S. Boris and S. Glebe, which artists copy. When officiating, the patriarch holds it high up in the tribune.

" In the chapel behind the altar are affixed to the wall the upper slab of the Lord's sepulchre, the hammer, the gimlet, and the saw, with which the cross of the Lord was made ; also the iron chain which was hung to the gate of S. Peter's prison, and the wood of the cross which Christ's neck touched. This is inserted in a reliquary in the form of a cross. In this chapel above the door is painted S. Stephen, protomartyr, and a lamp is hung before him ; when any one has bad eyes, they put round his head the rope by which this lamp is hung, and his eyes are healed.

" There is also the figure of Christ whose neck the Jew struck,[1] and the bronze trumpet of Joshua, who took Jericho, and the marble mouth of the well of Samaria.

[1] See this story in *Golden Legend*, " Exaltation of the Cross."

Near it Christ said to the woman of Samaria, 'Give me to
drink ;' the well mouth has been cut in half, and the
Samaritans still draw water [from the other half].

" There lie also the bodies of S. Abercius, S. Gregory, and
S. Sylvester, and the heads of Cyrus and John, and many
other relics.   There also is the Baptistery, upon which is
painted all the history of the baptism of Christ by John in
the Jordan : and how John taught the people, and how
little children and men threw themselves in the Jordan : all
this was executed by Paul the Skilful during my lifetime,
and there is no painting like this.   There are there wooden
supports, upon which the patriarch has had placed the figure
of Christ, thirty cubits high ; Paul first painted the Christ
with colours made of precious stones and crushed pearls
mixed with water ; this image is still at S. Sophia.

" And when they sing matins at S. Sophia, they sing first
before the great doors of the church, in the narthex, then
they enter and sing in the middle of the church ; then they
open the paradise gates, and sing the third time before the
altar.   Sundays and saints' days the patriarch assists at
matins and at mass, then he blesses the singers from the
ambo, they stop singing and then say the *polykronia :* then
they begin to sing again, and sing as harmoniously and
sweetly as the angels till the Mass.   After matins are
finished, they put off their surplices and then go out and
ask the patriarch's benediction for the mass.   After matins
the prologue is read in the ambo till the mass ; when the
prologue is finished, the liturgy is commenced, and, after the
service is over, the chief priest in the sanctuary recites the
prayer called 'Of the ambo,' while the second priest recites
it in the church on the side of the ambo, away from [the
sanctuary] : both, when the prayer is finished, bless the
people.   In a similar way vespers are sung.   There are no
bells at S. Sophia, but a little hand-bat [*hagiosidère*] which
they strike for matins, though they do not strike it for mass
and vespers, as in other churches : they follow the precepts of
the angel in having this bat ; the Latins have bells. . . . . .
When they built S. Sophia, they inclosed holy relics in
the walls of the sanctuary.   There are also many cisterns at

S. Sophia. Above [evidently *under*] the galleries are the cisterns and storehouses of the patriarchs and of the Church. Vegetables of every kind [suitable for the table] of the patriarchs, melons, apples, and pears are preserved at the bottom of the cisterns in baskets hung by cords : when the patriarch wants to eat, they bring them up quite fresh : and the emperor eats them also. The bath of the patriarch is also above [under] the galleries ; the water of the fountains mounts by pipes, and the rainwater is preserved in cisterns. On the galleries are painted all the patriarchs and emperors of Constantinople, and those who shared their heresies. In the choirs of the church are five heads ornamented with pearls like a silver [word indecipherable] . . . . . Lazarus, the image painter [1] . . . first painted at Constantinople, in the sanctuary of S. Sophia, the Virgin holding Christ and two angels. . . . . S. Sophia has 3,000 priests ; 500 share in the benefices of the church and 1,500 have no share ; when one of the 500 priests dies, his place is taken by one of the 1,500."

Frankish Occupation and After.—Three years after the visit of Anthony, Constantinople was taken by the Latins. One of the Crusaders, Villehardouin, writes, "Of holy relics I need only say it contained more than all Christendom combined ; there is no estimating the quantity of gold, silver, precious vessels, jewels, rich stuffs, silks, robes of vair, gris, and ermine, and other valuable things —the production of all the climates in the world. It is the belief of me, Geoffrey Villehardouin, maréchal of Champagne, that the plunder of this city exceeded all that has been witnessed since the creation of the world."

Much of the accumulated wealth of six centuries—the gifts from emperors and private individuals of "sacred vessels of gold and pearls and precious stones" [2]—was removed by the Venetians and Franks. Many of these precious objects are lost beyond hope of recovery ; such are

[1] Lazarus was a martyr in the cause of image-worship. See Bayet, *L'art Byzantin.*

[2] Cedrenus, ii., p. 609. Irene gave a cross "distinguished for its pearls" : Theo. Cont., p. 703.

the candlesticks and crosses.   As some representation of
these we give a figure of a gemmed processional cross, with
its *seizae* of jewels, from the *Menologium* of Basil (Fig. 15).

In the treasury of S. Mark's
at Venice there is however a
rich hoard of vessels, lamps,
and other objects, which were
taken from the churches of
Constantinople ; and many of
these crystal lamps, agate cups,
and enamelled book-covers
doubtless belonged to S.
Sophia.

Amongst these may be men-
tioned an agate chalice with
the name Sisinnius.   This may
probably be referred to a
Patriarch of Constantinople of
that name in 996 ; another
with the name Ignatius to a
patriarch in 877 ; a third with
the inscription "Lord help
Romanus, the Orthodox Em-
peror" to Romanus Lecapenus
(919—944).[1]   Extracts from
the Venetian historians men-
tioning objects brought from
Constantinople are given by
Riant.   Paulus Maurocenus
speaks of "the many holy
relics, and small figures, and
chalices and patens and other
beautiful things from the

Fig. 15.—Jewelled Processional Cross. church of S. Sophia ;" also,
"the very same doors which
now close the church of S. Mark's . . . . and two censers
of gold from S. Sophia of such grace and beauty that
one cannot see them without being astounded."   He also

[1] Ongania, *Il Tesoro di San Marco*, pp. 57, 59. Rohault de Fleury, *La Messe.*

mentions, though it is not quite clear if he associates this with S. Sophia, " The palla of silver-gilt with the figures of our Lord, the Virgin, the Apostles, prophets, doctors, and martyrs, which is now placed in the church of S. Mark." [1]

The head of S. Pantaleon was taken by Henrich Ulmen to the church of the saint at Cologne.

After the interregnum, S. Sophia was visited by several other Russian pilgrims, who have left accounts of the church which agree very closely. Of the fullest of these, which is by an anonymous Russian writer, 1424–1453, we give a condensed abstract, as it contains one or two more points, shows the acquisition of other relics in the place of those lost, and is useful for comparison with the anonymous Greek author translated in the next chapter:—

Near the west door in the middle of the narthex are the doors of the ark of Noah and the chain which bound the apostle Paul. Above the door is the miraculous image of the Saviour, and a lamp is suspended before it. In the sanctuary is the life-giving Cross on which the Jews crucified Christ. The stone on which He sat and conversed with the woman of Samaria is in the chapel on the right. Here is the table of Abraham. At the bottom of the church against the wall to the right of the altar is the bed of iron on which martyrs were burnt. Here is a stone coffer with relics of Martyrs and the Innocents. To the left is the tomb and the whole body of Arsenius : the doors of the ark : the bench where Jeremiah the prophet wept, and a column by which Peter wept. To the left are buried S. George and S. Theologos. On the left is a little shrine beautifully built ; it contains the image of the Virgin which wept when the Franks held Constantinople. Her tears, resembling pearls, are kept in a coffer before the image. The instruments of the Passion are exposed from Thursday to Saturday. Beyond is the image of Christ in marble, and the cross of S. John chained to the wall. Near the Holy Table in the bema is the tomb of S. John Chrysostom, covered by a plank overlaid with gold and gems. To the right on entering the church are situated a well and large basin of marble in which the patriarch baptizes. One

---

[1] *Exuviae Sacrae Constantinopolitanae.*

leaves S. Sophia by the south door ; at some steps from the gate,
to the left, is the Church of the Holy Saviour ; above the door
is suspended an image which an emperor attempted to destroy.
Behind the bema of S. Sophia is the church of S. Nicholas.
Near by in front of the door which is behind the altar of
S. Sophia is the place where they bless the water, plunging
in the Cross ; a roof covered with lead surmounts the basin
of green marble.   It is here they baptize the emperors ;
four cypresses and two palms form a crescent in this place.
Some distance in front of the ambo of S. Sophia is a
pedestal of marble which supports the holy chalice ; it is
within a stone inclosure, and is covered by a vault of gilt
copper.   From the entrance of the church to the ambo is 66
cubits, and it is 30 beyond to the sanctuary, which is 50 long
by 100 wide.   The church is 200 cubits wide and 150
high.   Above the first door is Solomon in mosaic in a circle
of azure.

That these accounts accurately relate the stories of the
guardians of S. Sophia is sufficiently proved by La Brocquière,
who was told in 1433 that S. Sophia possessed " one of the
robes of our Lord, the end of the lance that pierced His side,
the sponge that was offered to Him, and the reed that was put
in His hand.   I can only say that behind the choir I was
shown the gridiron on which S. Lawrence was roasted [the
iron bed], and a large basin-like stone on which they say
Abraham gave the angels food when they were going to
destroy Sodom and Gomorrah."

§ 2.—LIGHTING.

The description by the Silentiary [1] of the lamps and candelabra which illuminated the Great Church forms one of the
most fascinating parts of the whole poem.   Although the
multitude of lamps which once lit up the interior have long
disappeared, the main features of the lighting may be brought
back to our imaginations by comparing the description with
illustrative examples.   First then in the central space under

[1] See our p. 49.

the great dome, chains fell from the height of the upper cornice, where they were probably attached to strong bronze arms which projected far out like the present metal stakes which project in the exedras on the first-floor cornice. These chains all terminated at some height above the floor in supporting the great sweep of a metal circle to which were suspended flat circular discs of silver, each of which was pierced with holes into which were dropped glass oil vases with rims which prevented them falling through.   With these discs were associated crosses of metal which also carried lamps. These, cross and disc together, or alternately, hanging round in a great circle made a " circling chorus of bright lights " within which was a large corona of other lamps and above it a large central disc.

Then along the sides of the church were rows of lamps in the forms of silver bowls, and ships ; other rows of lights were attached to beams supported above the floor by metal standards, and to projecting metal arms, or suspended rods. Upon the beam of the iconostasis was a row of candelabra, each with a series of horizontal circles diminishing upwards about the stem, like a fir-tree, issuing from a silver bowl. Above the centre of the iconostasis was a great standard light-bearing cross. Round about the ambo similar light trees were placed.

Light coronae, crosses, or single lamps were favourite gifts to a church, and in these objects S. Sophia probably became much more wealthy as time went on.   Michael III., for instance, gave to the church in 867 "a circle (*kuklos*) for lights which they call a polycandelon, as big as any of the others but all of gold weighing sixty pounds. To it was given the first and most holy place." [1]   " A chalice and paten superior to all the others, as well as a polycandelon in the form of a cross with many lamps," are also mentioned as given by Michael. His successor Basil I., " as there was a danger of the sacred lamps being extinguished for want of oil," assigned for the use of the church "the tribute called mantea, so that the light might never be quenched." [2] The

[1] Theoph. Contin., ed. Bonn, p. 211.
[2] *Ibid.*, *Life of Basil*, ch. 79.

Anonymous doubtless exaggerates beyond belief with his
300 polycandela and 6000 lamps all of gold, but the kinds

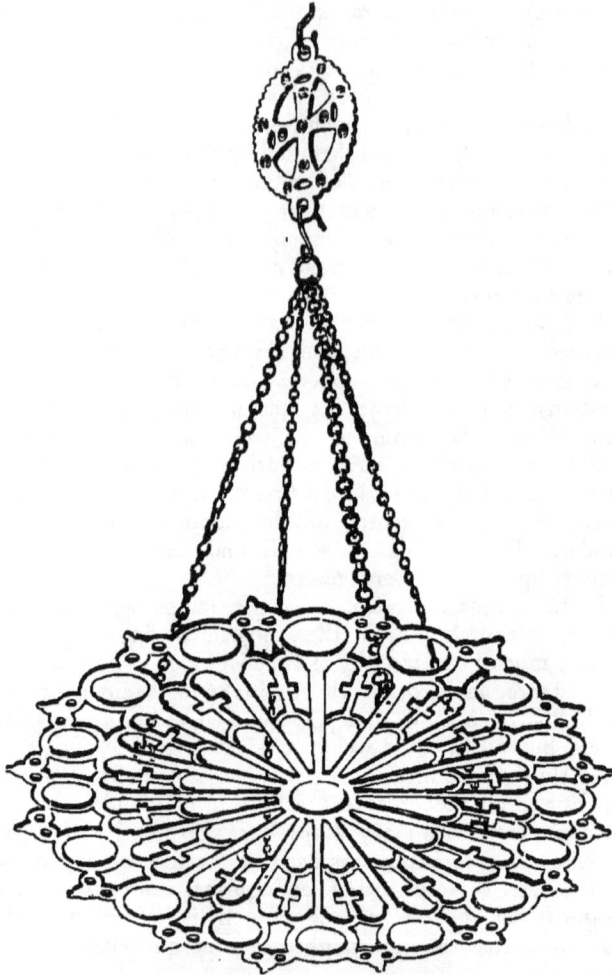

FIG. 16.—Polycandelon or Disc, for Seventeen Lamps, in the British Museum.

of candelabra he speaks of must have been perfectly well known (p. 140).

At the end of the twelfth century, Robert de Clari, the knight of Amiens, wrote—"Throughout the church hang one hundred candelabra, and there is not one which does not hang from a silver chain as thick as a man's arm, and each candelabrum has quite twenty-five lamps or more, and there is not a single candelabrum which is not worth two hundred silver marks." Benjamin of Tudela mentions "candelabra, lamps, and lanterns, of gold and silver more than any man can name;" and Stephen of Novgorod (1350) speaks of "a multitude immense, innumerable, of lamps."

Of the great brilliance of illumination obtained in the early churches there can be no doubt. Paulinus writes that at his church at Nola the lights were suspended in such profusion that they seemed to float in a sea. An interesting account of the method of lighting followed at the Lateran, illustrated by a plan of the circles, is given by Rohault de Fleury.[1]

A Byzantine lamp-holder lately sent to the Louvre from Constantinople is probably almost identical in general form with the "discs" of Paulus. This polycandelon is a broad flat ring of bronze pierced with eight holes for as many lights, and suspended by four chains. It bears a votive inscription which reads, "Lord, remember thee of Thy servant Abraham, son of Constantine." [2]

In the British Museum is a much more ornate example of the same kind of disc. This is also of bronze, about sixteen inches diameter, pierced with seventeen holes for the lights, the interspaces being cut away to form a radiating pattern. We give a drawing of this interesting lamp, with which we have associated a small pierced plate for a lamp chain in the same collection (Fig. 16). In the Archæological Museum at Granada there is an ornamental disc closely resembling the example in the British Museum. It came from the mosque of Elvira, and probably belongs to

---

[1] La Messe, vol. vi., p. 78.
[2] See fig. in Byz. Zeitschrift, 1893, p. 142.

I

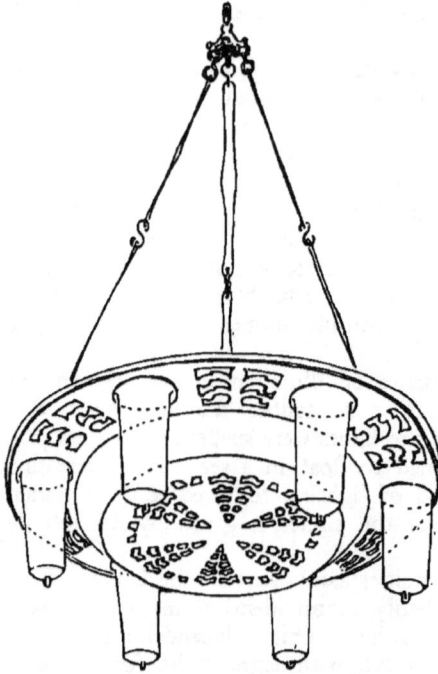

FIG. 17.—Silver Polycandelon from Lampsacus,
in the British Museum.

the ninth century. We mention this because the bottom plate of the modern mosque lamp with the small holes which take glass tubular vessels eight or ten inches long and only about two inches in diameter, continues the tradition of the Byzantine polycandela, and the oil vessels well represent those like spear shafts mentioned by the Poet.

In another example in the British Museum the disc is not quite flat but of the form of a dinner plate, the holes for the lamps being around the rim. This lamp-holder is of silver, and was brought from Lampsacus near Gallipoli with several altar vessels inscribed with a monogram which reads MHNA or AMHN. In Fig. 17 we have restored the oil vases. Another bronze polycandelon has recently been brought from Egypt by Professor Flinders Petrie: this is about eight inches across (Fig. 18 [1]).

[1] In the figure 18 the attachment for the chain is shown at A, the chain of monograms is taken from Rossi, B shows the provision for the chains in the last example (Fig. 17), where there is a slight mistake, the alternate piercings in the rim being crosses as here shown.

On Mount Athos we probably find the best existing parallel to the circle of discs at S. Sophia in the monastery of Docheiareiu (see Fig. 19).[1] In the words of the Silentiary, "these discs form a coronet."

The second crown of lights, which hung within the great circle of discs at S. Sophia, would also have had a circular rim supported by chains with lamps suspended beneath, or attached to arms projecting from the rim.   S. Bernard

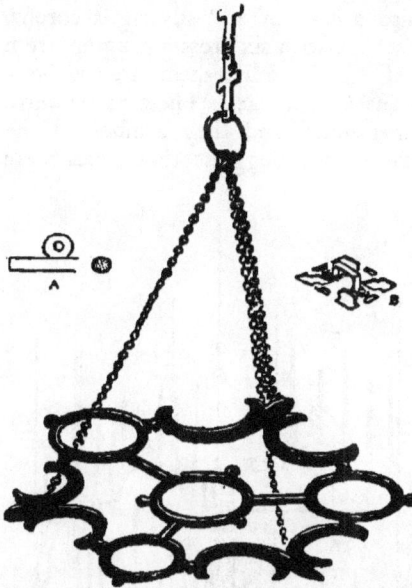

FIG. 18.—Coptic Polycandelon for Four Lamps.

speaks of a church where were placed " not crowns but wheels with precious stones and lights around them."   To these circular candelabra ecclesiastical writers usually give the title of coronae.   Leo III. gave to the basilica of S. Andrew at Rome a " gold corona of lamps set with gems."   Other authors call crowns with lamps of this kind *phara ;* we read in Leo Ostiensis of a " pharum or large crown of silver with six and thirty lamps hanging from it." [2]   They are also spoken of as *cycli*, but more generally as *polycandela*.   The *Chronicon Cassinense* mentions " a pharos or crown of silver, weighing a hundred librae, twenty cubits round about, with twelve towers projecting from it, and thirty-six lamps hanging from it.   This was fixed outside the choir, before the great cross, by an iron chain adorned with seven gold apples." [3]

[1] Adapted from a photographic view in A. Riley's *Mountain of the Monks.*   [2] Du Cange.   [3] Lib. iii.   This was at Milan.

The same chronicle also speaks of a "silver-gilt corona, coloured with precious stones, with six crosses hanging from it." The great circles of Aix and Hildesheim are the best-known examples of the ancient coronae. These have twelve towers like that just mentioned, and they symbolised the New Jerusalem. R. de Fleury suggests that relics were

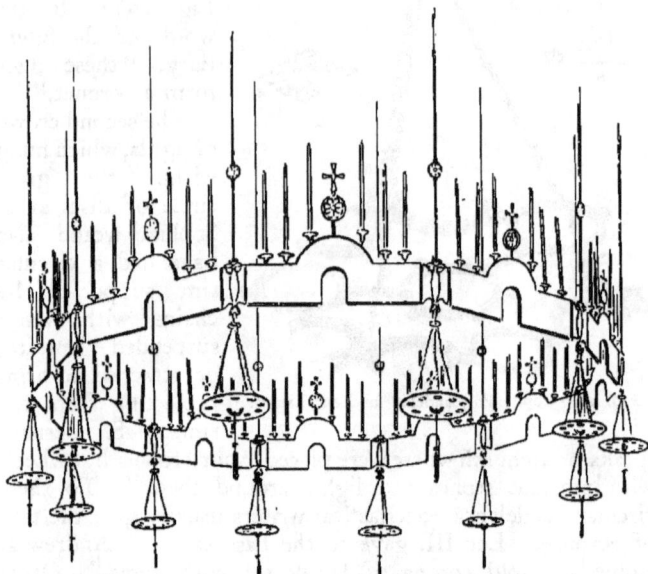

FIG. 19.—Corona with Lamp Discs, Mount Athos.

contained in such turrets. An extremely beautiful pharos in the Hermitage Museum represents a basilica.

The light crosses were very generally known throughout Christendom, and the historian Socrates mentions that crosses of silver with burning candles upon them were carried in processions in the time of Chrysostom. According to Anastasius, at S. Peter's there was a large pharos "in the form of a cross which hung before the presbyterium having 1,370 candles;" this was lighted four times a year;

also "a gold carved cross hanging before the altar with twelve candles," and "a cross lamp with two little ships and three fishes." The lamp cross hanging in S. Mark's is the best-known example remaining. It is possible that those at S. Sophia mentioned with the discs hung horizontally to four chains.

At S. Sophia, in addition to the discs, crosses, and circles, there were, according to Du Cange, lamps hung from nets. The word which he interprets in this way is that translated "skiff" (line 480), as it means a small row-boat. How he

FIG. 20.—Single Lamp with Votive Inscription.

gets his interpretation of nets it is difficult to see. We mention it here for its intrinsic beauty only : it was a familiar arrangement for lamps. Anastasius in his Lives of the Popes speaks of one of the churches at Rome having "a pharos in the form of a net," and again of a large pharos "like a net with twenty baskets," and also "a bronze net with silver baskets."

The hanging lamps in the form of ships mentioned by our poet would have carried the oil vessels round their sides. A most interesting example of a lamp of this kind is given in the *Dictionary of Christian Antiquities* (Smith and Cheetham). It represents a small vessel with a mast and sail, containing two figures, one steering, and the other looking out from the prow. These figures are either Peter and Paul or more probably Christ and Peter. The symbolism of the ship for the Church is too familiar to need comment ; the mast in the centre, without which the ship is unsafe, as S. Ambrose says, typifies the cross without which the church is unable to stand. The galley form of lamp was well known also in antiquity. In the Christian era it was only one of the many beautiful and suggestive forms in which lamps were made ; some resembled birds, crystal fish, or shells, others again were bowls of white or emerald glass.

In the sanctuary there would have been suspended large single lamps which burnt perpetually (*Akoimetoi*). A very fine single Byzantine lamp of this kind is shown in the fifteenth-century picture by Marco Marziale in the National Gallery, in which the interior of S. Mark's figures as the temple. In Fig. 20 we give a restoration of fragments of a beautiful early Christian bowl-shaped lamp bearing a votive inscription figured by Rossi. On Mount Athos Dr. Covel noticed a lamp of beaten gold set with jewels.

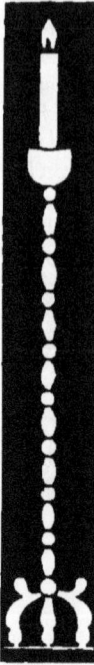

Fig. 21.
Sixth-century
Candlestick.

The treasury of S. Mark's probably still contains lamps which hung in S. Sophia : one of especial beauty is a glass bowl with circles cut on the outside and attached to a metal rim on which is inscribed in Greek, "St. Panteleon, succour thy servant Zacchariah, Archbishop of Iberia, Amen."[1]

In illustration of the tree-like candelabra which stood above the beam of the iconastasis, and round the ambo, we may mention the well-known classical examples. A lamp-bearer in the museum at Brussels is described as "an *arbuste* of considerable size and irregular trunk and branches with lamps suspended from the extremities of its boughs."

[1] For this and other lamps see especially *La Messe* and *Il Tesoro*.

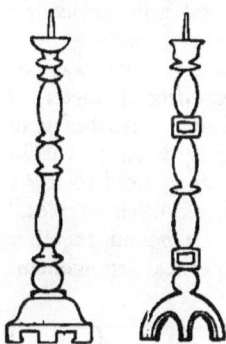

FIG. 22.—Candlesticks.

Anastasius mentions a "tree of bronze with candlesticks to the number of fifty in which were placed wax candles, thirty-six lamps as well hung from the boughs." Paulinus also speaks of hanging candelabra at Nola "with branches like a vine bearing little glass cups which resembled burning fruit ; when they were lighted it was like the sudden burst into life of spring flowers."

Besides all these oil lamps there would have been a great number of standing candlesticks in the sanctuary. The Anonymous speaks of some the height of a man. One constant type is represented in Fig. 21 ; this is inlaid in mother-of-pearl on the apse walls at Parenzo, and is of Justinian's time. Fig. 22 shows two others from the *Menologium*. Wax candles, which are frequently mentioned, were patterned and coloured.

The miracle of the moving cross of lights mentioned by Anthony reminds us of a remarkable custom in regard to the great coronas of lights in Byzantine churches which is observed on Mount Athos, and also at Sinai, and is probably ancient. A part of the great festival service at Vatopedi consists in singing the *Polyeleos*. "When the last of the multitude of candles had been lighted in the great coronas under the domes, the monks fetched long poles, with which they pushed out the candelabra to the full extent that their suspending chains permitted and then let them go, the result being that in a few minutes the whole church was filled with slowly swinging lights." [1]

The method of lighting described by the Silentiary has not changed in the unchanging East. S. Sophia is still lighted by a myriad little lamps arranged in rows, or suspended in circles. The single lamp is a small glass vessel of oil on which floats the wick ; the two typical forms being like a bowl or an elongated tumbler. These cups are hung by three chains,

[1] A. Riley, *Mountain of the Monks.*

or inserted in a ring, at the end of a metal arm, projecting
from the wall or from the rim of a suspended circle.

Up to the time of Fossati's restoration there was an
immense polygon of probably some sixty feet diameter of
iron rods suspended from the dome.   Grelot[1] described it in
1680 as a large circle of iron rods hanging down to within
eight or ten feet of the pavement and having fixed to it "a
prodigious number of lamps, ostrich eggs, and other baubles."
In the mosque of Achmet, several rings are bound together
by straight rods, making overhead a geometrical arrangement

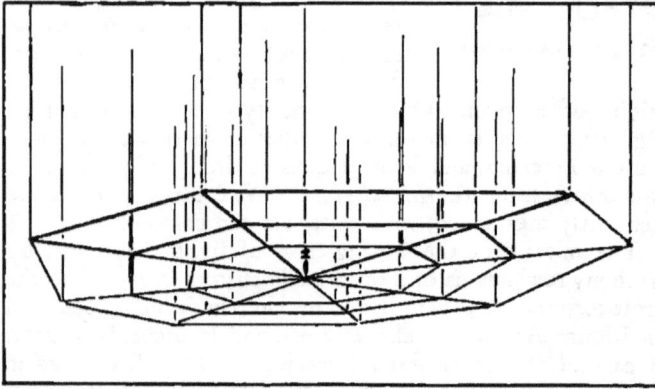

FIG. 23.—Hanging Rods for Lamps in S. Sophia until 1850.

of bars, from which the lamps are suspended ; although
these are all Turkish, the system remained from Byzantine
times.   Fig. 23 is re-drawn from Fossati.   (*Aya Sophia*,
Constantinople, 1852.)   One of the most beautiful methods
is that of suspending the lamps to long straight iron bars
running the whole length of the building as at S. John
Studius.

In the mosque of Damascus, before the recent fire, there
were hanging assemblages of circles one above another somewhat similar we may suppose to the trees of the poet.   At

[1] P. 154.

Salonica a network of lamps which hangs almost like a curtain before the bema of S. Demetrius may illustrate the "nets," if nets there were. During Ramazan festoons of lamps are hung from minaret to minaret arranged in inscriptions; in 1676 Dr. Covel of Cambridge saw illuminations before the Sultan at Adrianople which represented "castles, mosques, peacocks, Turkish writings, &c., extremely pleasant and wonderful to behold." These were formed by lamps hung to light frames; the method was probably derived from Byzantine illuminations such as the fireworks mentioned as being exhibited in the Hippodrome.

The four marble pillars that stand up out of the parapet at the western gallery of S. Sophia (Fig. 41) must always have carried lights on metal branches at the top, much as at present; and the long metal stakes with hook ends, that project from the first cornice at the angles of the exedras, and from which chandeliers hang, are possibly original in some cases.

The multiplication of small lights is the most brilliant system of illumination, for not only is there light everywhere but flame, and hence no shadows. Whoever sees the great church lighted for the solemn services of Ramazan, when, according to Fossati, "six thousand lamps are suspended at various heights," may imagine the splendour of the lighted interior in Byzantine times. When, after one of the services, the lamplighters walked round and extinguished the lamps with a whisk from long fan-shaped brooms, we saw the need of the passages above the different cornices; and leaving Constantinople one April evening, as we slowly wound round the point, while the circle of windows in the lighted dome seemed to hang above the city, we realised that it was no idle saying of the poet's that the mariner guided his laden vessel "by the divine light of the church itself."

CHAPTER VII

LATER HISTORY AND LEGENDS

§ I. HISTORY.

FROM the date of the completion of Justinian's restored church it has had to withstand the frequent earthquake shocks which, as we have so recently seen, devastate the city from time to time Von Hammer [1] calculates, from the accounts of the Byzantine historians, that from the beginning of the seventh to the middle of the fifteenth century there were twenty-three severe earthquakes, one of which, in 1033, lasted intermittently for 140 days. In the Turkish records, from 1511 to 1765, ten earthquakes are mentioned. It is remarkable that in this length of time the delicately poised construction of the church should only have required restorations which are relatively unimportant.

It is difficult to say how far the church suffered during the struggles about image worship, which raged for more than a century. The question will be considered more fully when we deal with the mosaics of the vaults. The restoration of images was finally accomplished in 842,[2] by Theodora and Michael.

A belfry was built in the centre of the west front about the year 865 : [3] and the eastern walk of the atrium was probably transformed into an exonarthex at the same time.

---

[1] *Constantinopolis und aer Bosporus*, vol. i., pp. 36-44.
[2] The images were restored in S. Sophia on the 19th of February. Pagi. Critica in *Universos Annales Baronii*, vol. iii., p. 587.
[3] Goar's *Euchologium*, 1647, p. 560.

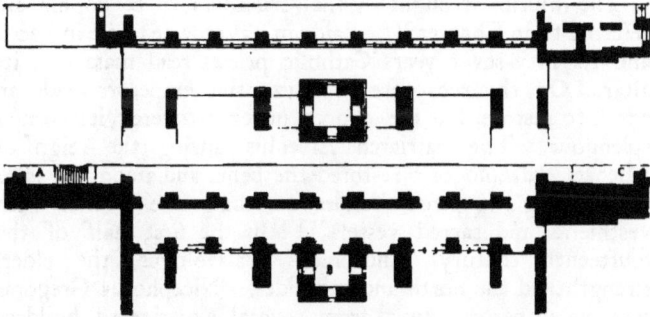

FIG. 24.—Plans of Additions to West End.   A and C North and South
Porches ; B Belfry.

The first regular restoration was also undertaken in the
second half of the ninth century, under Basil the Macedonian : " For the wide and lofty western arch of the great
church called S. Sophia was showing rents and threatening to
fall.   With the help of the workmen he girded it round and
rebuilt it, so that it was safe and strong.   And on it he
figured the Virgin with her Child on her arms, and Peter
and Paul, the chief of the apostles, on either side." [1]

The north and south porches and great lateral stairways,
which injuriously altered the exterior, must also have been
built by Michael or Basil, as we find them mentioned in the
Book of Ceremonies.

In October 975 an earthquake caused the " hemisphere
with the western arch (*apsis*) to fall." [2]   They were restored
again by the same emperor in six years : he spent, Scylitzes
says, " on the machines for mounting for the workmen to
stand on, and for raising the scaffolding, to build what was
fallen ; ten centenaria of gold." [3]   According to Glycas,
Romanus Argyrus (1028) beautified the capitals ; Scylitzes
also says this emperor " made bright with silver and gold
both the capitals of the great church and of our Lady of
Blachernae." [4]

[1] Cons. Porph. *Life of Basil*, ch. 79.
[2] *Leo Diaconus*, ed. Bonn, p. 176.
[3] Du Cange, *S. Sophia*, § 35.   [4] Paspates, *Byzantinae Meletae*.

The injuries wrought by the Crusaders to S. Sophia are
referred to in Chapter V. Baldwin was crowned here in 1204,
and for fifty-seven years Catholic priests read masses at its
altar. On the recapture the Byzantine emperors made an
effort to restore, but the church never recovered its former
splendour. The patriarch Arsenius during the reign of
Michael Palaeologos " restored the bema and ambo and solea
at the king's expense, besides enriching the church with
vestments and sacred vessels."[1] In the first half of the
fourteenth century, Andronicus Palaeologus, the elder,
strengthened the north and east sides. Nicephorus Gregoras
says the emperor " heard from several experienced builders
that in a short time the parts towards the north and east
would give way, and fall unless strengthened. And he
built pyramidal structures from the foundations and prevented the threatened destruction," but bricks and mosaic
continued to fall.[2] The pyramidal structures to the east
must be the four great sloping buttresses which stand over
the low attached buildings on that side ; they are shown on
Fossati's plan. Gregoras also inveighs against the Empress
Anna as having, in the reign of Cantacuzenus, robbed the
church of furniture and ornaments, and says that tyranny
and oppression were the chief causes of the destruction of
the church. Cantacuzenus, in his own history,[3] speaks of the
damage caused by an earthquake in 1346, when about a third
of the roof fell, destroying " the great stoa by the side of the
bema " (perhaps the iconostasis). This is also referred to by
Gregoras, " the easternmost of the four arches which rival
heaven fell, dragging with it the part of the house which
rested on it. The hidden beauty of the bema was destroyed
as well as its ornaments of sacred icons."[4] The stoa and bema
were restored by the Empress Anna, the wife of Andronicus
Palaeologos, Phaceolatus being prefect of the works, but the
upper parts with the roof had to wait until the accession of
Cantacuzenus in 1347. He restored the decoration both in
marble and mosaic, a work which John Palaeologus finished.

[1] *Pachymeres*, ed. Bonn, i., p. 172.
[2] *Hist. Byzan.*, ed. Bonn, p. 273.
[3] Ed. Bonn, lib. iv., p. 29.   [4] Nicephorus Gregoras, p. 749.

Both emperors were helped "by one Astras, in many things a clever man, but especially in building, and by John, surnamed Peralta, one of the Latin subjects of the emperor." [1]

The church was necessarily much neglected in the last days of the Empire. Clavijo, who gave a careful account of the church in 1403 (see Chapter IX.), says "the outer gates by which the church was approached were broken and fallen." He notes that "the Greeks do not call Constantinople as we name it, but speak of it as *Escomboli*." This clearly proves that the derivation of the Turkish name Istambul from εἰς τὴν πόλιν, "to the city," is correct.[2]

The Florentine Bondelmontius, who was there in 1422, says that "only the dome of the church remained, as everything is fallen down and in ruins." This exaggeration is probably explained by a story given by the Chevalier Bertrandon de la Brocquière, who visited the city eleven years later, in the course of his remarkable ride from Damascus to Dijon along the route of the present Oriental express. He attended service in the church, and writes :—"There the patriarch resides, with others of the rank of canons. It is situated near the eastern point, is of a circular shape, and formed of three different parts, one subterranean, another above the ground, and a third over that. Formerly it was surrounded by cloisters, and was, it was said, three miles in circumference.[3] It is now of smaller extent, and only three cloisters remain, all paved and inlaid with squares of white marble, and ornamented with large columns of various colours. The gates are remarkable for their breadth and height, and are of bronze." [4] The visit of the Chevalier Bertrandon brings us within twenty years of the fall of the great city.

The incidents of the later years of the empire, the vain efforts to get help from Europe, and the schemes for uniting the Greek and Latin churches, are described by Chedomil

---

[1] Cantacuz., ed. Bonn, p. 30.
[2] Compare Tozer's *Turkey*, i. 97. He says Constantinople is still constantly called "the City" all over the Levant.
[3] Gyllius reports a similar story.
[4] Wright's *Early Travels in Palestine*.

Mijatovich.[1] In the year before the Fall the negotiations
with the West had proceeded so far, that, on the 12th of
December 1452, a *Te Deum* after the Latin rite was sung by
Cardinal Isidore in S. Sophia, but this did not meet with
favour from the populace. Ducas speaks of the church after
that time as being nothing better than a Jewish synagogue or
heathen temple. Five months later, on the 28th of May
1453, the last Christian service was held within its walls.
At the vesper service on that solemn evening, the emperor,
after praying with great fervour, left his imperial chair, and,
approaching the iconostasis, prostrated himself before the
figures of Christ and the Madonna on either side of the
great central door. He then asked for pardon from any
whom he might have offended, and the ritual proceeded.

On the morrow at the first capture of the city the Janis-
saries rushed to the great church, which they conceived was
filled with gold, silver, and precious stones. They found the
doors fastened, but broke them open, and at once began to
pillage. The sultan as soon as possible rode to S. Sophia.
Dismounting on the threshold, with the mystic symbolism of
an Oriental, he stooped down, and, collecting some earth, let
it fall on his turbaned head, as an act of humiliation. Then
he entered the edifice, but stopped in the doorway some
moments, and gazed in silence before him.

"He saw a Turk breaking the floor with an axe.
'Wherefore dost thou that?' inquired the conqueror. 'For
the faith,' replied the soldier. Mahomet in an impulse of
anger struck him, saying, 'Ye have got enough by pillaging,
and enslaving the city, the buildings are mine.' "

A letter to Pope Nicholas V., written in 1453, describes
how "the profane heathen broke into the marvellous temple
of S. Sophia, unsurpassed by Solomon's ; they reverenced not
the sacred images, nay, rather broke them in pieces; they put
out the eyes of the priests, scattered the relics of the saints,
and seized on the gold and silver." [2]

Ducas, who died eleven years after the Fall, bewails " the
Great Church, a new Sion which has now become an altar of

---

[1] "Constantine, the last emperor of the Greeks."
[2] Brit. Mus. MSS. Add. 6,417.

the heathen, and is called the house of Mahomet." "The dogs hewed down the holy ikons, tore off the ornaments, the chains, the napkins, and the coverings of the holy table. Some of the lamps they destroyed, and others they carried away. They stole the sacred vessels from the skeuophylakium. Everything made of silver and gold or other precious materials was taken away, and the church was left naked and desolate as it had never been before."

With the exception of the removal of much of the treasure, the church did not immediately suffer great harm from its new masters.

On the outside however the destruction of many of the low attached chambers, and the addition of the minarets, have very much changed its appearance. The first minaret, which was indeed the first in Constantinople, was built at the south-east corner by Mahomet the Conqueror. Selim II., who reigned from 1566 to 1574, built the second at the north-east corner, and also restored the eastern apse which had been again damaged by an earthquake : Amurath III. erected the last two minarets at the western corners.[1]

"The description of the church of S. Sophia as it now appears," which forms one of the chapters in Gyllius' († 1555) *Topography of Constantinople*, describes the church before the addition of these three last minarets. It is interesting to note that he remarks how little the building had been altered, "and it is despoiled of nothing, except a little of the metal work [mosaic ?] which shows itself in great abundance through the whole church. The Sanctum Sanctorum, formerly holy and unpolluted, into which the priests only were suffered to enter, is still standing, though there is nothing remaining of the jewels and precious stones which adorned it, these having been plundered by its sacrilegious enemies." This is later supported by Grelot,[2] who writes, "It is decorated with everything that human industry and skill could devise to render the work absolutely perfect. . . . . I say nothing about the beautiful pictures, the faces of which have been destroyed by the Turks." It is clear

[1] Salzenberg, *Altchristliche Baudenkmale.*
[2] *Relation d'un Voyage de Constantinople*, 1680.

from Tournefort (1702) and Lady Mary Montagu (1717)
that the mosaics were not wholly obliterated ; the latter writes,
"the figures were in no other way defaced but by the decays
of time : for it is absolutely false that the Turks defaced all
the images they found in the city." On the other hand, an
Italian MS. description of S. Sophia in the British Museum,
written in 1611, says, "The Turks took away all the
beautiful work and covered everything with whitewash."[1] It
is evident from Dr. Covel's MS., quoted later, that much
was destroyed, defaced, and plastered over. Dr. Walsh tells
us that one of the smaller vaults fell in about 1820, scattering
its mosaic over the floor.

§ II. THE ANONYMOUS ACCOUNT.

We must now examine the description of the church by
the writer generally called the Anonymous of Combefis
(otherwise of Banduri or Lambecius). Codinus, who is
believed to have died soon after the capture of Constantinople
by the Turks, has so closely copied the Anonymous that
the accounts differ only in a few minor particulars. Combefis
says that the text of the Anonymous was collated by
Lambecius, "who produced it from the royal archives" with
the *Chronography of the Logothetae*, a tenth-century work
to which the same account is added as a separate treatise.
Labarte however considers that it was written in the eleventh
century : Choisy assigns it to the fourteenth, a view with
which we are inclined to agree ; but in any case we cannot
think it earlier than the twelfth century.

The description by Paulus is so precisely accurate where
we can—as is so largely the case—check it by the existing
work, that there cannot be a doubt of his entire accuracy.
With the Anonymous this is not so ; and it must first of
all be borne in mind that he professes not to write of the
church as he saw it, but to celebrate its splendour when first
completed by Justinian ; in this his account differs entirely
from the Silentiary's, which there is no sign to show that he

[1] MS. Harl., 3,408.

had ever read. The Anonymous has been very largely used by scholars of the ability of Labarte and Bayet, but we believe him to be entirely unreliable where he speaks of the former state of the church. He simply gathers the legends which had grown up, because facts were forgotten, and enumerates the relics.

"The great church,[1] known as S. Sophia [formerly a place of heathen worship—Codinus], was first built of an oblong (*dromica*) form, like those of S. Andronicus and S. Acacius. On its completion it was adorned with many statues. This building lasted seventy-four years. But in the reign of Theodosius the Great, at the time of the second synod of Constantinople, an Arian uproar arose, during which the roof of the church was destroyed by fire. The most holy patriarch Nectarius took up his office at S. Irene, a church which was also built by Constantine. Then for two [Codinus and Glycas say sixteen] years S. Sophia was without a roof, until Theodosius, with Rufinus as his master workman (*magistros*), covered it with cylindrical vaults. After this it remained unhurt for thirty-nine years, making altogether eighty-five years (*sic*) from the time of Constantine, until the fifth year of Justinian's reign. This was after the massacre in the Circus, in which thirty-five thousand men were killed, when a faction elected Hypatius emperor. However, in the fifth year of Justinian's reign, the Most High God put it into his mind that he should build a temple to surpass all that had ever been built from the time of Adam.

"He wrote therefore to the strategi, toparchs, judges, and satraps of the different provinces, that with all zeal they should look for materials—columns, piers, panels, and lattice-doors—everything in fact that would be useful for building. Obeying the emperor's letter, they quickly sent all that could be found from the shrines of the pagan idols, from baths, and private houses, from every province of east, west, north, and south, and from all the islands.

[1] From *Originum Rerumque Constantinopolitarium, variis auctoribus, manipulus*, F. Franciscus Combefis, Paris, 1664. The same anonymous description is also given by Banduri, *Imperium Orientale*, ed. 1711, vol. i.

K

"Eight porphyry columns from Rome, which, according
to Plutarch, Justinian's secretary, a widow Marcia had
received as dowry, were transmitted to Constantinople.
They had formerly stood in a temple of the Sun built by
Valerian, who surrendered himself to the Persians. Eight
others of green, of marvellous beauty, were quarried and
sent from Ephesus by the praetor Constantine. The Marcia,
whom I have just mentioned, wrote to the emperor as
follows : ' I send thee, master, eight columns from Rome
of equal length and size, and the same weight, for the
safety of my soul.'

"Of the other columns some were brought from Cyzicus,
some from the Troad, others from the Cyclades and Athens.
And when sufficient was collected for the work seven and
a half years had been spent. Then in the twelfth year of
Justinian's reign, the church built by Constantine was
destroyed with the foundations ; the old materials were put
aside, as a sufficient amount of fresh had been prepared ;
and Justinian began to buy up the neighbouring houses.
The first of these was one belonging to a widow named
Anna, of which the price was estimated at eighty-five librae.
She was however unwilling to sell it to the emperor, and
refused to give it up under five hundred librae ; nor did the
emperor gain his purpose by sending the nobles of the court
to win her over. He finally went himself and begged her
to sell her house at any price. But when she saw him as a
suppliant, she fell at his feet, saying, ' Lord and King, I can
accept no moneys for my house from thee ; I ask only that
I may obtain reward in the day of judgment, and that I
may be buried in a tomb near the future church, so that the
memory of my gift may live for ever.' The emperor
promised that when the church was finished she should be
buried there, for the land which she had given up, that the
memory of it might live for ever. The part which she gave
to the great church is that now occupied by the skeuophylakium, and the chapel (naos) of S. Peter.

"Then the part which is occupied by the Holy Well, and
all about the thysiasterium, and the place of the ambo, and
the middle of the nave, was the house of a certain eunuch,

Antiochus, which was valued at thirty-eight librae. He was offended because the emperor had not offered him a proper price for it. Now the emperor was much distressed, wondering what to do. But the Magister Strategius—a guardian of the treasures, the adopted brother of the emperor—promised that the emperor should gain his point by a little guile, and that the other should sell his house. Now this Antiochus was an eager frequenter of the Circus, and especially favoured the blue faction. When the games were about to be given, he was arrested and imprisoned in the Praetorian prison. Then Antiochus called out from the prison that if he could only witness the games he would do whatever the emperor wished. He was then led by the emperor's orders to his empty seat, and made to sell his house before the games commenced, the Quaestor and the whole Senate being witness. Now there used to be the custom, that as soon as the emperor ascended to his seat the charioteers should begin, but because they stopped then, until the eunuch had accomplished his deed of sale, even to the present day the chariots for the races are accustomed to enter at a slow trot.

" The whole of the right-hand part of the Gynaeceum[1] up to the column of S. Basil, and some portion of the nave, was the house of an eunuch, Chariton, nicknamed Chenopolus, who sold it as a favour for double its value, which was twelve librae.

" The left part of the Gynaeceum[1] up to the column of S. Gregory Thaumaturgus was the house of one Xenophon, a cobbler. When they wanted to buy this house, besides asking twice the value, which was fourteen librae, he also demanded that, on the day of the games, the four chariot-eers of the four factions should do obeisance to him as well as to the emperor. The emperor decreed that it should be done as he had asked, but made him a laughing-stock for ever. For on the day of the games he was set midway in the boundaries, so that the charioteers, by way of joke, bowed to his back before beginning their courses, and so it

---

[1] Evidently meant for lower aisles.

is still done, and the man is styled 'Chief of those below.'
He wears a white chlamys, woven with byssus.

"On the area of the naos, the four nartheces, the louter,
and the parts adjacent, was the house of Damianus, a noble
of Seleucia, the value of which he estimated at ninety librae,
and gladly gave to the emperor.

"Now Justinian, when he had measured out the site, and
found a stone to act as centre, from the thysiasterium as far
as the lower [western] apse, laid the foundations of the
great dome in circle-wise.   Now from the apses right away
to the most outside narthex, the foundations were laid in
marshy and spongy ground.   And when it had been begun,
he urged Eutychius the patriarch to offer up prayers to God
for its safe building, and then, taking with his own hands
lime and stone, giving thanks to God, he himself laid the
first stone in its place.   Now before the church was built
he constructed the oratory of S. John the Precursor with a
gilt vault, and various ornamentations of precious stones.
This is generally call the Baptistery, and is situated near the
Horologium.   He built at the same time the adjacent
portion of the Metatorium, that he might frequently rest
there with his court, and refresh himself with food.   Then
also he built the whole of the portico, which leads from the
palace up to the Great Church, so that, as often as he liked,
he might cross over and devote his time to the building,
without being seen by any one.   There were one hundred
master workmen, and each had a band of a hundred men
under him, making ten thousand men altogether.   Fifty
bands took one side, and fifty the other ; and by the
emulation between them, the work quickly progressed.

"The form of the church was shown to the emperor in a
dream by an angel.   And the first Deviser (*mechanikos*) of
the builders was skilful and full of sound wisdom, and well
versed in building churches.   Barley was put into cooking
pots, and its decoction, instead of water, was mingled with
unslaked lime (*asbestos*) and tiles [crushed].   The mixture,
when warm, became viscous and sticky.   At the same time
they cut slips off willow trees, which were cast into the
cooking pots with the barley ; they then made solid masses,

having a length of over fifty feet, and fifty feet broad, and twenty feet deep, and placed them in the foundations. They were put there, not hot, nor yet quite cold, that so they might bind better, and above these masses they placed large square stones.

"When the foundations had arisen from the earth two cubits, they had spent four hundred and fifty-two miliarisia of gold. Money was brought daily from the palace, and placed in the Horologium, and each of those who carried stone received a piece of silver, lest any slackness should come upon them, or they should be tempted to complain. Some of them, when carrying stone, gave way under the weight, and fell head foremost and were hurt. Strategius, whom I have mentioned, distributed the wages : he was a Count of the royal treasury, and foster-brother of Justinian.

" Now when the piers (*pinsoi*) had been finished, and the great columns, both those from Rome and the green ones, had been put in their position, the emperor left his noon-day sleep and devoted himself to the work, and inspected, with Troilus, a count of the household, all the polishers (*lithoxooi*), stonecutters (*laotomoi*), carpenters (*tektonikoi*), and labourers (*oikodomoi*), promising them each week a nummus more, or as much as each might ask, above their fixed wages. He used to come to see how the work was proceeding, clad in a white linen garment, his head covered with a kerchief, and holding a stick in his hand.

"And when they had raised the vaults (*apsides*) of the upper floor, those on the right and on the left, and had covered over these vaults, the emperor decreed that no miliarisia should be carried from the palace on Sundays. Now it was the third hour of the day, and Strategius ordered the men to go to their dinners. As Ignatius, the first *mechanikos* of the builders whom I have mentioned above, came down, he left his son on the right-hand side of the upper floor, where he had been working, with strict orders to watch the workmen's tools. He was a boy of about fourteen. As he was sitting there, a eunuch, clad in shining garments, and fair to look upon, like one sent from

the palace, appeared to him and said, 'What is the reason
why the workmen do not quickly finish the work of God,
but have left it and gone to eat?' To him the boy
answered, 'At the earliest hour, my lord, they will be
here.' But he cried, 'Go quickly and bring them.'
When the boy said that he was not to leave, lest the
tools should disappear, the eunuch said, 'Go quickly and
summon them here, for I swear to thee, my son, by the
Holy Wisdom, whose temple is now being built, I will not
depart, since, by the command of the Word of God, I am to
minister and guard here until you return.' When he heard
this, the boy quickly set out, leaving the angel of God as
guard. And when he had got down, and gone to his father
and the rest, he related everything in order; then the father
took his son and led him to the emperor's table. For the
emperor was then dining in the oratory of St. John the
Precursor, by the Horologium. When he heard the story,
he summoned all his eunuchs, and showed each in turn to
the boy. Then the boy calling out that he saw none like
the one that had appeared, the emperor knew that it was an
angel of the Lord who had addressed the boy, and this was
made more clear, as the boy said that he was clothed in a
white robe, his eyes glittering like fire; then the emperor
praised God, saying, 'God has accepted my temple.' And
as he had been wondering what name to call it, he named
it S. Sophia, according to interpretation 'Word of God.'
And the emperor took counsel with himself and said, 'I
will not allow the boy to return, so that the angel may
guard it for ever, as he promised by his oath. For if the
boy return, the angel will depart.' Having consulted with
the principal senators and the bishops, the emperor commanded that the boy should not be sent back to the temple,
so that, by the grace of God, it should have a guardian till
the end of the world. And then the emperor loaded the
boy with gifts and honours, and, with the consent of his
father, sent him to the Cyclades. Now the conversation of
the angel with the boy happened on the right-hand side of
the pier of the upper arch, as one ascends towards the dome.
[Codinus says, "near the Syllagonum," for this it has

been suggested to read Syllagoeum, or "the place of the council"].

"When the workmen had continued the work up to the second catechumena, and the upper columns and arches were built, and they were roofing the adjacent parts, the emperor began to be anxious for want of funds. But as he was standing in the upper part of an arch, as they were about to begin the dome, at the hour of the Sabbath just before dinner, an eunuch appeared to him, clad in white, and said, 'Why are you distressed for money? To-morrow bid some of your nobles to come, and they shall have as much gold as they wish.' On the following day the eunuch came and showed himself to the emperor. The emperor sent to follow him Strategius, and Basilides the quaestor, and Theodorus the patrician, and Colocyns who was a praefect, besides fifty servants, twenty mules, and twenty paniers. With all these he marched out of the Golden Gate. And when they had come to the Tribunalium, there seemed to those who were sent to be built there palaces of stupendous beauty. But when they had dismounted, the eunuch bade them ascend a wonderful stair, and then, producing a splendid gold key, he opened the door of a room, and, as Strategius says, the whole floor was heaped with gold coins. Taking a shovel, the eunuch filled each panier with four hundred pounds of gold, amounting altogether to eight thousand, and with these he sent them back to the emperor ; and having closed up the room with the key, he said to them, 'Take the gold to the emperor, and bid him spend it on the work.' The eunuch left them there, and they came and showed the emperor the gold they had received. He was astonished, and asked them where they had been, and where the eunuch dwelt. They told him all in order. and how the wealth of gold was spread on the floor of the room. The emperor hoped that the eunuch would return, but as he was disappointed he sent a slave to the place. When the slave had found the place where the palace had been, and saw that there were no houses there, he returned, and told all to the emperor. He was then astonished, but understanding how it was, said, 'Truly this is a miracle as all may see ;' and he praised God.

"Now when they were going to build the thysiasterium
and let in the light through glass windows, the Deviser
(*mechanikos*) suggested that the apsoid (*muax*) should have
one light.   Then he changed his mind, and suggested that
it should have two, so that it should not be heavy, because
no wooden ties (*ikriomata*) were placed there as in the
narthex, and on the sides of the church.   But the rest of the
craftsmen were opposed, saying that one arch (*kamara*) would
light the holy place.   Then the chief builder (*protooikodomos*)
was at a loss what to do, because the emperor said at one
time that there should be one arch (*apsis*), and at another
time two.   Whilst the master (*maistor*) was thus pondering
and anxious, on the fourth day, at the fifth hour, appeared
an angel of the Lord, like the emperor, with royal robes and
red shoes, and said to the craftsman.   ' I will that there be a
triple light, and that the conch be made with three windows,[1]
in the name of the Father, the Son, and the Holy Ghost.'
He then disappeared quickly.   Then the master, struck with
wonder, rushed to the palace, and said to the emperor, ' You
keep not to your word.   Until to-day you wanted one
window, and then two, to light the bema ; but now, when
the work is all but finished, you come to me and say, three
windows shall light the bema, as a symbol of the Trinity.'
Now the emperor knew that day that he had not left the
palace, and he recognised that an angel of the Lord had
spoken.   He said, ' As I have bidden thee, so do.'
    "All the piers (*pessoi*) inside and outside were made
strong by iron bars (*mochloi*), so that they were bound
together, and made immovable ; the joints of the piers
were made with oil and *asbestos ;* and upon them was placed
a plating of many marbles (*orthomarmarosis*).
    " The emperor sent Troilus the Cubicular, Thedosius the
Prefect, and Basilides the Quaestor, to Rhodes to have bricks
(*besala*) of Rhodian clay, made all equal in weight and
length, with the words engraved on them, ' God is in the
midst of her, therefore shall she not be moved ; God shall
help her, and that right early.'[2]   And they sent bricks of

----

[1] If this interpretation can be accepted for στοαί.
[2] Bricks stamped with long inscriptions of this kind were frequently
used : one from Sirmium is mentioned in *Byzantinische Zeitschrift* for

measured sizes to the emperor, twelve of them weigh one of
ours ; for the clay is light, spongy, fine, and white ; hence
arose the common idea that the dome is built of pumice
stone (*kiserion*) ; but this is not so, though it is light and of
a white colour.

"Thus the four great arches were built; and when they had
been raised to the level of the dome (*troulos*), on the completion of every twelfth course, prayers were uttered for the
church, and relics of the saints built in.   Thus arose the
building ; it was then adorned with marble and covered
with mosaic.   And into the piers, arcades, and larger
columns they placed relics of the saints.   And when the
marble plating had been finished, they applied gold to the
margins of the slabs, and to the capitals of the columns.
And the carved work, and the ornaments of the upper
galleries, both of the parts with two stories, and with
three (*diorophoi* and *triorophoi*), were all covered with pure
gold.   The thickness of the gold plating (*petalos*) was two
inches.[1]

"But all the vaults (*orophoi*) of·the upper galleries, of the
parts with two stories on the sides, and the vaulting of the
nave, and of the parts adjacent, and of the four nartheces,
he gilded with glass mosaic.   He gilded even the proaulia,
with their upper chambers, and columns, and marble slabs.

"The floor of the nave was adorned with various marbles,
both with the Roman of a rue-green colour and others of a
rosy red ; and these were all laid down and polished.   The
walls outside and all round were covered with large and
valuable stones.

"The thysiasterium was of shining silver, the barrier
(*stethea*), and its large columns, with the doors, were all of
silver.   All the silver was dipped in gold.   Four tables were
set up in the thysiasterium supported on columns, and these
were gilt.   The seven seats of the priests, on which they sat
on either side, with the throne of the patriarch, and the four

1894, p. 222 : "O Lord Christ, help this city, keep off the Avars and
guard Romania and him who writes this, Amen."
    [1] This may mean the thickness of the marble wall lining in some
places gilt—if it has a meaning.

columns, were all gilded. And it was forbidden to go up
into the holy place, the *Kuklios*, also called the Holy of
Holies, which is above the steps.

" He set up also large columns of silver-gilt, and the lilies
with the ciborium. And the ciborium he made with silver
and nielloed (*arguroencauston*). Above the ciborium was a
globe of solid gold, weighing 118 pounds, and golden lilies,
weighing six pounds, and above them a golden cross, with
most precious and rare stones, weighing eighty pounds. Such
was the design he made.

"And as he wished to make the holy table more beautiful
than the rest, and more precious with gold, he collected
numerous craftsmen, and consulted with them. Their
opinion and advice was to cast into the melting pot
(*choneuterion*) gold, silver, stones of every kind, and pearls,
copper, electron, lead, tin, iron, glass, and every other
metallic substance. And they ground them all together and
formed them into masses (*olboi*), and poured them into the
pot ; and when it had been melted, they took it from the fire
and poured it out into a mould (*tupos*). Thus the holy table
was made. And it was then set up by the emperor on solid
columns of gold, studded with precious stones. And the
' sea ' (*thalassa*) of the holy table was ornamented with gold
and precious stones. Who can see the holy table without
being astonished ? and who can gaze at it on account of the
many glinting surfaces ? so that at one time it all appears of
gold, from another place all of silver, and in another of
glittering sapphire ; and altogether there are eighty-two
different colours of metals and stones and pearls.

"He made also, above and below, carved ivory doors overlaid with gold, to the number of 365. In the first entrance
into the louter he made the doors of electron ; doors also of
electron were in the narthex, two of them smaller than the
middle one, which was much larger, and of silver dipped in
gold (*chrusembaphos*). The architraves also were overlaid
with gold. Three of the doors inside, instead of being made
of new wood, were made of wood from the Ark. He wished
to make the pavement entirely of silver [Codinus says gold],
but his advisers dissuaded him, saying that in the future

poor emperors might have it taken up. And those who persuaded him were Maximian and Hierotheus, Athenian philosophers and astronomers, saying that in the latter days poorer rulers would come and take it all away. And following these counsels the thought was given up. And every day the emperor had 2,000 miliarisia put in a heap and mingled with earth ; and when work was finished, in the evening, the craftsmen dug out the mound and found the miliarisia, and this the emperor did that they might be eager for their work. And collecting the materials, as was said, took seven and a half years. But the completion of the temple, even with the crowd of workmen I have mentioned, all labouring with the greatest eagerness, took nine years two months.

" The ambo with the solea he paved with sardonyx, and inserted precious stones ; its columns were of solid gold, with carbuncles and crystals and sapphires ; and he overlaid the upper part of the solea richly with gold. The ambo had also a golden dome studded with pearls, lychnites, and emeralds.

" The gold cross of the ambo weighed 100 pounds. It had also seizae,[1] and lychnites, and was embroidered with pearls. And the ambo above had a hat-shaped covering (*petasion*), upon [2] supports (*stethea*).

"The top of the Holy Well was brought from Samaria. It was considered sacred, because Christ had sat on it, and talked to the woman. And the bronze trumpets, which stand by the Holy Well, were brought from Jericho ; they were those at whose blasts by angels the walls of Jericho fell down. The honoured Cross, to-day in the skeuophylakium, which was the measure of our Lord's height, was eagerly sought for in Jerusalem by the faithful and brought hither. And for this reason they surrounded it with silver, and all kinds of precious stones, and overlaid it with gold. And to this day it works healing wonders, and drives away diseases and demons. And in every column [of the church] both above and below is placed one sacred relic.

[1] σειζαί, a network, studded with jewels, suspended from processional crosses, and from the sides of crowns, see Fig. 15.
[2] Reading ἐπί for ἀντί.

" He made also golden vessels for the twelve solemn feasts, according to the sacred Gospels: basins (*cherniboxeses*), ewers (*orkioloi*), chalices (*diskopoteria*), and patens (*diskoi*) ; they were all of solid gold, set with precious stones and pearls. And the number of the sacred vessels was 1,000 ; altarcloths (*endutai*), with rows of jewels, 300 ; crowns, 100. Every festal day had its own chalice covering (*poterokalumma*). There were paten covers (*diskokalummata*) of gold, with pearls and precious stones, to the number of 1,000 ; four-and-twenty gospels, each worth two centenaria ; thirty-six censers of solid gold with precious stones ; 300 lamps (*luchnitai*) weighing forty pounds ; 6,000 candelabra (*polycandela*), and clustered lights [1] of solid gold, for the ambo, the bema, the two gynaecea, and the narthex.

" The revenues of 365 farms in Egypt, India, and all the East and West were devoted to the maintenance of the church.   For each holy day was set aside 1,000 measures of oil, 300 measures of wine, and 1,000 sacramental loaves. Similarly for the daily services, the clergy, including the lowest, numbered 1,000, with 100 singers divided into two for alternate weeks.   For the clergy there were cells round the building ; for the singers there were two monasteries.

" He made five gold crosses, each weighing 100 pounds, which were adorned with all kinds of precious stones, so that they were each valued at eight centenaria : also two candlesticks of gold incrusted with pearls and precious stones, valued at five centenaria, as well as two other large carved candelabra (*manoualia*) of gold ; these had golden feet, each worth 100 pounds, to stand below the golden candelabra. He made fifty others too, of silver, of the height of a man, to stand by the altar.   On the adornment of the ambo and solea was spent 100,000 pounds, which was the tribute levied by Constantine on Saroboris, King of the Persians, and on many others.   The whole church with the parts outside and around —with the exception of the vessels and ornaments, which were given by the emperor—cost 800,000 pounds.

" Now Justinian alone began and alone finished the church

---

[1] βοτρυιδόν, "like bunches of grapes."

with no other helping him, or even building a part of it. Its beauty is wonderful to behold ; all kinds of pearls glitter there like the sea, and one seems to see the ever-flowing waters of great rivers. Now the four boundaries [1] of the church he called after the rivers that flowed from Paradise, and he made a law that whosoever was excommunicated should stand there for his sins. And for the phiale in the centre he made twelve arcades, and lions belching out water for the people to wash in. On the right side, however, of the right-hand gynaeceum, he made a basin (*thalassa*) of one cubit for the water to come up in, and one flight of steps (*klimax*) for the priests to cross above the water. He placed too in the front of the basin (*dexamene*) an open tank for the rain (*ombusia*), and carved twelve lions, twelve pards, twelve deer, and eagles, and hares, and calves, and crows, twelve of each, and these spouted out the water for the use of the priests alone. The place was called the place of the lions (*leontarion*) and metatorion, because there was a golden couch there, that the emperor might rest on his way to the temple. But who can describe the comeliness and beauty of the temple, overlaid with resplendent gold from the crown to the pavement ?

" When the temple and the sacred vessels had been all completed, on the 24th of December he marched in solemn pomp from the palace to the Gate of the Augusteum, opening into the Horologium ; and he killed 1,000 oxen, 6,000 sheep, 500 deer, 1,000 pigs, 1,000 fowls, and gave them to the poor and needy, as well as 30,000 measures of wheat. And the distribution of these on that day took three hours, and then the emperor entered with the cross, and the patriarch Eutychius, and at the royal entrance he left the patriarch and walked alone to the ambo ; then, stretching out his hands to heaven, he cried, ' Glory be to God who has thought me worthy to finish this work. Solomon, I have surpassed thee.' And when the ceremony was over he distributed largesse, and with the help of Strategius gave away three hundred pounds of gold. But on the following day he solemnly opened the temple, and killed even more oxen, and

[1] φίνες, Graecised form of the Latin *fines*.

feasted every one for fifteen days until the feast of Epiphany,
praising God.   In such a way as this was the great work
completed.

"Now the new dome which was built by Justinian, and
the gorgeous and wonderful ambo, with the solea, and the
patterned pavement of the nave, lasted seventeen years.   But
after the death of Justinian, his nephew Justin succeeded, and
in the second year of his reign, and the fifth day, at the sixth
hour the dome fell, and destroyed the wonderful ambo with
the golden supports, and the solea, and all the sardonyx, and
choice pearls and sapphires.   But the arches, and the columns,
and the rest of the building remained unhurt.   Then the
emperor summoned the skilful mastermen, and inquired what
had caused the fall of the dome.   But they answered and
said to the king, 'Your uncle took away too quickly the
supports (*antinux*) for the dome, which were of wood, to
cover it with mosaic ; and made it too high so that it should
be seen from everywhere, and thus the craftsmen, by destroying the scaffolding (*skalosis*) before the foundations had been
sufficiently set, caused the fall of the dome.'   Thus spake
they to the king, and they added that if he wished to build
a dome like a hollow cymbal he should follow his uncle's
example, and send to Rhodes, and should order bricks made
in the same way and of the same weight as the previous
ones.   The emperor gave the order, and bricks were brought
from Rhodes, similar to the previous ones.   So once more
the dome was built, with fifteen fathoms taken from its
height, and formed like a drum so that it should not again
fall.   The supports were left for a year, until they knew that
the dome had become well set.   But the ambo and solea,
which they were not able to build of an equal magnificence
to the former ones, they are made of marble, with columns
covered with silver, and there was a silver inclosure (*stethos*),
round the solea.   But the dome of the ambo he did not
build again, frightened by the expense.   And for the pavement, as he was not able to find slabs of such beauty and size
as heretofore, he sent Manasses, a Patrician and Praepositus,
to Proconnesus, and marble was worked there as is seen
now, of a green colour, like rivers flowing into a sea.

" But when they wished to cut away the scaffolding of the dome, and to take away the timbers, they filled up the church with water to a height of five cubits, and threw down the beams into the water, and thus the lower parts of the walls were uninjured. And he covered it all with mosaic. Hence there are some who say that Justin, Justinian's nephew, built the church, but in this they lie. Let us rather give thanks to our God who has willed that the great structure should remain untouched, so that we can enter it, and give the praise that is due to Christ ; for He is worthy of all glory, honour, power, and worship, now and for ever, Amen."

§ III. LEGENDS

Many of the points in this celebration of the wonders of S. Sophia seem to be traceable to the writer's absorbing traditions of the work of Basil—who built like a goldsmith at his new church—into his account. In the destructive rapacity of the Crusaders and the interregnum that followed while they occupied S. Sophia we find such a satisfactory cause for this half-mythical retrospect undertaken in all good faith that we cannot think it was written until after the Frankish ascendency.

We need not suppose that the Anonymous invented even the wildest of these stories ; such stories grow up as a matter of course, and to-day various forms of some of them are told within the walls of many other buildings. The accounts given by the Russian pilgrims (see Chapter VI) agree so closely in many respects with the Anonymous description that we might think the writer had been their guide in the church. That the stories were widely told in Constantinople at this time is proved by the account of S. Sophia given by El Harawi, an Arab traveller, who visited the city in the thirteenth century. " Here is also Agia Sophia, the greatest church they have. I was told by Yakub Ibn Abd Allah that he had entered it : within are 360 doors. And they say one of the angels resides there ; round about this place they have made fences of gold, and the story they relate of him is very strange." [1]

[1] Quoted in Ibn Batuta, Orient. Trans. Socy.

This story of the angel recalls the Wingless Victory of the Athenian acropolis, but it is probably more closely related to the "Angels of the Churches" in the Revelation. An interesting reference to this thought is made by Palladius in his Life of Chrysostom. Before he left S. Sophia for ever the patriarch entered it saying, "Come let us pray and say farewell to the Angel of the Church;" but, adds his biographer, "the Angel departed with him." We give here an account of the church from a thirteenth-century English MS., in the British Museum, *Vit. A.* xx. 14, which refers to the more commonplace part of the story as told by the Anonymous. "That famous city is endowed with wonderful and inestimable wealth. In it may be seen the famous church Agia Sophia, that is the Holy Wisdom ; an angel of God appeared and taught the workmen as they were building. Underneath the church in its cisterns there is refreshing water, some of which is salt and some of it rain-water. The church below is borne on one hundred and seventy-three columns of marbles, and above on two hundred and forty-six. Round the choir from the top to the bottom it is covered with silver gilt. And this same choir has an altar 'starred' (*stellatum*) all over with most wonderful and precious stones. In the church are lamps of the purest silver and gold, and their number cannot be counted. The church is opened and closed by seven hundred and fifty-two double doors, and there are windows innumerable. There are seven hundred prebendary priests, of which three hundred and fifty take each week in turn. Now the Patriarch of Agia Sophia has in that city one hundred metropolitans and archbishops, and each metropolitan has seven suffragans in the same city."

The idea of competition with Solomon's Temple and the Tabernacle would be sure to suggest itself, and, once received, it would be justified by many assertions ; indeed a tendency to imitate the biblical accounts may be detected in the Anonymous author. For instance, we have Justinian's intention to cover the floor with silver, the description of the gold vessels for the altar, and the "sea" for the priests. Justinian's oft-quoted speech on entering the completed church may be assigned to this leading idea, which we find expressed as early as the sixth century by Corippus, the poet-bishop, who says, " Praise of the temple of Solomon is now silenced, and the Wonders of the World have to yield the pre-eminence. Two shrines founded by the wisdom of God have rivalled Heaven, one the sacred Temple, the other the splendid fane of S. Sophia, the Vestibule of the Divine Presence." [1] Glycas, who tells many of the stories given by the Anonymous, continues the idea further. Justinian, he says, set up a statue " representing Solomon as looking at the Great Church and gnashing his teeth with envy." [2]

In the Book of Proverbs we read, " Wisdom hath builded her house, she hath hewn out her seven pillars." This was also seized upon, and Michael Psellus speaks of S. Sophia as " the very beautiful temple, the incomparable home which the Divine Wisdom built in His own name and which He raised on seven pillars." [3] Modern writers, Tournefort, Von Hammer, &c., have delighted to point out that the church has 107 columns ; indeed, with a little humouring, 108 may be counted. The symmetrical number of the workmen employed according to the Anonymous may be matched in a legendary account of the building of S. Luke's, according to which there were twenty-four protomaistores, each of whom had twenty-four workmen under him.

The story of Justinian mixing money with the earth is parallel to the account, given by Vasari, of Brunelleschi's scheme for building the dome of S. Maria del Fiore in Florence. It is impossible that the church should have been flooded with water, as described by the Anonymous. There appears to be no basis for the supposition that the great dome was gilt outside. In the texts of Codinus the dome is said to be of ivy-wood (κισσηρίνος) : this is evidently some-body's misreading for pumice-stone (κισήριον).

The stones were actually supposed to be specifics for diseases by the Russian pilgrims and others. Clari the Knight of Amiens [4] (1200) speaks " of the Minster

---

[1] Du Cange, notes on Bondelmontius.
[2] Glycas, *Annalium, Pars V.*, ed. Bonn, p. 498.   [3] Du Cange, *op. cit.*
[4] Hopf, *Chroniques Gréco-Romanes*, Berlin, 1873, p. 67.

L

(*Moustier*) of S. Sophia, and the riches which were there.
. . . . There are vaults all round over the church, which
are carried on large columns, very rich ; for there is not a
column but is of jasper, or porphyry, or some precious
marble, and every column has a medicinal quality ; some
keep off *Mal des rains*, some *Mal du flanc*, and other
diseases : and there is nothing in this minster such as a
hinge (*gons*) or band (*verveles*) generally of iron, which is
not of silver."

Codinus concludes his account of the church with a story,
which may be classed with a large series, as " the gratitude
of employers to their architects ; " imprisoning and blinding
them, or cutting off their hands. It is in a sense one of the
truest of stories ! The master workman of the great church,
" Ignatius (*sic*), owing to the great favour which his work
won for him from the people, was shut up by the emperor in
his statue in the Augusteum." To parallel other tales this
must be the artist's own work which is the instrument of
his torture. Here he would have died of hunger had it not
been for his faithful wife, who threw to him a rope
besmeared with liquid pitch ; afterwards fire destroyed all
evidence of his flight.

We have also the customary tales of statues found in the
ground when the church was begun. Gyllius, quoting from
Suidas, says that Justinian discovered more than seventy
statues of the Greek deities, the figures of the twelve signs
of the zodiac, and eighty statues of Christian princes and
emperors. The travels that bear the name of Sir John
Mandeville relate that once when an emperor made a grave
in S. Sophia, " they found a body in the earth, and upon the
body lay a plate of gold, that said thus in Hebrew, Greek,
and Latin, ' Jesus Christ shall be born of the Virgin Mary,
and I believe in Him.' It was laid there 2,000 years before
the birth of Christ, and is still preserved in the treasury of
the church. And they say that it was Hermogenes, the
wise man."

The legends were not forgotten after the taking of the
church. Sandys, the English traveller, who was in Constantinople about 1610, tells us that " one of the doors was

famed to be the ark of Noe, and is therefore left bare in some places to be kissed by the devoted people," and "the total number of doors was said to be as many as the days of the year."

When this, the church of the world, fell into the hands of the Turks, many stories came to the West, or arose there without coming. The poetry of the Fall required the miraculous salvation of the priest celebrating mass, and the prophecy of his return as told by Theo. Gautier. It also required a massacre in the church, the riding in of the proud conqueror, and the mark of his blood-stained hand, which indeed is still pointed out some twenty feet above the pavement! Mijatovich, in his history of the last of the emperors, regards the massacre as unhistorical.

An English romance almost contemporary with the Fall tells us how the Turks took possession,

"For to let theyr hawkys fly
In the chirch of Saint Sofy."

CHAPTER VIII

SANCTA SOPHIA seems really to have been in a dangerous condition when, in 1847, the Sultan Abdul Mesjid began a much-needed work of reparation which was carried on under the guidance of the Italian architect Fossati, who appears to have taken great pains, and notwithstanding some alterations and "restorations" in the worst sense he deserves our gratitude for probably saving the building.   In the preface to his lithograph views published in London in 1852 he says, "The portions of the building that looked most threatening were reconstructed, and the lead roofs were repaired.   The dome was relieved of four heavy buttress arches, whose function was taken by a double ceincture of iron around its base.   Thirteen columns of the gynaeceum, which were inclining under the thrust of the great arches that support the dome, were put straight again."   The marble work of the interior was cleaned, and the gold mosaic vaults were cleared of the crust of limewash which concealed them. All representations of figures were however covered again. The sultan's tribune was built, Fossati says, "in the Byzantine style."   The walls outside, after being repaired, were covered with a coating of plaster on which red stripes were painted.

Since this time various remains of the Great Court, which existed as late as 1873, have entirely disappeared, and the broad bare space, in front of the exonarthex, has little now to recall the atrium with its fountain and quadriporticus.

All study of the church in its condition at that time must

be based on the exhaustive plates and text of Salzenberg.[1]
M. Texier had in 1834 made some drawings at Constantinople, which are now preserved in the library of the Royal
Institute of Architects ; and several coincidences seem to
point to Salzenberg's having had the use of Texier's ground
plan. In any case Texier was the first to make correct plans
including the upper floor, also the atrium, baptistery, and the
circular building at the north-east. As Salzenberg made full
use of the unique opportunity afforded by the scaffolding,
when the building was given over to the workmen, we have
thought it wise to give a condensed paraphrase of his
account where it is descriptive of the structure, even at
the risk of some repetition. Our remarks in other places
where they may overlap are the result of our own observation, from different points of view. The rest of this chapter
is an abridgment of Salzenberg's text and descriptive of his
plates, and we add nothing unless in notes or square brackets.

Design.—The exterior walls of the atrium, with several
entrances, were built of brick, but the inner sides had marble
columns between square brick piers, two columns to one pier.
These carried semicircular arches. The atrium walks, as
remains showed, were barrel-vaulted, and the vaults were
formerly covered with mosaic. The parts for which there was
evidence remaining are shown in darker hatching in Salzenberg's plate vi. The outer wall on the north side, with
several arched openings ; and traces of the western boundary
still existed.

The long vestibule in front of the narthex has groined
vaulting, and large windows in its west wall ; there are some
Turkish additions to this part. A door from each lateral
cloister, and two others from the open atrium, led into it.
On either side of the two doors from the court are strong
projecting piers, connected above by a wide arch, forming a
porch-like shelter over the doors. These four piers rise
above the roof of the vestibule.[2]

[1] *Altchristliche Baudenkmale von Constantinopel*, published by the
Prussian Government, Berlin 1854, with metrical version of the Silentiary's
poem by Dr. Körtum.

[2] Salzenberg here suggests that these formerly supported equestrian
statues. See his plates ix.-xii. and compare our fig. 29.

Double tiers of buttress arches spring from each of these piers to the west wall of the church. A close examination of the wall and piers led to the conviction that they are not contemporary with the church, but were built later, though partly of old material.[1] The upper cornices for instance differ. [Modifications here can be explained by removal of Bell Tower, see p. 194.] The piers were probably erected by Byzantine builders, to strengthen the western vault.

Five doors lead to the narthex, the windows of which are above the roof of the outer vestibule. The walls are covered with marble, and the vaulting with mosaic ; while the walls and ceiling of the exonarthex, are quite plain. Two other doors enter the narthex at its north and south ends, and nine lead from it into the church ; the large central entrance being the Royal Door.

The walls of the church form approximately a square, the length of which in the interior, exclusive of the apse, is 241 feet, and the breadth 224.[2]

The dome measures 100 feet across from the edge of the cornice, but above the cornice the vaulted space is 104 feet across ; it is 179 feet from the floor to the vertex, The dome rises above the square area on four huge arches, with a large semidome to the east and another to the west, each of which embraces three smaller spans. The lateral openings which thus pierce the east and western semidomes are covered by *conchs*, but the middle opening in each case has a cylindrical vault, that to the east being prolonged into the eastern apse.

At the corners of the central square of the nave rise four large piers, which are joined by arches to four buttress piers in the northern and southern walls behind them. The arched openings connect the three parts into which the aisles are divided by the piers. On either side of each of the central openings from the eastern and western hemicycles rise other piers, which are pierced by narrow arched passages, running from north to south. The piers, eight

[1] Salz. xx., figs. 9 and 10.
[2] All dimensions in this chapter are in Prussian feet, 100 of which = 103 English.

altogether, carry the whole vaulting of the nave, as well as a part of that of the side aisles. Between the middle division of each aisle and the nave are four large columns with five arches on the ground floor, and on the first floor six smaller columns with seven arches. Above again is a wall with windows, filling up the great arches on the north and south sides under the dome. Each exedra has, on the ground floor, two large columns with three arches, and, on the floor above, six small columns with seven arches.

The vault of each division of the aisles is supported on four columns. Those next the east and west walls of the church, eight in all, are square, the others are round. The divisions of the galleries follow those of the aisles underneath. The four main piers however were pierced by additional arched openings [now filled up] between the galleries and the nave. The part over the narthex opens to the nave by three arches, on coupled columns. Above is the immense semircircular window which fills up the central barrel vault at the western end.

All the openings towards the nave in the upper aisles have marble parapets. The vaulting of the lower aisles rests on forty round columns and eight square ones, and in the galleries on sixty round columns, not including the coupled columns at the west ; this makes in all a hundred round columns. Possibly the eight square pillars in the aisles were employed, so that this number should not be exceeded.

In the walls are numerous large windows, and the dome is pierced by forty just above the cornice ; thus light streams into the church from every quarter. Much of the dome, including the central circle of mosaic at the crown, can be seen from the Royal Door.

The greater number of the buildings which formerly surrounded the church are either destroyed, or so altered by Turkish minarets and buttresses that it is difficult to conjecture their original form.[1]

On the north and south of the narthex are long porches of Byzantine workmanship, with cylindrical vaults. In the northern one is a flight of fourteen steps leading down from

[1] See Salz., plate vi.

outside to the narthex. The southern porch is called by Von Hammer the Vestibule of the Warriors. It is mentioned by Nicetas as the place where the Archangel Michael was represented in mosaic. It was through this porch that the emperor passed to the church, and here some of the bodyguard would remain. The vaulting still bears the remains of mosaics which are now covered up.

On the east sides of both the northern and southern porches are accesses to the gynaeceum, formed of a series of inclined planes. The entrance to the northern one is from the porch, but the southern stair is reached from a narrow passage between it and the baptistery. To the west of the northern and southern porches, in the angles between them and the outside walls of the atrium, are the two minarets built by Murad III.

On the first-floor level, above the southern porch and part of the adjacent staircase, is a series of chambers,[1] of which the purpose is not known. The walls of the two larger chambers are covered with marble, and their ceilings with mosaic.

Only one stairway is now extant at the east. The minaret built by Mahomed II., which helps to buttress the south-east corner of the church, occupies the position of a second. Salzenberg's Plate xiv. shows the stairway restored, but in Plate xiii. the northern one is removed to explain the arrangement of the part of the building to the south of it. On entering at the door of this north-eastern stairway one can either mount the ascending planes which wind round a well for light, or go to the left through a small lobby into the church. On the right steps ascend to the round building adjacent. The light ' well ' once ascended the whole height of the staircase, which seems to have been formerly still higher, as the eastern wall of the church, which is here prolonged northwards, rises about four feet above the present roof of the stairway, and shows the remains of a window. These stairways may have been built by Andronicus Palaeologus in the fourteenth century, when he erected the buttress masses which are called pyramids by Nicephorus Gregoras

[1] Salz., plate vii.

All these stairways however were additions to the building, probably built when the dome abutments were strengthened. The original staircases to the gynaeceum were in the four piers by the northern and southern walls of the church, and the steps from the gynaeceum to the base of the dome still remain.[1]

In the eastern buttress pier on the south side is a portion of one of the original staircases, leading *downwards* from the gynaeceum, though beneath on the ground floor there is now a vaulted passage.[2] In the western buttress pier on the south side, at the ground-floor level, is a vaulted passage adorned with mosaic, and a door leading to an external addition. In the similar position on the gynaeceum level, the staircase, which formerly led higher, has been destroyed, to make a way to the upper floor of this same late annex.

The south-east porch may have been used by the emperors on non-festal days, as it was close to the southern aisle where they sat. Three columns are now placed on each side of this porch; the two outer ones are of porphyry, and have capitals with a design of a basket and doves.[3] These capitals are fine Byzantine work, although the arch above may be Turkish. Here seven steps descend into the church. The other porch on the north of the east end was destroyed at the last restoration to make an entrance for the Sultan. Remains of a series of chambers can still be traced on the east side between the porches : their roofs must have been below the lower windows of the eastern wall. The chambers are now built up ; but their original plan may be conjectured from the lead saddle-roofs, which have gutters that conduct the rainwater through the outer wall. Two doors from the porches, and two doors from the church— all four now blocked up—show the previous communication with this row of chambers, which probably contained the priests' vestments, and the vessels for the altar.

Amongst the buildings that surrounded the church must be mentioned the skeuophylakium, in which was kept the sacred furniture. Here were placed biers for the state funerals :

---

[1] Salz., plates vii., viii., and illustration of stairs in text.
[2] Salz., plate vi.   [3] *Ibid.*, plate xx.

conspicuous amongst them was one quite covered with gold, the gift of Studios and Stephanos. This probably was the isolated round building at the north-east of the church, reached by the steps previously mentioned. It now has two floors of wood ; for security there were no windows, but only twelve niches in the wall, in one of which is the door. This building now serves as a storehouse for the army kitchen (imareh) adjacent, and is much injured. Windows have been made in the walls, and the door altered.[1] The baptistery [south-west building] is square outside, but octagonal with four niches within. It is vaulted by a dome without ribs. On the east side is an apse, and on the west a porch. The Anonymous says that the baptistery was formerly called the Chapel of S. John, and that it was built by Justinian. [Entrance to this is now obtained by a door, which has been pierced in its north-eastern angle. The western wall has a semicircular-headed opening, of the same size as the niches, leading to a narthex or vestibule to which there is now no access from the outside.]

In addition to the western entrance, a door on the north, now blocked up, led through an open porch into a small court. The large cylindrical arch of this porch had a screen at its northern side, the columns and door-frame [2] of which are still extant, but the marble lattice is destroyed. Through an arch in the east wall of this porch the addition which was made outside the south-west buttress pier could be reached, where there was a passage into the church. Salzenberg's plan [3] of this addition is taken at the level of a landing reached by a staircase from the passage through the south-west buttress pier. This landing seems at one time to have been connected with a chamber above the north porch of the baptistery, and from thence with the stairway at the south-west angle of the church. Leading upwards from this landing is the original staircase to the gynaeceum, and at this level there is a small chapel vaulted with a cupola.[4] The vault is

---

[1] Only a short time was allowed to Salzenberg for its examination. He was convinced it was not a baptistery, but gives no reasons.

[2] Salz., plate xviii., figs. 9, 13.

[3] Salz., plate vi.   [4] Salz., plate vii.

adorned with mosaic ; figures of angels stand in the four pendentives. Originally the chapel was not lighted ; but at
the last "restoration" a hole was made in the roof, which
was filled with glass ; a passage from this chapel to the
gynaeceum is probably Turkish. The chapel is supposed
by the Greeks to be the one into which the officiating priest
disappeared at the capture by the Turks.

The Turks turned the baptistery into a storeroom
for the oil used in lighting the church, but on the sudden
death of the Sultan Mustapha I. it was converted into a
turbeh. Almost the whole of the church is raised above
vaulted cisterns. An opening in the south aisle [1] gives access
to the water, and there is another opening in the north-
west exedra. The depth of the water prevented a close
inspection.

· Of the two additions made in Byzantine times to the
centre of the north and south walls on the outside, and
intended to buttress the aisles, the southern one has been
further lengthened by the Turks. To preserve the use of
the door and window in the wall of the church, each addition
was pierced by a passage. Remains of stairways and side
passages have also been found here.[2] Other remains of
buildings existed on the north and south sides of the church,
but they were too insufficient to base any conclusions on
them.

Materials.—The principal materials employed are brick,
and a kind of peperino stone. The latter is used in those
parts of the building which have to stand great pressure,
such as the four large piers in the nave, the piers to east and
west, and the extra projections from the buttress piers in the
side aisles and gynaeceum. In addition a horizontal course
two feet deep runs round the whole building four feet from
the floor.

The outside walls of the original building, like the
vaulting, were entirely of brick, but in the later additions
they are formed of alternate layers of brick and stone, and
some of the later buttress masses are almost entirely of stone.

The bricks are as a rule about fourteen inches long and

---

[1] Salz., plate vi.   [2] Salz., plates vi., x.

two inches thick ; some vaulting bricks brought from the
ruins by the porch on the east measured fourteen inches
square and two inches thick; on one side of them were
scratched lines probably made by the three fingers of the
maker, and on the other was an oblong label inclosing an
inscription (1) ; another had a different inscription (2) ;
and a third, not from this vault, but of the same size,
was also inscribed (3).

		+ΚΥΡΙΕΒΟ
+ΚΟϹΤ	+ΗΕΓ ∽	ΗΕΙφΗΔΙ
ΑΝΤ+	ΕΚΚΛ ∽	ΜΟΙΝΔ ∽ Ζ

[(1) Reads Constantius or Constantine. (2) May be
rendered " the church which is being erected," by reading
a participle of ἐγείρω for the second and third letter. (3)
This is also given in the *Revue Archéologique*, 1876, with
some slight differences in second and third lines ; it is there
said to have been found between SS. Sophia and Irene. It
probably reads, " Lord, help Philemon : Indiction 7." The
two first vowels of Philemon have changed places, and the
contraction form after " ΙΝΔ " is also turned the wrong
way.]

At the base of the dome the bricks are 27 × 9 inches,
and two inches thick. Some appear to be twenty-seven
inches square ; but at the apex of the dome, by the hole
intended for the lamp-chain, the thickness is twenty-four
inches. There was no trace of the light bricks made in
Rhodes which the Anonymous mentions ; although in the
pendentives a light substance, whitish, with impressions of
plants in it, was used in irregular masses. The mortar
has a red colour, and was evidently mixed with crushed
brick ; the joints are from one to two inches thick.

The marble of Proconnesus, which somewhat resembles
the architectural marble of Carrara, is employed for the
cornices, capitals, and bases of the columns, and for the
windows.

In Salzenberg's plans the materials are expressed by
different depths of tint ; the darkest being marble, slightly
lighter is stone, and a still lighter brickwork ; the additional

buildings are represented in the lightest tones, and the Turkish buildings with strokes and dots.

Construction.—The outside walls average a height of seventy feet : those on the north and south have a thickness of three and a half feet, that on the east is four and a half feet, and that on the west between the nave and narthex five feet. Where the arches rest on the walls there are piers which project about two feet: thus the west wall, for instance, has in parts a thickness of seven feet. As a general rule, the interior vaults of wide span continue through the walls, and appear as arches on the outside face. The window and door openings are semicircular. The marble finishings were inserted after the completion of the walls.

The dome at first sight seems to rest upon four arches each of -100 feet span ; it is, however, only on the east and west that these arches are open. From north to south the main piers are 106 feet apart, and their breadth in this direction is fifteen feet eight inches ; but on either side of the nave there are projections, narrowing the opening to 100 feet, and giving the open arches abutments of eighteen feet eight inches.

Behind each of these main piers again, at a distance of twenty-nine and a half feet from them, stands one of the buttress or staircase piers, which, including the outside wall, is seventeen feet four inches by twenty-four and a half feet in area. Round arches, which appear below the vaults, transmit the thrust of the great arches from the main piers to these buttressing piers. Above these each of the immense buttress masses which stand right across the aisles, and rise to within eighteen feet of the springing of the dome, bear upon two relieving arches of different radii, so as not to load the vaulting beneath.[1]

---

[1] It is probable, writes Salzenberg, that originally the buttress masses reached only up to the roof of the gynaeceum, level with the springing of the great arches ; as Cedrenus describes how Justinian, at the restoration after the fall of the dome, made outside the building, in the neighbourhood of the main piers, above the roof of the gynaeceum four staircases, "cochleas" which reached up to the dome "to strengthen the vaulting." Theophanes also speaks of new piers which Justinian erected to strengthen the dome. The circumstances mentioned by

The cylindrical arches, which, at the ground-floor aisles and the gynaeceum, connect the great piers with the outer buttress piers, are each reinforced by two extra arches, standing on stone additions to the main piers, from which they project five feet.[1] These arches, though thus strengthened, are almost all out of shape ; those by the two northern main piers have been pushed out nearly fifteen inches.

A drawing given in Salzenberg's text shows the south arch which supports the dome with the mosaics removed. The piers from east to west are seventy-two feet apart, and accordingly the span of the arch is seventy-two feet, its soffite being fifteen feet eight inches. The arch is five feet deep, formed of two unconnected rings, and on each side the lower part is laid in horizontal courses so that the portion with radiating joints is only three quarters of the whole arch. The window wall which fills the arch opening is four feet thick, and is bonded with the horizontal courses, but a movement of the arches has caused a fissure, which is shown in the diagram. These window walls on the south and north sides have cracked in several places. The upper part of the window wall on the north side is only twenty-nine inches thick. The windows have been reduced and strengthened by inserting stone jambs.

On the north and south side are also two large arches, which project on the inside three feet from the window wall and rest on the main piers, having the same height and span as the arches on the east and west. They complete the

Procopius seem to indicate that the abutments of the great arches were not sufficient. See our chap. x., § 1, for another interpretation.

[1] These Salzenberg thought later additions, "for the stone projections are not bonded to the piers, and the Silentiary says columns stood in these positions." We do not so interpret the lines of the poem, and, although Choisy here follows Salzenberg, it is impossible to see, if there were additions subsequent to the completion of the building, how it is that the perfectly symmetrical disposition of the marble panelling shows no disturbance, and the beautiful carved cornice which mitres round these projections has had no additions made to it (our Fig. 47). The straight joints, which Choisy in another place specially notes as a method of Byzantine building, were here most wisely applied ; for on one side the great pier was of stone, and on the other the buttress pier is of brick.

square form under the cornice of the dome, and give the idea that the dome is carried on four arches of 100 feet span : whereas in reality, as has just been shown, the real supporting arches on the north and south side are concealed in the window wall, and are not suggested in any way in the interior decoration, being only visible on the outside.[1]

The four principal piers are very carefully built of shaped stones, the joints, according to Procopius, being run with lead, but the Silentiary mentions a cement as being used here.

The height from the floor to the springing of the great arches is seventy-three feet.

The arches of seventy-two feet span have abutments of twenty-four and a half feet, which are increased above the vaults of the gynaeceum to twenty-nine feet.

The great arches under the springing of the dome are about four bricks, or five feet, thick. The depth at the top, including the cornice of the dome, is about six feet and three quarters. The centre of the arches is two and a half feet above the springing, so that they are more than semi-circular. In the internal angles formed by them are the four pendentives. The cornice has a projection of about two feet nine inches. The lead mentioned by the Silentiary may be found in the interstices of its stones.

The dome springs from the cornice on forty piers, about three feet five inches broad on the inside, and about eight and a half feet deep in the direction of the radius. They are connected by arches which form windows four feet nine inches wide. On the outside the piers project beyond the arches, and may perhaps at one time have been connected with other arches, forming a drum for the dome : within they form part of the ribs of the dome.

In the interior the ribs project at the springing six inches from the surface of the dome, which is there twenty-nine inches thick, but their projection gradually diminishes, till

---

[1] Salzenberg conjectures from Agathias that these arches were a later addition made when the dome was restored by Justinian. But without them, as he remarks, there would not have been originally a square base for the circle of the dome. See explanation of original form, p. 210.

they are lost in the great circle of thirty-seven and a half feet diameter in the centre. In the interior from rib across to rib is 104 feet, so that all round on the cornice is the passage two feet nine inches wide, which, according to Paulus, was used by the lamplighter. The dome rises forty-six feet nine inches above this gangway, so that it is considerably less than a semicircle in section. The original dome, according to Agathias, must have been even flatter. Theophanes states the increase in height to have been twenty feet, and Zonoras twenty-five.[1]

The dome has now many swellings and depressions which are not visible from the ground. At the same time we see how immovable domed vaulting is, if only its supports remain uninjured.

At the east and west ends of the nave the two cylindrical vaults are each forty-seven feet across. They rest on the four lesser piers, and have an abutment of fifteen and a half feet. The four exedras are each forty-one feet across. All the conchs and semidomes have drums outside, which are pierced by the windows. The conchs which cover the exedras have strong arches, where they intersect the semidomes. The weight of the exedra conchs is chiefly supported by the columns ; the upper columns of the south-east exedra, at the time of the last restoration, were much inclined, and had to be brought back to the vertical, by propping the arches, cutting away the old bases, and inserting new pieces —the columns being surrounded and supported by wooden cradling. The thickness of the western barrel vault is four feet ; the eastern apse is about three feet thick. The western semidome received an additional thickness at the restoration.

Vaulting of the Aisles.—The three principal divisions of each aisle are covered by domical vaults. The vault arches rest partly on columns ; and the spaces between these columns and the outside wall are also vaulted. The middle division of the north and south aisles has two domical vaults, separated by a barrel vault that opens towards the

[1] Salzenberg assumes from Paulus that " the dome was surmounted by a cross " : the cross was of mosaic inside.

nave arches, and to the window in the outside wall. The arches have iron ties four inches thick, which stretch from the outer wall to the columns of the nave, and grip them tightly. The four columns in the aisles which carry the vault are much lower than those between the aisles and nave, and for this reason the narrow vaulted space, which joins the aisle vault to the nave arcade, is formed by a stilted quadrant.

This arrangement only applies to the lower aisles : above is a stilted cylindrical vault, running lengthways between the main gynaeceum vaults, and the arcade towards the nave.[1] Here, besides the iron ties, there are wooden beams.

The large arches in the aisles are twenty-nine and a half feet from column to column. The domical vaulting of the aisles is very flat—a combination of cross groining and a dome. For, though it starts with angles at the four corners, it gradually merges into a dome at the apex. The vaulting bricks are arranged in horizontal circles.[2] A diagonal band of mosaic starts from each corner, and merges into a central circle.[3] In the gynaeceum the vaulting is higher and consists of spherical domes, the radii being half the diagonals of the spaces covered. The mosaic decoration here again follows the form.[4]

Narthex.—The narthex is covered with vaults, similar to those of the lower aisles of the nave. Each vaulted space is separated from the next by a segmental arch, six and a half feet wide with a span of twenty-six and a half feet, which abuts on the west wall of the nave, and the piers of the outer wall. The vault spaces vary from sixteen and a half feet in the middle to thirteen and a half feet towards the ends. The piers of the outer wall are connected together by arches above the window openings, and the spaces below

---

[1] See Salz., plate x. The right-hand side is a section through one of the domical vaults, and the left through the barrel-vault which connects two domical vaults. The plans, plates vi. and vii., and the section plate xi., show how close some of the columns stand to the piers, to which they are joined by small barrel-vaults, intersecting the domical vaulting.

[2] A mistake for vertical circles ; the large number of cisterns where the vaults are uncovered make this certain. See our p. 221.

[3] Salz., plate xxiv. [4] Salz., plate xxiii.

M

the windows are filled up with thin 'screen' walls. The upper floor of the narthex is covered with a semicircular vault, intersected by the window arches between the piers of the outer wall. These piers are the continuation of those beneath, and have a width of six feet, and a depth of seven. They had to bear the thrust of the barrel vault of twenty-six and a half feet span : the buttresses previously mentioned, springing from the piers of the propylaeum, were subsequently added to strengthen them.

In the exonarthex there are cross groins with arches between. The arches have a span of fourteen and a half feet and an abutment of seven feet. This seems to be of a later construction than the rest of the vaulting, and not improbably, as well as the piers, belongs to a reconstruction of this porch, undertaken to strengthen the west wall of the narthex.

All the arches of the nave which stand on columns have iron ties ; and to the three large openings of the gynaeceum at the west end of the nave there are wooden binders as well. In the lower rows of windows beneath the dome on both the north and south sides of the nave iron ties can be seen, which seem to stretch across the whole width of the large arches which support the dome.

Roofs.—All the exterior vaults are covered with lead about a quarter of an inch thick, which rests on a layer of wooden battens placed immediately upon the brick vaults. There are several passages and staircases for access to the roofs. Access to the exterior of the side aisles and narthex is gained by the staircases in the buttress piers : the stairs are supported on brick arches. In the north-east pier the stair space is only four feet eight inches by six feet seven inches, and in this are placed the flights of stairs two feet eight inches wide, with a space of fifteen inches between.[1] At the top of each flight spaces are hollowed out in the wall, which serve as landings from one flight to another.

These stairs ascend above the roofs of the side aisles to the upper part of the buttress piers, from which open passages, with breast-walls on either side, lead above the

[1] See figure in Salzenberg's text.

buttress piers to the angles at the base of the dome. There were two flights of steps leading to the platform of the dome: one of these on the south-east, which Salzenberg shows dotted in Plate viii., is still quite preserved, though injured at the upper end ; remains too can still be traced of the north-west stair. A door now built up, on the north side of the south-east stair, and remains of vaulting in the north-west stair, seem to show that other passages must have existed.

The roof of the cylindrical vaulting at the west end of the nave is reached by means of stairs in the small round towers, which flank it on the outside.[1] These turrets can also be reached from the roof of the narthex. Another passage runs along under the narthex roof at the west (Salz., Plate ix.), which has an opening close to the upper surface of the vaulting, and from thence any part above the nave can be reached. Probably this was formerly used for the lighting of the church. To reach the cornice at the foot of the dome there was an opening in the wall under one of the dome windows.

Decorative Work.—All the constructional forms were shown boldly on the outside without any adornment ; the west front of the narthex next to the atrium was alone covered with slabs of Proconnesian marble, some of which are still preserved, but the upper wall surfaces were perfectly plain.

In the interior the whole of the walls are plated with rare variegated marbles, and the vaults are covered with glass mosaic. Two chief masses of colour in the nave are separated horizontally by a cornice, and another cornice forms the springing for the vaulting. There are also cornices at the foot of the dome, and around the walls of the aisles. All these are of carved white marble in simple profiles. The lower range of arch spandrils between the piers of the nave is formed of slabs of white marble completely covered with carving: the upper spandrils above the gynaeceum arches have sectile work of coloured marbles. The carving is sharply cut, but conforms very

[1] Salz., plate xi.

closely to the general surfaces; according to the old descriptions it was gilt, and remains of colour still extant show some of the leaf-ornament coloured with a dark red.[1]

Columns.—Amongst the columns are beautiful examples of the dark green Thessalian marble, now called *verde antico.* Of this are formed all the round columns in the nave and ground-floor aisles, with the exception of the eight in the four exedras, which are of dark Theban porphyry. It could not have been always possible to find a sufficient number of columns of the same height and diameter, and the transport of them must have been frequently accompanied by injuries of one kind or another. There are differences between similarly situated columns, and in many cases mended fractures appear on the surface of the marble. In no cases are antique capitals placed on these columns. All the capitals and bases are of Proconnesian marble, and were wrought by Byzantine chisels.

The greater part of the capitals are similar in design, though their size varies in proportion to the height of the columns which support them. Salzenberg, in Figs. 1 and 3 of his Plate xv., shows one of the capitals of the great order. The leaf-work on them—partly acanthus and partly palm—is very deeply undercut, and lies almost clear of the ground underneath. In the middle of front and back are monograms.

Under the capitals are bronze rings eleven and half inches high; each is composed of three members, with a wrought lock on the side towards the nave, on which is repeated the monogram of each capital. At the foot of the columns above the bases are similar rings nine inches high. These rings occur on all the old columns, with the exception of the two dual columns of the west gallery. They seem to be let into the shaft, and, according to the description of the Silentiary, they were gilded. In addition to these rings, there are on other columns—as, for instance, the porphyry columns of the exedras—simple rings, rectangular in section, in positions where cracks and injuries appear; there being three or four

[1] Preparation for the gold.

such rings on a column at different heights. It is possible
that some of these are of Turkish origin.

The bases as a rule have much the same form as the
Attic base; the porphyry columns of the exedras have
pedestals[1] below them, because the shafts were not long
enough.

Each of the great verde antique shafts has a height of
twenty-five and a half feet, and the bronze base-ring has an
inside diameter of three feet seven inches. The capital is
three feet ten inches high, and the upper part five feet eight
inches wide, the whole height, including base and capital,
being thirty-three and a half feet.

The porphyry columns of the western exedras have a
total height of thirty-one feet; the shafts are twenty-two
feet and three-quarters long, and the diameter at the bottom
is three feet one inch. The capital is four feet high, and the
abacus above measures towards the nave four feet nine inches,
and towards the aisles four feet eleven inches. In the
direction of the thickness of the arch the side of the
abacus measures five feet, the variation being due to the
circular plan of exedras.

The columns of the upper storey, which separate the
gynaeceum and the nave, also of verde antique, stand nearer
to one another and are smaller than those below. The total
height of those in the middle division is twenty-two feet
five inches; those in the exedras are twenty-one feet, with a
diameter at the bottom of two and a quarter feet. The
capitals are three and a half feet high, and the bases, including
a six-inch bronze ring, two feet one inch.[2]

The parapet is three feet ten inches high, and of white
marble.[3] It stands between the columns, and like them is
set on a stylobate one foot six inches high, above the lower
cornice. It should be noticed how the wide vaulting of
the aisles is contrived, so as not to interfere with the view
through the arched openings of the lower range of columns.

The columns in the interior of the ground-floor aisles

---

[1] Salzenberg's plate xv., fig. 6. The inclination of the sides of that
shown is much exaggerated, if in any case it exists.
[2] Salz., plate xvi., fig. 1, 5.   [3] Plate xvi., figs. 5, 6.

are about twenty-four feet seven inches high. These capitals
are similar to those already described. Those in the interior
of the gynaeceum, with shafts of Proconnesian marble, have
capitals of quite another form.[1] They are very similar to
others in the church of SS. Sergius and Bacchus ; the twin
columns in the gynaeceum at the west end of the nave have
similar capitals ; the columns being verde antique. In these
capitals, however, the volutes are not arranged diagonally,
but show " cushions " at the side.

The capitals in the atrium resembled those of the twin
columns ; though the cushion was shorter and the top had
less projection, and it was crowned with a flat egg and
tongue moulding. The capitals and shafts were of white
marble. The beautiful square capitals of the eight square
white marble pillars in the aisles are shown in Salzenberg's
Plate xvi.

The arches of the great order have an elaborate leaf-
ornament round them, continuing above the capitals in a
horizontal line, resembling in fact an architrave. [In the
centre above each capital is a cross, and at the crown of the
arch is a four or six-armed cross.] The spandrils are filled
with acanthus-ornament, and in the centre of each is a disc
of coloured marble—surrounded by a carved circle in the
white marble. The ornament of the intrados of the arches
consists of five divisions in the width: these are covered with
a continuous pattern, seven slabs casing the intrados of
the arch. [The five bands are only carved alternately, the
centre and lateral ones being plain.] See our Fig. 50.

The respond on the main pier at each end of this arcade
is a kind of pilaster strip,[2] surmounted by a capital in low
relief, and surrounded by a notched border.

The two cornices running round the nave, which serve as
galleries for the lamplighters, have an extremely simple profile.
The slanting under-surface, divided horizontally by a row of
beads, has acanthus-leaves in the upper part forming a cym-
atium, and in the lower modillions carved with ivy and

[1] Salz., plate xvii., figs. 12 and 13. Fig. 14 gives the base, fig. 2 a complete column.
[2] Salz., plate xv., figs. 7, 8.

acanthus, and between them, panels with different leaf-ornaments. Beneath the aisle cornice is a frieze of marble mosaic. The base mouldings or skirtings are worked out of thin slabs.[1]

Salzenberg's Plate xx. contains a collection of architectural details, which seem to belong to different periods ; Figs 1, 2, 3 represent one of the white marble capitals which adorn the two porphyry columns of the south-east porch. The arch above them is Turkish, and hence it may be questioned if this was their original position : they seem more intended for an ornamental structure than to support a load, and they may perhaps have belonged to a ciborium above the holy table. The two marble capitals (Figs. 4 and 5), only three inches thick, were found in the chamber in the north-east buttress mass, above the gynaeceum roof, together with broken pieces from a window. They may originally have belonged to the upper part of the building, such as the window wall under the north arch of the dome.[2] The workmanship is very different from that in the rest of the church, and is more closely allied with ancient treatment. Perhaps they are fragments from the earlier church which found a fresh application in Justinian's building. The parapet pillars between the twin columns of the western gynaeceum, with tall pedestals, are each formed in one piece of verde antique. Their capitals resemble those of the windows,[3] with the exception that the former are rounded underneath instead of being square.

[1] See Salz., plate xv., figs. 1, 4, 5 for lower cornice ; plate xvi., 2 and 3 for upper, figs. 3, 4 for dome cornice, fig. 9 aisle cornice. This last, says Salzenberg, "is mended in many places with gypsum, and comes from an earlier building." We do not know what earlier building could have furnished a quarter of the quantity used in S. Sophia. Is it possible that the whole of it is of gypsum ? (See our chapter xii.) The marble skirtings are shown on plates xv. and xvi.

[2] In a note Salzenberg draws attention to Paulus speaking of eight windows in this wall, and conjectures that instead of the five upper windows there was one large opening here.

[3] Salz., plate xx., fig. 4. Fig. 6 is a capital that was found on one of the four parapet posts, and removed at the "restoration"; fig. 7 was not found in S. Sophia ; fig. 8 was an isolated capital in north aisle ; figs. 9–11 show upper mouldings to the piers of the propylaeum.

168 S. SOPHIA

The wood ties which span different arches are adorned on the sides and beneath with carvings.[1]

Windows and Doors.—The lighting of the church is most brilliant ; wherever space or construction permitted, windows of considerable size were opened, so that light floods the whole church. At the foot of the dome the light streams in through forty windows, and each of the seven apses has five openings. The eastern sun sends its first rays through the six windows in the apse, and the setting sun shines through the great west lunette. There are twenty-four windows in the two great tympana, besides large windows in the aisles.

The windows in the conchs of the exedras are now closed up, the grouped windows in the great tympana on the north and south are diminished to insignificant openings, and the large arched openings at the sides or the end divisions of the aisles seem even in Byzantine times to have been reduced in size ; at least the remains of piers, shown in Salzenberg's Plate xiii., indicate that there was originally an opening with pilasters, similar to those at the eastern end of the side aisles.[2]

It is said that Justinian gave instructions that combustible materials should be avoided. If so, these instructions were followed even to the windows and doors, for the lattice-work of the former is of marble, and the panels of the latter are of bronze, or rather they are covered with bronze.

Salzenberg[3] gives the inside elevation and section of a window on the south side of the gynaeceum, with details on a larger scale. The opening in the wall is brick-arched, and the framework consists of upright posts, with a thin horizontal architrave dividing the window into two parts. Between these posts were fitted the breast-wall and lattice-work. The posts are narrow towards the outside, and the ends of the architrave rest on thin pieces against the jambs.

The 'breast-wall' at the bottom of the opening and the 'lattice-work' are formed of marble, three inches thick.

[1] Salz., plate xx., fig. 12 shows the underside of the beam in the middle of the west gynaeceum ; fig. 15 is the side, and fig. 16 the underside of one in the south gynaeceum ; figs. 13 and 14, one in the north gynaeceum.

[2] Salz., plate xiv. [3] Plate xvii., figs. 1–7.

The openings pierced in the slabs are about seven or eight inches high, filled with panes of glass. Between the panes the marble has a width of three and a half inches, slightly splayed on the inside. A second row of slabs fills the lower part of the windows pierced with openings, surrounded by wider margins.[1]

The great semicircular west window is divided vertically by two columns with plain capitals and bases ; the horizontal division from column to column is similar to the crowning member of the breast-wall of the other windows. The lower part is filled with marble slabs, which conceal the roof of the western gynaeceum. Each panel is ornamented with a cross upon a circle, and within the latter is a monogram.

The small windows are simply filled with marble lattice for the glass. Inside the apse windows of the east end are other windows having coloured glazing ; but these are evidently Turkish.

Marble door jambs were placed in the openings left in the walls, just as the posts were inserted in the windows ; the middle, or Royal Door, from the narthex to the nave, is of bronze. All the frames were moulded, and above are fixed door-hooks, like bent forefingers ; these held rings and leather fastenings, from which were suspended the customary door-hangings.

The lintel of the bronze door-frame bears a relief. This represents an arch, supported by columns above a throne with the book of the Gospel and the descent of the Holy Ghost in the form of a dove. On it are the words of S. John, 'The Lord said, I am the door of the sheep ; through me if any man enter, he shall enter and shall go out, and shall find pasture.' The simple bronze door-plating now remaining does not seem to be original. [See p. 265.]

Salzenberg,[2] as an example of the marble frames, gives the east door of north aisle. Like all Byzantine door-frames, the head does not cut across the jamb, but mitres. This perhaps

---

[1] See Salz., plate xvii. Fig. 3 is the upper capital, fig. 4 the lower, figs. 5 and 6 the base, and fig. 7 the under side of the architrave. Figs. 8, 9, 10 are details of large west window.
[2] Salz., plate xviii.

made it easier for fixing within the openings left in the walls. Salzenberg[1] also represents the arched opening, which stands between the Baptistery and the small court on the south side of the church.[2] There are two tiers of columns, with a thin architrave band between them. The door stands between the lower columns ; to avoid concealing them the frame is made as small as possible, as the plan shows. A similar arrangement is found in the earlier church of S. John Studius.[3]

The bronze door-plating on the exterior of the south porch entrance is extremely interesting.[4] A wooden foundation four or five inches thick is covered with ornamental bronze casings. The borders to the panels are beautifully modelled, and must be ancient. The other outer margins, with knobs and rosettes, and the four panels, which are decorated with monograms, belong to the Byzantine school. In the more ancient parts the metal is one-eighth to one-fourth inch in thickness, in the latter it is three-eighths to half an inch. Antique doors must have been enlarged and fitted with new panel plates.

Marble Plating.—Broad horizontal bands run round the nave at different heights, and the spaces between them are filled with single panels and vertical sheathing. All the bands and panels have notched fillets, $1\frac{1}{2}''$ wide, of white marble as borders. The more important panels have sculptured white marble frames, eleven inches wide with a " pater noster " and notched-fillet borders on either side.

The spandrils of the upper arches and the bands beneath the topmost cornices are incrusted with designs of leaves, flowers, fruits, and birds formed of different kinds of marble.

The marble casing to the walls of the nave is arranged as follows.[5] Above the skirting is a $[3'.10'']$ band of verde antique, then the notched fillet, then a $[1'.5\frac{1}{2}'']$ yellow band [oriental alabaster] ; above this is a vertical sheeting $[7'.10'']$ formed of Pavonazzetto marble, alternating with a yellowish brown marble ; then another horizontal band of yellow.

Above this stretches a series of panels round the whole

[1] Plate xviii., figs. 10-14.   [2] See plates vi. and xi.
[3] Salz., plate iii., fig. 7.   [4] Salz., plate xix.
[5] See Salz., plate ix.

nave—a panel of *rosso*, with two vertical slabs of a dark marble like *porto venere* on either side, each surrounded by the sculptured frames. The space from the top of this series to the lowest cornice is adorned with two bands of yellow [alabaster], and between them is sheathing similar to that below.

The upper division of the nave starts above the cornice with horizontal bands of white and verde antique ; above which are vertical panels of porphyry, set in a frame of yellow [alabaster], with slabs of the russet marble on either side. [Then follows another horizontal band of oriental alabaster, and above it a range of vertical slabs of verde antique alternating with Synnadan.]

Beyond this again, and immediately below the upper cornice, is the band made up of different marbles[1] [*opus sectile*]. A dark brown marble forms the groundwork, the tendril ornament is white, and the rest is of red, like rosso antico, and of green serpentine. Similar work incrusts the spandrils of the gynaeceum arcade. The centre of each is a disc of green marble, and the whole spandril is edged by a three-inch strip of pale red. Above the centre of each arch in this spandril decoration are discs containing crosses, from the arms of which hang seals.[2] The soffites of the arches are covered with glass mosaic. The aisles are lined with marbles similarly arranged to those in the nave.

The walls of the bema are covered with panels of inlaid marble.[3] These panels in pairs are separated by a plain slab of porphyry. By the side of the arched opening into the gynaeceum is a panel of porphyry with a pattern in slight relief, and surrounded with yellow alabaster. The arched opening into the gynaeceum is closed with a parapet of white marble, with a carved framework above, formerly fitted, as holes show, with a metal lattice.

The lower division of the bema walls is decorated by two rows of panels, divided by a horizontal band of verde antique. Salzenberg's Plate xxii., Fig. 6, shows the frieze directly

[1] Salz., plate xvi., fig. 4. [2] Salz., plate xvi.
[3] Salz., plates xxi., xxii. Plate xxii., fig. 1 shows the upper frieze and the panels beneath.

below the bema cornice, and the top of a porphyry pilaster-strip with a capital of white marble ; a similar pilaster fills the narrow space on each side of the apse.

The walls of the apse are shown on Salzenberg's Plate xxi. The frieze beneath the cornice is given in Plate xxii., Fig. 8. The porphyry ground has an inlaid pattern which slightly projects : the serpentine in the frieze, Fig. 6, also projects from its rosso ground. The lower portion of the apse, formerly occupied by the seats of the priests, is now plated with a white gray marble. This is probably Turkish. The height of this probably gives the height of the iconostasis, as there is no sign of any change in the decoration above.

The marble is fixed to the wall with a dark brown resin. In the opus sectile, pieces of coloured marble about a quarter of an inch thick were cut to the forms of the design, and then laid with their polished faces downward at the bottom of a mould ; on this was poured a three-quarter inch backing of resin mixed with bits of stone and brick. When set, the slabs so formed were attached to the wall with cement. The large marble slabs are one to two inches thick, and, besides the cement, are fastened to the walls by iron [? bronze] clamps. The pavements of ground floor and gynaeceum are of white marble with dark gray stripes. [Proconnesian.] In the south-east angle of the square area under the dome is a square of marble mosaic, of which details are given in Salzenberg's Plate xxii., Figs. 9–15. It is formed of a circular centrepiece of a gray brown granite, ten feet two inches in diameter, round which are arranged coloured marble discs of various sizes, set in a mosaic of marbles, with a little glass mosaic in the angles.

In the centre of the west end of the gynaeceum is a square [of about twenty-four feet] in the pavement laid with slabs of "gray cipollino" [Proconnesian], having a border of verde antique, with a patterned edging [1] of giallo and rosso on one side, and giallo and serpentine on the other. [Between this and the parapet is a circular slab of verde antique four feet seven inches in diameter.]

[1] Salz., plate xxi., fig. 18, and our fig. 9.

CHAPTER IX

Palace.—Before entering on particulars of the exterior of
the church, it will be well to have a clearer view of the
edifices in its immediate neighbourhood as they appeared in
the time of Justinian.

The group of buildings of which the Augusteum was the
centre was profoundly modified by the fire of the Nika
Sedition, and by the building energy of the emperor. The
researches of Labarte and Paspates have been almost entirely
confined to the elucidation of the palace as it existed in the
tenth century.

A restoration of the relative position of the several parts
of the palace, unless by the discovery of remains positive
evidence is obtained, is certainly impossible ; the attempt of
Labarte was worth making, but Paspates, in bringing forward
another scheme, seems only to have succeeded in showing
how conjectural the whole matter is, although he speaks of
certain scraps of walls as belonging to this or that part of
the palace with as much confidence as if he had found them
labelled.   His work carries internal evidence of the greatest
inexactness and confusion, and has proved most misleading,
although his citations are valuable. .

It should not be assumed that wherever a palace is
mentioned by the historians the "Great Palace" is the one
referred to, and it must be remembered that the palace
described in the *Ceremonies* was the result of gradual growth :

indeed, what is required is a chronological analysis of its history. We have seen in the first chapter that according to the *Paschal Chronicle* Constantine built a palace by the hippodrome, and the *Notitia* mentions the palaces of Placidia and Marina in the same neighbourhood. According to Procopius the palace was almost rebuilt by Justinian, but he only specifically mentions the Chalké.

Remains of a palace now on the sea-wall, exactly to the south of the curve of the hippodrome, are thought to be portions of the palace "Hormisdas" which Justinian occupied before he came to the throne (B, on Plan, Fig. 2). Close to the sea-wall farther to the west was the double church of SS. Sergius and Bacchus and SS. Peter and Paul, of which the first survives as Little Sancta Sophia (A, on Fig. 2). These were early works of Justinian, and his monogram and that of Theodora appear on the capitals of S. Sergius.

Procopius tells us that the church of S. Sergius was "close to the king's palace which was formerly called by the name of Hormisdas. This was once his own private house," and when he became emperor "he joined it to the other imperial apartments." The Great Palace was higher up the slope, against the hippodrome and Augusteum, to which its gates opened.

It was long after Justinian that the great palace reached its maximum development; the Chrysotriclinum was erected by his successor Justin II. The houses of Marina and Placidia were still in use at the end of the sixth century, although this is mentioned by neither Labarte nor Paspates. The wedding of the daughter of Phocas was celebrated in the former,[1] and "the Royal palace of Placidia" is referred to by John of Ephesus. The writer tells us that Tiberius II., the successor of Justin II., made large additions to the palace. Before he reigned alone the wife and daughters of Tiberius occupied the house of Hormisdas, "as it was situated just below the palace, and he would go down and spend the evening with them and return early in the morning to the palace." [2] Justinian II. also added to the palace, and in the ninth

[1] Bury, vol. ii., 202.
[2] I. of Ephesus wrote *circa* 590, R. Payne Smith's translation.

century Theophilus built the Triconcha. Basil the Macedonian still further increased the assemblage of buildings.

It is clear that in the time of Justinian there were at least four more or less separate palaces grouped together—the Great Palace, Hormisdas, and those of Marina and Placidia.

Hippodrome.—The information in regard to the hippodrome brought together in the works before mentioned, and by Gyllius, cannot be recapitulated here.[1] As the ground fell away steeply towards the south, that end had to be raised high on vaults, and this retaining wall, perhaps forty feet high, forming a semicircular curve, still exists.[2] On either side rose the tiers of the marble seats. At the north end was the royal stand, called Kathisma, from which the emperors watched the games ; this was raised above arched chambers, where the chariots for the arena were kept. The south-west end was called *Sphendone*—The Curve. A rough draft of Constantinople, made early in the fifteenth century for Bondelmontius, reproduced by Mordtmann, shows columns standing on the retaining wall around this curved end. A clear representation of this semicircle of columns is also given in the *Nuremberg Chronicle*. Banduri reproduces from Panvinius, who wrote in the middle of the sixteenth century, a drawing of the hippodrome which seems to have been made with considerable care. Beneath it is written, "The ruins of the circus or hippodrome of Constantinople as they were a hundred years before the capture of the city by the Turks."[3] But that it should have been in a ruinous state at this time is not borne out by the accounts of writers like Clavijo and Bondelmontius, who described it in the generation before the Fall : on the contrary, we should suppose this to be one of the draughts for the Venice view of the city published about 1570, with which it agrees in many respects.[4] This bird's-eye view shows the monuments on the Spina, the Grand Stand and its

[1] See also Rambaud, *Revue des Deux Mondes*, Aug. 1871.
[2] See plan and view in Strzygowski und Forchheimer, *Die Wasserbehälter von Konstantinopel*.
[3] *Imperium Orientale*, p. 664.
[4] See *Ancien Plan de Constantinople imprimé entre 1566 et 1574, avec Notes explicatives par Caedicius*, 1890.

"Podium" of vaults, and also the high external retaining wall of the curve, above which the columns again appear, but set back from its face, so as to leave a passage outside the columns, the outer wall being finished with a battlement. It is true that in the engraving it is rendered as if these columns were attached to a wall, or rather as if a wall were built between the columns, for they appear both inside and out ; but this interpretation cannot be given to a description of this colonnade by Gyllius.[1]   "In the front of the hippodrome facing the Propontis there was a range of seventeen pillars of white marble standing when I first came to Constantinople, going round that part of the hippodrome which lies between south and west."   They stood on a low wall, about two feet six inches high towards the hippodrome, but outside it was fifty feet to the ground.   They were of the Corinthian order, three feet five inches in diameter and twenty-eight feet high, standing eleven feet apart on pedestals; above them was an architrave to which rings were fixed for curtains.   "Above was another range of pillars, which were remaining some time after the taking of the city by the Turks."   These last were only reported to Gyllius ; and if we accept such a second tier we may suppose that it ranged with a colonnade surmounting the containing wall of the terraces of seats.   Paspates makes from this account a wonderful and impossible arrangement ; he supposes the first-mentioned columns to have been continued along the external sides of the hippodrome, he further rears the second range on them, and this, he thinks upheld the immense mass of the rising seats.   "If we suppose," he says, "the height of those in the upper row to have been twenty-one feet, we have about fifty-six feet as the height of the wall on which the seats for the spectators were built."

These columns probably formed an open screen through which the spectators might see the sparkling waters of the Propontis, set with the blue jewels of Prince's Islands and the white peaks of Olympus rising far away to the left—one of the most beautiful scenes in the world.   This addition of a natural spectacle behind the scene was frequently obtained in ancient theatres : the best known is that at Taormina.

[1] Ed. 1562, p. 91.

Clavijo[1] speaks of the hippodrome as being "surrounded by white marble pillars," but he adds "thirty-seven in number." The anonymous Russian who wrote about the same time says "thirty columns and their summits are united by an architrave." See Fig. 2. An "open hippodrome" and a "covered hippodrome" are mentioned by the Byzantine writers. Labarte distinguishing them, placed the latter within the palace. Byeljayev, however, conjectures that the covered hippodrome was a part of the Great Hippodrome. Be this as it may, the "rings for curtains" of Gyllius suggest that portions were sheltered by a Velarium.

Bondelmontius[2] writes thus of the hippodrome : "In it those of noble birth joust in the presence of the people, and there are combats and tournaments. It is 690 bracchia long and 134 wide, and it is built above vaults, in which a cistern of the best water covers the whole of the space mentioned. At the head of the hippodrome are high pillars [of Kathisma] where the emperor sits with his nobles, and on both sides in its length are seats of marble arranged in steps where the people sit and see all the games." On the outside towards S. Sophia there was the church of S. Stephen, "from the galleries of which the ladies watched their chosen champions." On the Spina he notices a fountain where the wounded were laid, the two obelisks, and the three serpents " with open mouths from which, it is said, on days of jousting water, wine, and milk used to spout." At the end of the Spina were four small marble columns where the emperor sat on feast days.[3]

Besides the bronze serpentine column from Delphi, there still stands in the hippodrome an Egyptian obelisk, set up by Theodosius I. on a pedestal sculptured with a representation of the emperor viewing the games from the Kathisma, and a record of the methods used in erecting the obelisk by means of ropes and winches. Nicetas in his life of S. Ignatius

[1] Hakluyt Society, 1859, p. 34.
[2] Migne, S.G. vol. 133, p. 695.
[3] Texier figured in the *Revue Archéologique*, 1845, a small fountain found near the hippodrome to which it probably formerly belonged.

says that a brazen pine-apple surmounted this obelisk. A
third monument is a large built-up obelisk of stone, pitted
all over where pins which attached bronze plates were inserted. An inscription often quoted, records that Constantine, father of Romanus, repaired it and added to its
beauty. The casing of bronze was probably covered with
reliefs and ornament, as was the case with the pillar in the
Augusteum, and the anemodulium, which was set up by
Theodosius in the Forum Tauri. This last was an obelisk
entirely cased with bronze, "having reliefs[1] of cattle, sheep
and skipping lambs ; peasants labouring or playing on their
pipes, and birds ; there was also represented the sea, and
sea-gods, and cupids playing at ball. On the point was a
statue of a woman which turned to the slightest breath of
the wind."

Among the statues in the hippodrome mentioned by Nicetas
as having been destroyed was the colossal bronze Hercules,
and a sundial which was in the form of an eagle with wide
expanded wings trampling on a serpent. The twelve hours
were marked out beneath its wings, six on either side, and
the sun shining through a hole in each wing marked the hour
or the day. Near the eastern goal was a row of statues of
charioteers, driving their chariots and turning the goal.
Besides these there were many other statues of persons and
animals ; an elephant with a proboscis that moved is mentioned, but it is not clear however that this last was in the
hippodrome.

Sigurd, King of Norway, saw the games given here in
1111 ; there was a spectacle in which people appeared as if
riding in the air, some sort of fireworks, also music with
playing of organs, harps, and other instruments.[2] Benjamin
of Tudela (1161) says, "lions, bears, and leopards were shown,
and all nations of the world were represented, together with
surprising feats of jugglery." The hippodrome was used
for spectacles after the change of masters. An Italian MS.
of 1582 in the British Museum describes the ambassadors
and princes sitting on staging, with a large stand for the

[1] Nicetas, ed. Bonn, p. 857.
[2] An organ is shown on the sculptured base of the obelisk of Theodosius.

band in the "piazza" of the hippodrome ; the Sultan and his son sat on an inclosed and covered throne.[1]

Augusteum.—" In front of the palace," says Procopius, "there is a forum surrounded with columns. The Byzantines call this forum the Augusteum. On the eastern side stands the Senate-house." Other writers speak of it as the Agora of the Milion, or simply as the Milion, from the building which adjoined it. Zonaras seems to call it the Proaulion of the Great Church. Round its sides were peristyles, and the buildings mentioned in the first chapter, most of which were re-built by Justinian. It was laid with a marble floor of long slabs, a portion of which was discovered many feet below the present level, together with the inscribed base of the silver statue of Eudoxia, when Fossati built the new government offices in 1848.

"Outside the palace the public baths of Zeuxippus and the great porticoes and all the buildings on either hand as far as the Forum of Constantine are the work of the emperor Justinian."[2] Large pillars have frequently been found which appear to have formed part of colonnades in the Augusteum. Gyllius saw seven large Corinthian columns, forty-six feet high over all and "twenty foot ten digits apart." On the shaft of one was cut the name of Constantine, with the signal of the cross he saw in the heavens, and the inscription ЄΝ ΤΟΥΤѠ ΝΙΚΑ. These, he seems to suggest, may have belonged to the Milion. On this is built up a characteristic piece of restoration by Paspates, who sees in the seven columns, standing over twenty feet apart, and obviously in a straight line, " a square building resting on seven columns," to which he adds an upper range of pillars supporting a domed chamber. Bondelmontius, who is also cited for these columns, says there were six, and *all in a row.* They were almost certainly a part of the nine columns seen by Clavijo[3] before the Fall, when he was told that "a great palace used to stand on the top of them, where the patriarch and his clergy held their meetings."

1 MS. Mus. Brit., Sloane 2742, xvi. c.
2 Procopius.
3 Hakluyt Soc., p. 36.

This great square, surrounded by colonnades, contained so many statues and other works of art that Labarte well calls it an open air museum. To the north, opposite the south-west corner of the church, was the colossal bronze equestrian statue of Justinian surmounting a pillar, which, according to Procopius, stood on seven stages of steps and was covered with bronze reliefs. The king looked to the east, and carried the orb of the earth surmounted by a cross in his hand. The pillar had originally been erected by Arcadius to support a silver statue of Theodosius his father. The statue of Justinian, which replaced that of Theodosius, was destroyed by lightning in 1492.[1] The fragments were seen by Gyllius, and, from measurements which he gives, it seems to have been from twice to three times natural size. Bondelmontius says the pillar was seventy cubits high. A very good drawing of the statue, now amongst the MSS. of the Serai library, made about the year 1340, is reproduced by Mordtmann. This pillar and its statue is often called the Augusteum, and it probably gave its name to the place in which it stood.

The Milion.—It is probable that the city milestone existed before Constantine, who may have built the structure over it. According to Du Cange [2] the Augusteum, with which it was so closely associated, was often called by its name ; so that Codinus tells us that the church of S. Phocas was built "in the Milion." It appears to have formed the western boundary and gate of this forum, or at least of its inner part, if divided, and to have been connected with a colonnade running north and south as well as with the *Mese*. It is spoken of as a colonnade (*embolos*), as vaulted (*kamara* and *phournikon*), or as having many arches (*apsides*). Cedrenus and other writers speak of statues in the apsis or kamara of the Milion. It can hardly be doubted that it had four large arches facing different ways. A structure of this kind remains at Lattaquieh, which is about ten metres square and was surmounted by a dome. De Vogüé [3] compares it with ruins

---

[1] *Nuremberg Chronicle.*
[2] *Constantinopolis Christiana*, lib. i., ch. xxiv.
[3] *La Syrie Centrale*, p. 75.

of a similar erection found at Palmyra, the Mesomphalion of Nicaea, and the Umbilicus of Antioch described by Dion Chrysostom, and others. This last stood at the centre of the two great colonnaded streets that ran east to west and north to south through the city.

The principal reference to the Milion is the description by Nicetas[1] of the struggle with the insurgent troops in the reign of Alexius Manuel. "As many buildings as adjoined the Great Church and commanded the Augusteum were seized by the rebels, who scaled the large *apsis* which stands over the Milion, and also fortified the church of S. Alexius, which is joined to the Augusteum. But the imperial troops made a sally from the great palace and established themselves in the church of S. John called Diippus ; and the agora was full of men who were injured by those on the *apsis* of the Milion, and on the church of S. Alexius. But fresh troops from the palace filled all the thoroughfares and passages leading to S. Sophia. The rebels, coming out of the temple and passing by the Augusteum, became engaged with the others in the narrow ways, and the conflict remained uncertain, until the imperial troops drove back from the streets those who had come out of S. Sophia and shut them within the Augusteum. The imperial troops broke open the gates of the Augusteum, and the rebels were forced from the top of the Milion by the troops mounting the *apsides*, while the rest of them, being worsted in the Augusteum, gave way ; but a shower of missiles was kept up from the part called Macron, overlooking the Augusteum, and the neighbouring chamber of Thomais. They took refuge in the pronaos of the church, where is the Archangel Michael in mosaic standing with drawn sword as if on guard. The imperial troops, because of the narrowness, were unable to follow them with advantage, nor did the insurgents dare to trust themselves out again. The patriarch descended into the *proskenion* or *protekdikeion* of the church, and then harangued them to prevent further sacrilege."

In the *Ceremonies* we twice read of the emperor passing through the nave of S. Sophia and its Royal Gate,

[1] Ed. Bonn, p. 307 *et seq.*

then across the narthex, and, by the *louter* (fountain), reaching the steps of the *athyr* (atrium). "Then he passes through the Milion, and along the Mese and reaches the Forum, where is the Chapel of S. Constantine." Labarte, wrongly explaining this as the Forum Augusteum, instead of that of Constantine, makes the *louter* the baptistery, and the *athyr* its porch. Other processions from the Palace to the Church through the Milion have been given by Labarte.

The colonnades adjoining the Milion are mentioned in the account of a fire which attacked a part of the Great Church in the reign of Isaac Angelus. "The parts by the apsis of the Milion, and the Macron, and the place called the Synods were burnt. The porticoes of Domninus were reduced to ashes, as well as the two covered ways starting on both sides of the Milion one of which reaches to the Philadelphion." [1] The Philadelphion was towards Constantine's forum, and the other way probably led from the Milion north and south to the church and the palace gate.

We learn from Agatho the Deacon [2] that in the porticoes (*stoai*) of the Milion were represented the seven Œcumenical Synods of Constantinople ; this is probably what is meant by Nicetas, where he speaks of "The Synods" as quoted above (see, however, Mordtmann, p. 68). The seven synods is one of the iconographic schemes given by the *Byzantine Manual*, and they are represented in the mosaics at the Nativity Church at Bethlehem.

Horologium.—In close connection both with the Milion and the church was the court of "the time-measure"—a sundial or water-clock. At the triumphal entry of Basil "they passed along the Mese up to the Milion, and entered through the embolos of the Milion into the Horologium, and, having put off their crowns in the metatorium within the Beautiful Gate, they entered the narthex." [3] The Horologium is constantly spoken of as being near the baptistery, and was certainly on the south side of the church.

[1] Nicetas, p. 733.   [2] Quoted by Buzantios.
[3] *Ceremonies*, appendix *ad lib.* i., p. 502.

Baptistery.—In our first chapter we have given reasons for supposing that the round building at the north-east formed part of the earlier church and became the baptistery of Justinian's building. Buzantios considered that the former was the baptistery "perhaps also used as a sacristy." A knowledge of an earlier baptistery would seem to be implied in the way the south-west building is spoken of by Porphyrogenitus and later writers as the "Great Baptistery by the Horologium."

According to Codinus and the Anonymous the Great Baptistery was built before the church, and Salzenberg thought the style was earlier than that of the church. Is it possible that this was built as an independent church and only ultimately became the baptistery? It appears from the account of the Russian pilgrim Anthony that in the twelfth century its dome was painted with the baptism of Christ in Jordan, a scheme which agrees with the two baptisteries at Ravenna.

St. Peter's Chapel, &c.—To the east there were some detached buildings, at least in later times. The Anonymous we have seen mentions a chapel of St. Peter as near the skeuophylakium. Anthony speaks of this chapel, in which St. Peter's chains and the carpet of St. Nicholas were preserved, as behind the altar. The anonymous Russian says a chapel of St. Nicholas was behind the bema, and also speaks of a marble basin covered with a lead roof, "where they baptise the emperors" as being behind the altar, in a space set round with cypresses. Anna Comnena also mentions "the chapel of the Hierarch Nicholas" as part of the Great Church and a place of sanctuary.[1] The passage of St. Nicholas is also referred to. It is possible that this chapel was otherwise known as St. Peter's, and either this or "the place where they baptise the emperors" may be the present round building—the ancient baptistery as we suppose. That St. Peter's chapel was of some importance and detached seems clear from the *Menologium*. On January 16 was celebrated the adoration of St. Peter's chains. It is explained that after Peter's release, "the chains were found by some

[1] Ed. Bonn, v., p. 266.

believers and guarded from generation to generation until
they were brought to Constantinople by a pious emperor
and placed in the church (ναὸς) of St. Peter which is near
St. Sophia." We have given a picture of the chains in
Figure 8. A tradition of some of these buildings may be
preserved in an Italian MS. of 1611 in the British Museum.
" The ancient buildings round the church have been ruined
by the Turks except a small part of the close (*canonica*),
where they have made dwellings ; there is also the sacristy
and the place of the baptistery, which had originally three
vaulted ceilings, one above another. It was of wonderful
architecture and made with six angles. From the sacristy to
the base of the dome is an arquebus shot ; between it and
the Seraglio lies a road."

Boundaries.—Probably the fullest and clearest account of
the approach to the church through the Augusteum is given
by the Spanish ambassador Clavijo, who was at Constantinople in 1405, at a time when many of the buildings in the
precincts had been destroyed. In a court in the front of the
church, he saw " nine very large columns of white marble,"
and he was told that before his time a palace had been here,
where the patriarch met the canons in chapter. " And in
the same place before the church stands a stone pillar of
marvellous height, on the top of which is a horse of copper
as large as four horses put together ; on the horse was an
armed knight with a great plume on his head like a peacock's tail. The horse has chains of iron round its body
secured to the column to prevent it from falling, or being
moved by the wind. The horse is very well made, and one
fore and one hind leg is raised, as if it were in the act of
prancing. The knight, on its back, has his right arm raised,
with the hand open, while the reins are held with the left
hand. This marvellous horse is said to have been placed
here by the Emperor Justinian, who erected the column.
At the entrance to the church under an arch in front of a
gate, is a place adorned with four columns, and below is a
little chapel very rich and beautiful. And beyond this chapel
is the gate to the church covered with bronze very great and
high ; beyond again is a little court surrounded by high

galleries [horologium?]. Afterwards there was another gate of bronze [the south porch]. Beyond this gate there is a 'nave' vast and high, with a ceiling of wood [the exonarthex]. And on the left hand there is a cloister very large, and beautiful [the atrium], with many stones of jasper of infinite variety of colour. On the right hand under the said nave—covered as I have said—and after the second gate, you arrive at the body of the church, which has five doors, high and large, covered with bronze, of which that in the middle is the greatest."[1]

The present south porch we should suppose is the pronaos mentioned by Nicetas as that where the Archangel Michael stood on guard. The exonarthex is now vaulted, but not covered with mosaic; it is bare and rough, and it seems possible that at one time there may have been a ceiling of wood.

Stephen of Novgorod (1350) says that the first gate of the church was by the column of Justinian; then there was a second, a third, fourth, fifth and sixth and by the seventh you entered the great church. This may be exaggeration, but Gyllius speaks of the south entrance formerly being by six *valvae* of brass, " now there are only three, ingeniously worked," so that there would appear to have been at least one more double door in his time than the two now existing. If we consult the careful drawings made by Grelot, which take us half way back to the conquest, we shall see that the boundaries of the cypress garden on the south side agree entirely with the present walls. The first of the turbehs was built here about a hundred years after the conquest, and we may almost safely assume that it was backed against the outer wall, as at present. Now when we find Clavijo, some fifty years before the conquest, in approaching the church from this side, speak of an outer gateway and a court before the church was reached, we shall almost certainly be justified in placing this outer gate on the present boundary. The fountain in the south court we suppose occupies the site of an ancient fountain. A comparison of Grelot's plan (1680) with Fossati's (1850), will make clear the south boundaries

[1] Hakluyt Soc. series.

of the church, as they existed at the time of the conquest. The octagonal building attached to the south side of the church shown in Fossati's plan must be Turkish, probably the library of the sultan mentioned by Pococke.

The palace of the patriarch, with the library of the Thomaites, we would place on the ground between the south boundary and the church, the gardens which belonged to it occupying the ground of one of the courts. It had evidently been destroyed by the time of Clavijo's visit, and for what is known as to the buildings we must refer to Paspates.

The courts to the north of the church were probably occupied by the cells of the clergy and the college called Didaskalion (see our page 49); Bondelmontius speaks of "the way of a thousand columns in pairs" (the Mese) through which the emperor walked to S. Sophia "where the houses of the 800 clergy were round the church."[1]

The Atrium.—The street lying at an angle to the west wall of the entrance courtyard, rising steeply towards the hippodrome, is probably ancient.

Some considerable remains of the atrium colonnade were in existence in the present century, but they were finally destroyed in 1873.[2] The present boundary of the western court appears to occupy the position of the exterior west wall of the atrium. Outside it there is a level roadway, beyond which the ground falls rapidly to the street. As the church stands across a hill the ground had to be made up to a level, and this, together with the position of the street, would account for the court not having been square as was usually the case. As excavations have shown that the pavement of the Hippodrome and the Augusteum were eight or ten feet below the present level,[3] steps would have been required to attain the level of the church at the west. The *Ceremonies* show that the royal processions entered and left the church on the south side through the Augusteum, which served as a great forecourt to the church on

---

[1] Anna Comnena also speaks of the houses of the Great Church.
[2] See Curtis *Broken Bits of Byzantium*, part 2.
[3] Paspates, p. 40.

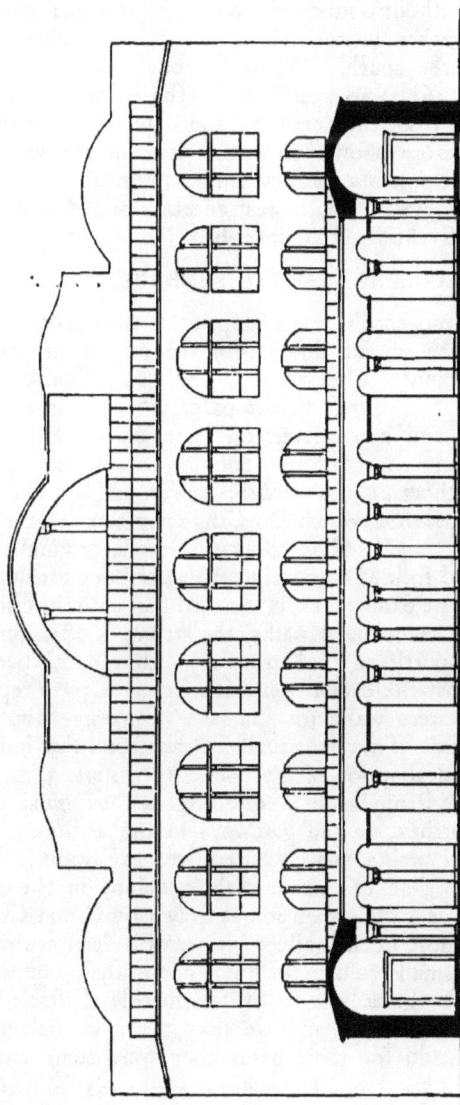

FIG. 25.—Original state of West Front as built by Justinian.

this side.   Without doubt this was the principal entrance.
Clavijo and other visitors all appear to have entered the
church from the south.   When Grelot's western view was
made (before 1680) no west doors to the atrium existed, but
it was entered from the north and south only.   In our plan
we have therefore shown only one door in the west wall
of the atrium, possibly there was none (Fig. 3).

Outside the present south-west entrance of the court there
remained until 1869 a stone inscribed

+CACΘCENΘΑΔEKATOIKIMHΔEI . . . .·

Its form suggests that it was a step, or it may have been a
lintel from one of the doors into the atrium or the rim
from a fountain.[1]   The words "The Holy God dwelleth
here let no . . . . " may be compared with the inscriptions
for fountains and gates given on pages 84 and 264.

This atrium court of S. Sophia was called by the
Byzantine authors *aule, mesaulion, aithria,* and by some late
writer, *garçonastasion,* which Du Cange explains as "the place
where pages wait."   The cloistered walk originally surrounded it and formed a quadriporticus; although the eastern
walk, the present exonarthex, is inclosed and entirely different
from the other colonnaded walks, the atrium is often referred
to as "Four-porticoed" (*Tetrastoon*).   It cannot therefore
be doubted that the exonarthex with its great piers replaced
the original eastern walk, for the sake of greater abutment
to the church.   This is equally clear from the building
itself and the description of the poet.   (See Figs. 3, 24, 25,
29).   The "Propylaeum" often spoken of must either
be this exonarthex, or the gateways in the atrium.

The cloister walks were vaulted, and the walls covered
with marble.   One of the capitals remained in the courtyard as lately as 1873, when it was drawn by Canon Curtis;
it resembled those in the gallery inside, with deep sculptured
dosseret and small volutes below.   More than one writer
remarks on the great beauty of the marble shafts.   They
were set in close order, and we may see from Salzenberg
that, when we add for their bases, they were some twenty-

[1] See Curtis, *Broken Bits of Byz.,* part 2.

two feet high, and must have made a fine portico to the
west front. In 1852 two of the pillars were represented on
the plan of Fossati as still *in situ :* now every evidence of
the atrium has entirely disappeared.

Phiale.—In the middle of the court was placed a fountain,
where, according to the Silentiary, was a "bubbling stream
leaping into the air from a bronze pipe." The name given
to such a fountain by Greek writers was phiale or colymbethra, and, by the Latins, cantharus or nymphaeum. At
S. Sophia it was also called "The Laver of the Atrium"
(λουτήρ μεσαυλίου).[1] The louter or loutron, with its
colymbethra, formed a sanctuary for the pursued : we read
in Procopius of their "fleeing to the church of S. Sophia,
and coming to the holy loutron, and laying hold of the
colymbethra which was there." [2]

According to the Anonymous author, on whom we place
no reliance, the phiale had twelve arcades or columns, and
lions spouted out the water. Canopied phialae it is true
still exist at St. Demetrius at Salonica, and in the monasteries of Mount Athos. The canopy of the phiale at old
St. Peter's was of bronze ; under it the great pine cone,
which still remains, threw out water in innumerable little
threads. On the canopy were probably placed the beautiful
bronze peacocks, which also still exist.[3] A very beautiful
fountain of this kind, at Constantinople, was placed before
the church built by Basil in the palace. The basin was
marble, from which rose a pine cone pierced with holes.
Above on the cornice were placed cocks, stags, and rams, of
cast bronze, from which the water flowed.[4]

In the Court of the Lions at the Alhambra, the basin of
the fountain rests on lions, and the water runs away from the
fountain in four open streams to the four sides of the cloister.

[1] It may be mentioned that an Italian cantharus, or font, of the twelfth
century, in the possession of Mr. Brindley, has the Latinised form of the
same word in an inscription around its rim which reads

Artificum summus cui nullus in orbe secundus Hunc luterem clarum
sollerer sculpsit aquae. . . .

[2] Quoted by Paspates, *Byzan. Mel.* Note on p. 340.
[3] Lanciani, *Pagan and Christ. Rome.*
[4] Labarte, *Pal. Imp.*

This work was certainly executed under Byzantine influence, and it is curious to find more than one small garden fountain at Constantinople in which the water issues from the mouth of lions. On the other hand it seems probable that the Anonymous imitated the description of the temple of Solomon and the laver, which stood on twelve oxen. The other washing place he describes (see page 141) with the different kinds of animals represented, seems to be founded on the description of that of Basil's church.

Porphyrogenitus speaks of the "cup of the phiale"; and it seems most probable, considering the simple description of the Silentiary, that, as in so many ancient churches, it was at first merely a bowl, standing on a pillar rising from a polygonal basin. In the time of Michael Palaeologus, there was such a basin on the sides of which "was engraved on the marble the honoured form of the cross." [1] A bowl figured by Gruterus [2] in 1602 as "newly found at Constantinople," has been spoken of by Du Cange and others as having belonged to S. Sophia, although the evidence of this is not very positive. [3] This was a circular bowl very similar to the well-known representation of a cantharus of Justinian's time in the Ravenna mosaic. The inscription around the rim read equally well in both directions. [4] This circle being horizontal, we cannot but think, as it would necessarily be read from outside, that Gruterus was mistaken in putting the bottom of the letters toward the centre; we have therefore reversed this in our figure. The words "Wash thy sins, not thy face only," almost certainly refer it to a phiale. Eusebius, for instance, speaking of one of these fountains, says, "it is not meet for an unclean foot to step on the sacred place within the temple," and Paulinus tells us that at Nola those who entered the church washed

---

[1] *Pachymeres de Michael Palaeol.*, ed. Migne, p. 703. See also Du Cange, *S. Sophia*, § 22.   [2] *Inscriptiones Antiquae totius orbis Romani.*
[3] Grelot is vague in regard to it. Banduri understood him to mean that the inscription was on the inner water vessels. The Greek patriarch Constantios accepts it as having belonged to the Phiale. Buzantios wildly says baptistery.
[4] An inscrip. in Baptistery Florence, reads—
EN GIRO TORTE SOL CICLOS ET ROTOR IGNE.

FIG. 26.—Inscription on Phiale from Gruter.

their hands in a similar place.[1] Probably, so accurate a writer as Du Cange had good reasons for referring the bowl in question to S. Sophia. Dr. Covel of Cambridge, who was at Constantinople from 1670 to 1677, and has left a valuable MS. now in the British Museum, which we shall have further occasion to quote, also gives the inscription, which he says came from the fountain of S. Sophia, but again, it is possible he derived this from Du Cange, or from Grelot, whom he appears to have met, for some of the Frenchman's drawings are included in the MS.

In this collection are drawings of two beautiful phiale cups, which existed at Ephesus when visited by Dr. Covel. From the simple elegance of their forms we suppose that these bowls cannot be later than the sixth century.[2] See Fig. 27.

Pavement of the Court.—When the Anonymous tells us that the four boundaries of the church were called after the rivers that flowed from Paradise, it is quite evident from the context that he is speaking of the atrium ; and it seems probable that immediately before, where he speaks of "ever flowing waters of great rivers," he is describing the pavement of the court as figuring four streams. This certainly would furnish a reason for the walks taking their names from the four rivers of marble which flowed towards them, like

[1] See p. 84 and Kraus for other similar inscriptions.
[2] The first, he says, "stands by the entrance to an old Bagno," it was 4' 3½" in diameter. "The second stands in the midst of the cistern in the square court of the supposed St. John's Church." This was 2' 6" in. diameter.

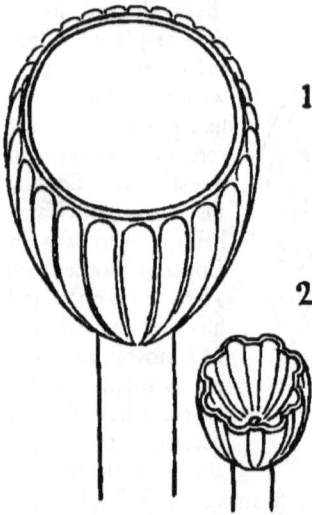

FIG. 27.—Phiale Bowls from Ephesus.

the four real streams flow in the court of the Alhambra. There is much to countenance this theory. For instance, the atrium of old St. Peter's was called Paradise : Symeon of Thessalonica tells us the part outside the doors of a church represented the creation, as the bema symbolised heaven; and the idea might easily be referred to the words used in the service for blessing the waters of the phiale.

This custom of blessing the waters on the eve of Epiphany, to which Paulus the Silentiary alludes (see page 44), was practised as early as the end of the fourth century.[1] Goar gives the ritual.[2] After the evening service the priest with the censer and candlestick proceeds to the "*luter* of the *mesaulion*," chanting "the voice of the Lord is upon the waters." Part of the ceremony of blessing included a prayer, " We beseech thee, O Almighty Father . . . . who fixed Paradise in Eden and bade its quadruple spring flow far and wide . . . . who blessed the waters for Jacob, and hast bidden us, through thy prophet Isaiah, to draw water in gladness from the fountains of the Saviour." The account of the Anonymous may be a duplication of his description of the interior, but outside Charlemagne's church at Aix there is a pine cone which formerly belonged to a phiale ; the water rained from it through little holes, and about the foot are verses referring to the rivers of Paradise and Baptism.

West Front.—On the east side of the atrium court,

[1] Migne, *Pat. Cur. Com. Series Graeca*, vol. i.
[2] *Euchologium*, ed. 1647, p. 463.

against the west wall of the exonarthex, rise four great piers
from which spring flying arches to the west wall of the church.
Salzenberg thought that the upper arches were Turkish, and that
the piers were originally intended to support equestrian statues,
which he therefore shows in his drawings. Other writers,
amongst whom is Fossati, say that the bronze horses now
on the gallery outside the west front of S. Mark's at Venice,
taken from Constantinople in 1204, came from this position ;
but there is not the least authority for this statement, and the
horses at Venice are not half the size of those that would be
required to justify the suggestion. Bondelmontius in 1422
describing the columns of the city, speaks first of that of
Justinian, "secondly of that of the Cross, where are seen
four upright porphyry columns ; and on them were placed
four bronze horses which the Venetians took to S. Mark's at
Venice, but the columns remain." Brocquière, writing ten
years later, says that "westward [in the city] is a very high
square column with characters traced on it, and bearing on
the summit an equestrian statue of Constantine in bronze.
He holds a sceptre in his left hand, with his right extended
towards Turkey in Asia and the road to Jerusalem as if to
denote that the whole of that country was under his government. Near this column are three [sic] others placed in a
line, and of single pieces which bore the three gilt horses
now in Venice." Brocquière has here certainly confused the
column of Justinian, and that of Constantine, but we may
safely accept Bondelmontius. The porphyry column of
Constantine, situated in the Forum Constantine, at this time
bore a cross with the inscription "Holy, Holy, Holy."
Many modern writers place the four horses in the hippodrome, as Nicetas speaks of "the arched starting-places for
the racers, above which are fixed powerful horses of gilt
bronze, curving their necks and facing one another as if
eager for the course" (Ed. Bonn, p. 150).

Between the four great piers of the west front there are
now three doorways. If, however, we refer to the plates of
Salzenberg, we shall find that only the two lateral ones are
there shown, and that the position of the central door is
occupied by a window ; this arrangement was seen by Texier

in 1834, and is shown in a MS. drawing of his, now in the library of the Royal Institute of Architects. Referring to the views and plan which Grelot published in 1680, we see the central bay occupied by a belfry, with a pyramidal top rising above the roof of the exonarthex. Now in Goar's *Euchologium* [1] there is a note to this effect, " The Greeks first took up the use of bells from the time when Urso Patricio, Doge of Venice, in the year 865, sent them to Michael the emperor, who greatly valued them, and built a tower for them against S. Sophia." We have already seen that large repairs were made to the west front of the church about this time (page 123), with a view of counteracting the thrust of the vaults. Before the belfry was built the Semantron would have been used ; this was a plate of bronze or wood suspended in the atrium and struck like a gong (see Fig. 28). It appears from the Russian pilgrims that the bells remained in use for only a short time. A sixteenth century French MS. in the British Museum speaks of the old square tower and bells. Grelot [2] says "this tower, formerly the belfry, is now void, the Turks having exchanged the music of bells for the noise of cannon." It was not fifty *toises* high, and could not have held many bells, or large ones. [3]

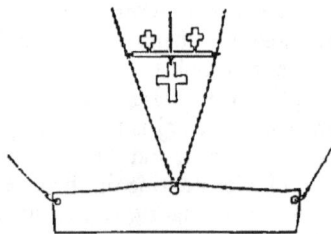

FIG. 28.—Semantron at Constantinople, from Lenoir.

The upper story of the narthex, Grelot tells us was supported by six flying buttresses, and both his exterior views show three complete piers and flying arches on each side of the tower. The bay next the belfry on the right was occupied by a low building with a pent roof, in which were descending

[1] Ed. 1647, p. 560.
[2] *Relation Nouvelle d'un Voyage de Constantinople*.
[3] In Fig. 29 we have followed his drawings disregarding his estimate of height.

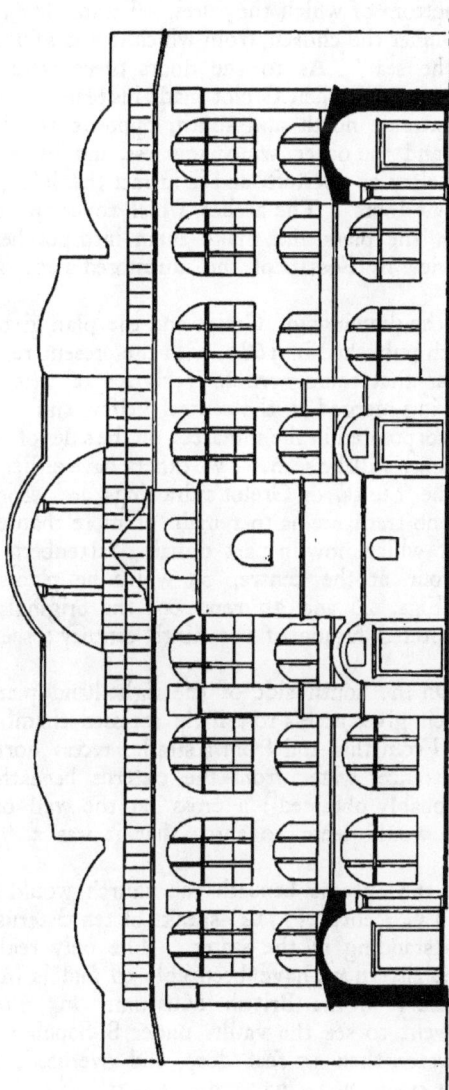

Fig. 29.—West Front as altered in the Ninth Century.

steps, at the bottom of which they drew off water from "the great cisterns under the church, from which it was said a boat might reach the sea." As to the doors there were three towards the west, used when Grelot made his plan, two being those at the extreme north and south, opposite the lateral atrium walks, and the other, which was less, and little used, was next the belfry on the left, and is in fact the left one of the three present doors. The arches, which cover two of the spaces between the piers and make them into porches, are shown in the view by Fossati of the unrestored state of the front.

Comparing the drawings of Grelot and the plan given by Du Cange, both published in 1680, with the present remains, it would appear that there were formerly ten of these buttresses ; two being merged in the central belfry, and the two outside ones incorporated in the minarets, on the sides of which traces of them may still be seen. Two others have either been destroyed by the Turks, or Grelot's drawings are wrong to this extent, as no trace seems to remain of more than eight. Of these eight which now in part remain, Salzenberg only reserves the four at the centre, on which he places the horses. Our Figs. 26 and 29 represent the original west front and the altered façade of the ninth century ; see also Plan, Fig. 24.

Cisterns.—On the south side of the right-hand pier is a small arch which gives access to a little recessed chamber in the buttress. From this and from a similar recess north of the central entrance, water from the cisterns beneath the church was probably obtained : a cross on the wall of the little chamber would seem to show that it was a "holy well." [1]

Clavijo says the cisterns beneath the church would float ten galleys, and C. Lebrun (1714) speaks of ten cisterns and forty columns standing in the water. The only real description of the cistern we have been able to find is in Dr. Covel's MS. diary in the British Museum. In 1676 he writes, "We went to see the vaults under S. Sophia ; they were full of water, then 17 feet deep, and overhead, from

[1] Curtis, *Broken Bits of Byz.*, Part II.

the water up to the top of the arch was about 2 yards and 6 inches. Every pillar is square ($4\frac{1}{2}$ feet), and distant from another just 12 feet. The bricks are very broad, thin, and well baked ; [it is] not plastered within, the mortar very hard. They say it goes under [the] At-Meidan, but we could not enter it. The waste water of the Aqueduct enters into it, and [going] out of it passing through the Seraglio, goes into the sea by the dunghill. [There is] severe punishment to [those who] have houses with offices [draining] into it ; or [for those who] throw any filth into it : the well of S. Sophia [opens] into it and many wells in the Seraglio." He gives a diagram plan, showing two rows of eight piers and a third row of three, although, as no boundary is shown, it is impossible to say if this is the whole extent (see below).[1]

Generally.—Some of the exterior was doubtless cased with marble like S. Mark's ; indeed some of the marble plating remained in Salzenberg's time. " The walls outside (the Anonymous writes) were covered with large and valuable stones." Where not so incrusted the narrow coursed brickwork showed in thin red lines, almost equalled by the thick joints of the mortar. From this brickwork the marble lattices of the windows, each with its slab at the bottom charged with a cross, shone out fair, and the gray lead of the many domes rose above all, curve on curve in pearly gradation of light. The courts were doubtless closely set with cypresses, like those which now rise about the turbehs on the south side.

Many passages in the Byzantine authors show how much beauty of site was regarded as essential for a fair church.[2] Procopius, describing the Church of the Fountain at Constantinople, says, " there was a grove of cypresses in a rich meadow of blooming flowers, a garden abounding in fruit, with a gently bubbling spring of sweet water, everything suggested the site of a church."

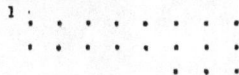

[1] . . . .
. . . .
. . .

[2] See P. D. Kouppas, *The Building of Byzantine Churches.* Ἑλλην. Φιλολ. Συλλ. παραρ. vol. 20-22, p. 38.

CHAPTER X

§ I.—ORIGINS.

It may be well to say a few words on the growth of the Byzantine architecture, of which Justinian's church is the perfect flower. This building is often spoken of as if it were at once the first and the maturest essay in this great style, but this we might know would have been impossible, even though the links that led up to it were lost, which is not entirely the case. It is perfectly true, however, as Mr. Morris says, that "the style leaps into sudden completeness in this most lovely building."

The new wants of the Church soon evolved the complete Christian basilica, which, it has been said must have been in the mind of the writer of the Apocalypse as the type of the entire arrangement of the altar, the twenty-four elders, and the great congregation, in his vision of the heavenly worship. In the time of Constantine, and in Rome, alongside of work which was entirely classic, the churches, with fewer ties to the past to limit development along truly rational lines, had developed a manner which was a more direct outcome of the necessities of building with a minimum of merely perfunctory "architectural" forms—those conventions for the thoughtless expenditure of the workers' labour, which in still worse times make architecture a burden to them instead of a delight.

This transitional style is rightly called early Christian, or Constantinian. In the East, the vital part of the empire at this time, a greater change was taking place that brought back life once again to the arts of decoration ; this may be expressed in a formula as the re-orientalization of classic art—the linking of simple massive Roman building to a new decoration, vividly alive and inventive, frank, bright, and full of colour, and yet as rational in its choice and application as the construction. In the modern sense the Romans may be said to have invented building, and the Byzantine-Greeks architecture.

The Roman system of arched building, covered with brick and concrete vaulted shells and domes, had been masked by non-functional pillars, tablements, and pediments in what was thought the true Athenian manner ; at the same time many beautiful decorative expedients were also in use, such as the lining of walls with large thin marble slabs, or small pieces of glass of various forms and colours. Mosaic of gold glass seems to have been known before the time of Constantine.[1]   Gold tesserae probably originated in an at first almost accidental use of portions of the Roman glass vessels which are decorated by patterns in gold leaf protected by a thin layer of glass over the surface.   Parts of such vessels are found used decoratively in the Catacombs.

Byzantine architecture was developed by the use of brick in the frankest and fullest manner, especially in domical vaulting. Wide spans were kept in equipoise by other smaller domes. The more concentrated supports were marble monoliths, and the wall and vault surfaces were covered by incrustations of marble slabs and glass mosaic.   Directness, an economy of labour relative to the results obtained, is perhaps the most essential characteristic of the art both in construction and decoration in the great period.   This freedom and rationality mark it out from all other styles of building, or rather make it include all other styles, for this reaches the universal.   M. Choisy rightly insists on the fact that the Byzantine builders endeavoured to suppress preparatory and auxiliary work, and to execute their vaults and domes without centring.   "The greater number of their vaults," he says "rose in space without any kind of support. . . .

[1] For gold tesserae of second cent. see *Bull. Soc. des Ant.*, 1893, p. 76.

Their method is not a mere variation of that of the West, but it is quite a distinct system, not even derived from a Roman source, but Asiatic. Byzantine art is the Greek spirit working on Asiatic elements." Here we have an extreme statement in one direction, and the word Roman must be used in a narrow sense ; for these Asiatic elements in construction, of which alone M. Choisy seems to be speaking, whatever were their remote origins must have been completely absorbed into the larger Rome of the Empire, and we have no knowledge of any other system of con-

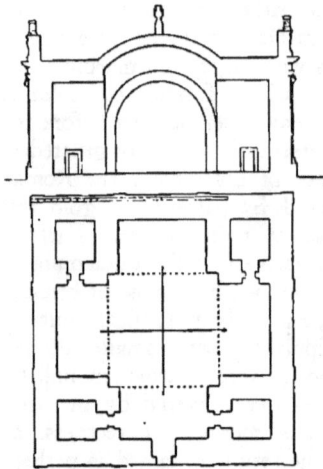

Fig. 30.—Roman Tomb in Palestine.

struction in western Asia from the first to the fourth century than " Roman," unless we subdivide this into Palmyrene, Herodian, or construct an imaginary Persian style out of what went before and came afterwards. Choisy himself shows that a large use of burnt brick was first made by the Romans, and that the system of building vaults in sections known in Assyria and Egypt had been adopted by Roman builders in the East in the time of Constantine. But this was the essential germ of Byzantine construction. It was the falling away of a dead scholasticism that left Roman building in the East free to be shaped into Byzantine architecture. Mr. Bury, who is extreme in the opposite direction, and makes the same claim for the continuity of Roman art as he does for the Empire, suggests that Romaic would be a better term than Byzantine. But whatever name is given to the political system we must remember that the arts are shaped by the people, and that the people were truly Greek who, in the age of Justinian, thought out and left to the

modern world the last great gift of Hellenic genius—
mediæval Greek architecture.

While the art of building in the East, particularly
in Syria and Asia Minor, and possibly in Egypt, was
still distinctly Roman, a ferment and change may be
detected which cannot be matched in Rome itself. Both in
construction and ornamentation there is much already at
Palmyra and Baalbec that belongs to the new, and repudi-
ates the rules of merely official art.

In Rome the dome never appears to have been finally
adapted to a composite building by being directly applied to a
square plan.   The dome on pendentives, so far as we know,
was invented and perfected entirely in the East.   M. Choisy
figures a building from Jerash, which may be of the third
or fourth century which he considers the earliest known
dome on pendentives.   This building, although it is plainly
early, has nothing characteristically Roman about it.   A
building of the same class however, recently discovered
by the Palestine Exploration Society at Kusr en Nûeijîs in
eastern Palestine,[1] is an ornate example of late Roman work ;
Ionic pilasters and carved entablature mask the outside, while
within we have a perfected dome on pendentives covering a
central square area, counterpoised by four barrel vaults.   We
agree with the Memoir that—"there can be little hesitation
in ascribing this building to the second century A.D."
This building, probably a mausoleum, in adjustment of
parts, and geometrical development might be a Byzantine
church of three hundred years later.   It is a little Sancta
Sophia, and taken together with the Jerash building it
makes a class invaluable as a fixed point to work from.[2]
This however like most Syrian buildings is of stone.

A church at Koja Kalessi in Isauria,[3] Fig. 31, which there
is a great reason to suppose of early fifth century work,
furnishes an important link.   We have here an approximation of the square domed building to the columned basilica
which is most interesting.   This church is substantially

[1] *Eastern Palestine Memoirs*, 1889, p. 172.
[2] See Fig. 30.
[3] From the Hellenic Society's supplement to their journal.

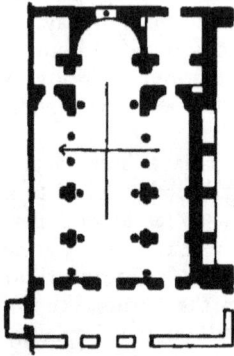

FIG. 31.—Plan of a Church in
Isauria.

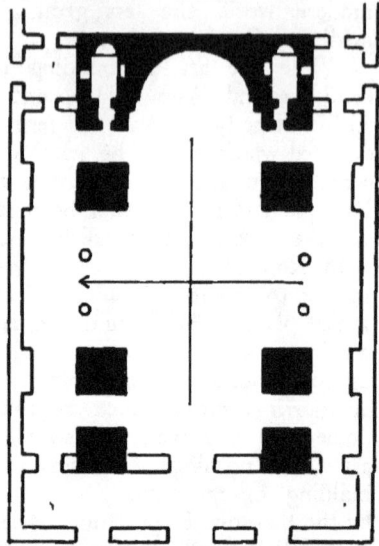

FIG. 32.—Church of the Trinity, Ephesus.

complete with women's galleries opening to the nave by a
second tier of arcades just as at S. Sophia.

The next building we should place in the sequence is the
church of the Trinity at Ephesus of which Hübsch, Wood
and Choisy give plans. The former furnishes a restoration,
and speaks of it as probably one of the earliest of Christian
churches, but there is no reason to suppose it earlier than
the beginning of the fifth century. Choisy speaks of it
as a curious monument of transition already Byzantine in
structure. Before seeing Hübsch's restoration, we had
placed an arcade in the lateral arches, agreeing in every
respect with his suggestions ; and that this was the original
form is strongly confirmed by the next church—as it seems
to us—in the development. This is the church of S. Sophia
at Salonica, which has long been assigned to Justinian's
reign at a time subsequent to the erection of S. Sophia, but
is now thought to belong to the fifth century. M. Petros

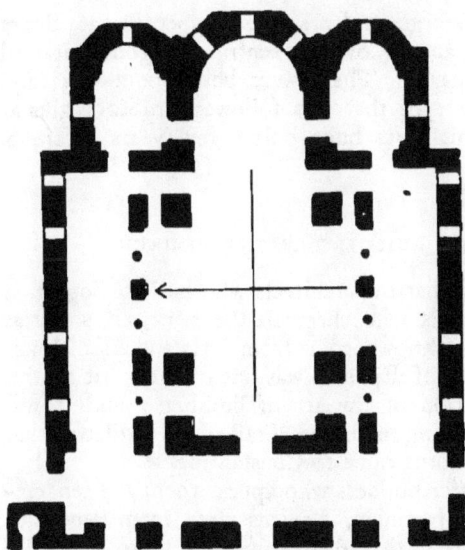

FIG. 33.—Church of S. Sophia, Salonica.   Scale about forty-five feet to an inch, for three plans.

Papageorgios in the *Hestia*[1] of Athens for October 3rd and November 14th 1893, gives the mosaic inscription of this church, which he thinks definitely fixes its decoration in the year 495.[2] The churches at Cassaba, Ancyra and Myra in Asia Minor engraved in Texier's *Asie Mineure*, and repeated by Salzenberg relate themselves so closely to this chain of development that we believe they will be found to belong rather to the fifth and sixth centuries than to the seventh or eighth as those writers thought. The square type with a central dome persisted independently without coalescing with the basilica. Such was the domed church at Antioch founded by Constantine and completed by Constantius ; here the central dome was surrounded by aisles, and formed an octagon. In the

[1] See also *Byzantinische Zeitschrift*, 1894.

[2] The inscription states that the work was done while Paul was archbishop. And—

ΜΗΝΙΝΟΕΜΒΡΙѠΙΝΔΙΚΤΙΟΝΙΤΕΤΑΡΤΗΕΤΟΥϹ
ΑΠΟΚΤΙϹΕѠϹΚΟϹΜΟΥϹ

The vital numerals were defaced, but there seemed no doubt that the last fragment was a part of S (6000) and as the writer states that there was only room for one more letter, SΔ or 6004 (495) is the only year that will fit the fourth indiction. "The architect Bubroff is about to show that the church was built in the fifth century."

churches of St. George at Ezra, and St. Sergius at Bozra
we have domes standing over a central octagon contained
in an external square. These were built about 515, and
they furnished the type that was followed at St. Sergius at
Constantinople which was built only a few years before S.
Sophia.

§ 2. THE BUILDERS OF THE CHURCH.

It is noteworthy that the architects who built S. Sophia as
well as the historians who chronicle the work, all, so far as
their birth-places are known, come from Syria and Asia Minor.
The flourishing city of Ephesus was one of the great centres
of the transformation of the art of building ; and it was
from the neighbouring cities of Tralles and Miletus, that
Anthemius and Isidorus came to Constantinople.

Of the two master builders who appear to have been employed together by Justinian, it seems clear, from Procopius
and the other writers, that Anthemius was more especially
concerned in the preparation of the first draft or model, and
that Isidorus, by birth a Milesian, was associated with him in
the conduct of the works.

"Anthemius," says Paulus, "skilled in setting out a plan,
laid the foundation." "Anthemius was the man who devised
and worked at every part," writes Agathias, and this author
gives some account of his life. "Now this Anthemius was
born at Tralles, and he was an inventor of machines ; one of
those who apply designs to material, and make models and
imitations of real things. He was distinguished in this and
had reached the summit of mathematical knowledge, just
as his brother Metrodorus was distinguished in letters.
Besides these there were three other brothers, Olympus,
famous for his knowledge of law, and Dioscorus and
Alexander, both skilled in medicine. Of these Dioscorus
lived in his native land and Alexander in Old Rome. But
the fame of the skill of Anthemius and Metrodorus reached
the emperor, and they were invited to Constantinople, where
they spent the rest of their lives, each presenting wonderful
examples of his skill. One taught letters ; the other raised

wonderful buildings throughout the city and in many other places; these, I think, even if nothing were said about them, as long as they remained unharmed, would be sufficient to win for him perpetual glory."

Stories of his mechanical ingenuity are told by Agathias one of which is as follows. Anthemius had a quarrelsome neighbour whose room overhung his ground. He placed here large kettles of water, with an arrangement of leather pipes and a tube like a trumpet up to the projecting part ; and making the other parts secure, "he heated the water so that the whole thing burst up like an earthquake."

As to the scheme prepared by the master builders for the building, an examination of the evidence seems to suggest the following antecedent conditions and governing ideas. 1. The ground levels required a short and wide church (ante, p. 186). 2. An old western apse possibly suggested the western hemicycle of the new church (ante, p. 19). 3. The plan, while a direct outcome of traditional forms as we have shown, seems a synthesis of the three types which were then current ; the Basilican like S. John Studius; the square church with a dome like S. Sergius, and the cross plan of the Church of the Apostles.

At S. Sergius, the expedient of planning columned exedras to fill out the angles of the square beneath a domed vault had proved its utility and beauty. For the influence of the cross type we need only turn to the plan, and observe that the width across the "transepts" is exactly the same as the length included by the eastern and western hemicycles.

The master builders not only designed the church, they came "and worked at every part," and lived with their building until their death ; they certainly graduated as workmen, and we hear nothing of their honours or position, only .of their genius.[1] In the words of M. Choisy, "In Justinian's time, to build was the essential *rôle* of the architect."

Both master builders are again mentioned as working together on the occasion of the fortifications of Dara in Mesopotamia, having been injured by floods. The emperor

[1] A book on mechanics (περὶ παραδόξων μηχανημάτων) has been ascribed to Anthemius.

on hearing of it at Constantinople "straightway summoned those most celebrated architects Anthemius and Isidorus mentioned before, and inquired what might be devised." The scheme of Chryses, the engineer of the works at Dara, was however adopted.[1]

The younger Isidorus who re-erected the dome of S. Sophia Procopius mentions as having been employed by Justinian in rebuilding the city of Zenobia in Mesopotamia with its fortifications, churches, baths and porticoes. "All this work was done under the superintendence of Isidorus and Joannes, of whom Johannes was a Byzantine and Isidorus a Milesian by birth, being the nephew of that Isidorus I mentioned before."

To the master builders Procopius, Paulus, and Theophanes give the names *mechanikos*, *polumechanos*, *mechanopoios*, to which other writers add *protooikodomos*—"first of the builders," *magistros* and *maistor*. The craftsmen appear to have been classed as *technitai* with a foreman over each subdivision. The Latin names of the different building crafts are given both in Theodosius' code,[2] and in the edict of Diocletian,[3] which fixed their wages. This edict is bilingual, but unfortunately the Greek synonyms for the workmen are wanting. In the description of the building of S. Sophia, Procopius speaks of the *lithologos* or "stone-layer," who built the big piers, Paulus and the Anonymous use *laotoros* and *laotomos* a " mason " and "stone-cutter," wherever marble workers are mentioned, to which must also be added *lithoxos* "stone polisher." The general bricklayers, &c. are comprised as *oikodomoi*. *Tektonikos* implies a carpenter. S. Gregory of Nyssa, in describing a church of S. Theodore, calls the craftsman who arranged the mosaic tesserae, ὁ συνθέτης τῶν ψηφίδων.

A list of the chief classes of workmen employed in the sixth century on a monumental building in Italy given by Cassiodorus,[4] names the following—Instructor-parietum, sculptor-marmorum, camerarum-rotator, gypsoplastes, and

---

[1] Procopius in *Pal. Pilg. Text.*, p. 48.
[2] Lib. xiii., tit. iv.   [3] Edit. by Waddington, p. 18.
[4] Giacomo Boni, *Il Duomo di Parenzo*, in *Archivio Storico dell'Arte*, 1894, p. 5.

musivarius. The instructor-parietum is probably the man who set out the work, the camerarum-rotator is he who turned the vaults. The gypsoplastes, a literal transcription of γυψοπλάστης, signifies a worker or modeller in stucco, corresponding to the plastes-gypsarius of the edict of Diocletian. The musivarius is the "putter together of tesserae" of S. Gregory. Workmen who understood the mysteries of "vault turning" seem to have been especially appreciated, as Theophanes tells us that Isaurian workmen were employed to build the dome of S. Sophia.

In the humblest work the personality of the maker is often delightfully expressed. A Byzantine brick in the British Museum is stamped "XP. made by the most excellent Narsis," and a late Roman glass cup bears the legend "Ennion made this. Think of it, O buyer."

In his inquiry as to the methods of workmanship, M. Choisy says the Byzantine Greeks did not efface from buildings all traces of the workman's individuality. "The workman is no mere passive instrument, obedient, without any regard to initiative or responsibility, to the workshop foreman ; he is treated as an intelligent power, and finds in front of him liberty, and a field open to his imagination."

In Roman times the system was that we call "division of labour." "*L'art roman est un fait d'organisation.*" The workman was not an independent citizen working at his own pleasure for his daily wants ; he was a *functionnaire*, and compulsorily a member of an association organised by the state on the model of military service. In the East an altogether freer system seems to have obtained. The guilds were independent associations, and in Palestine the Carpenter's Son and the tentmaker followed their callings irrespective of state authority. "In Byzantine buildings the same name occurs in turn upon columns, capitals, or simply squared blocks of stone, and there is nothing to show that the foreman of the works kept one man at one particular kind of work. The East never changes ; at present the absence of division of labour in Oriental buildings is most striking. The proprietor chooses a master workman (*protomaistor*) ; to this improvised architect he adds a certain

number of head workmen (*maistores*) and their companions,
and these same men will work at digging the foundations, at
the masonry of the walls, and at the carpentry of the roof;
even the ironwork and joinery is scarcely reserved for special
workmen." The terms masters and companions suggest an
arrangement which merits consideration. Like western workmen the Greek artizans were affiliated to corporations which
have lived to our days. These associations (*sunergasiai*) had
a council, composed exclusively of those, who, by appren-
ticeship and trial, had earned the title of masters (*maistores*).

Each society was presided over by a "protomaistor"
helped by secretaries (*grammateus* and *kerux*), to summon
the meetings. It was at once a corporation of workmen, a
religious brotherhood, and a mutual aid society : and such
societies engaged in mutual acts of hospitality and assistance
between one town and another.

All workers in the East seem to have been thus associated
into guilds, and municipal life was organised on the guilds.
This is evident at Constantinople as early as the *Notitia*,
see p. 11 above. The members of the guilds had to help at
fires, and Lydus gives the cry which brought them together,
"*Omnes Collegiati.*" Demetrius, the silversmith of Ephesus,
called together the *Sunergasia* when the craft was in danger ;
we even hear of strikes. Even unskilled labourers had their
guilds, and Mr. Ramsay has described the Guild of Street
Porters of Smyrna in Roman times (*American Journal of
Archæology*, Vol. I.). The existence of the guilds is the most
significant fact of the social history of the middle ages.
In such craft organisation of labour, free of the financial
middlemen who now rightly call themselves "Contractors,"
we see the only hope that building for service, and ornament-
ing for delight, can again be made possible.

Our studies have convinced us that "shop production"
went on side by side with the building organisation. This
shop production will be at once allowed for such things as
gold cups and altars, lamps and bronze doors, but we believe
that decorative marble work was largely produced in this
way, and that just as enamelled cups and damascened doors
were "ordered" in Constantinople, so also were sculptured

slabs and capitals. It would be possible to account for mere resemblance by "influence," but absolute likeness between the capitals and sculptured or inlaid slabs found in contemporary buildings, at cities so far apart as Constantinople, Salonica, Parenzo, Ravenna, and Rome show that in the fifth and sixth centuries such works were dispersed from a common centre. So early as the fourth century S. Gregory Nazianzenus speaks of a priest who came to Constantinople "from Thasos bringing with him the gold of the church wherewith to buy slabs (*plakes*) of Proconnesian marble." [1] These things were not only bought, but specially commissioned ; for instance, the marbles of St. Clemente, which are almost certainly Constantinople work, bear fine monograms of John, afterwards elected pope in 532. The great contributing cause for this, besides the political and artistic position of Constantinople, was doubtless its possession of an absolutely perfect material in boundless profusion—the coarse white marble, which we may see to-day so delightfully wrought in small shops into the tombs, each of which has its carved tree of cypress, palm, or rose.

§ 3.—ORIGINAL FORM OF THE CHURCH.

Dome, &c.—Agathias tells us that when Justinian rebuilt the dome it was made higher, and that large alterations were made to the sustaining arches on the north and south sides. Salzenberg cites Theophanes and Zonaras who give the increase of height as twenty and twenty-five feet respectively. If we examine the longitudinal section we shall see that the great semidomes of the hemicycles and the apsoid of the bema show much less of their curvature outside than the present central dome. The windows in these do not stand above a cornice, but are pierced through the vaults at middle height ; the domical surface being unbroken by any cornice from springing to crown. The cupola of the baptistery is also continuous with the pendentives. A dome of this kind, however, continuing the pendentives, would seem to be impossibly flat, and would be some thirty feet less than the

[1] *Migne*, S.G., vol. xxxvii., p. 1090.

P

present height—see A in Fig. 4, the existing dome rising to
B. If a curve between these two be obtained by lowering
the crown of the dome about fifteen feet to c, it may be
noticed that a straight line tangential to the curve of the
eastern apsoid, and also to the great semidome would form
similar contact with the dome.

Salzenberg, understanding an account of Cedrenus as to a
strengthening of the abutments of the dome to refer to the
great buttress masses which rise above the gynaeceum roof,
considers that the external parts of these masses were additions made at the time of Justinian's restoration. These
great vertical piles are so essential to the structure, to the
logical beauty of the design, and to the staircase service of
the building ; moreover the preparation for them beneath is
so adequate, that we cannot accept this suggestion, and
therefore follow Choisy in considering them original. Now
Choisy, examining the external base of the dome where it
forms a square, found that the four angles had been increased, and that it did not originally form a square, but
rose above the piers and the lateral arches as shown in Fig. 34,
and in Fig. 37, where the first base is shown by hatching and
the additions by dotted lines, A A. "This alteration,"
he writes, "is not hypothetical. I verified the entire absence
of bond between the first base of the dome and the added
work" (p. 138). These additions were built on the lateral
arches, and on the top of the piers, altering the form shown
in our Fig. 35 to the present form given by Salzenberg.
That Choisy is right, is borne out by seeing the resemblance
of treatment that there would have been between the
growth of the dome on the north and south and the semidome on the west (see Fig. 34.).

Again, Salzenberg hardly makes it sufficiently clear that
the large arches in the walls which fill the great vertical
semicircles over the arcades on north and south sides, are in
fact the inner surfaces of the arches which pass between the
pairs of piers on north and south sides (seventy-two feet apart
in this direction), and being the whole width of those piers
(fifteen feet eight inches) on soffite they form the immense
arches so well known on the outside. The semicircles of wall,

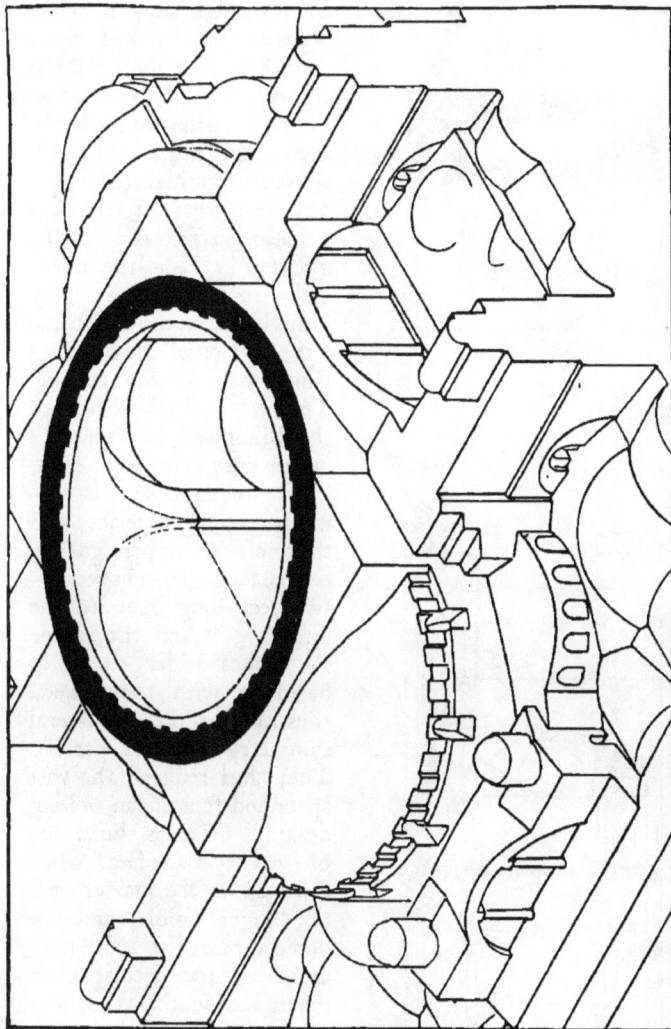

FIG. 34.—View of Vaulted System of S. Sophia, adapted from Choisy.

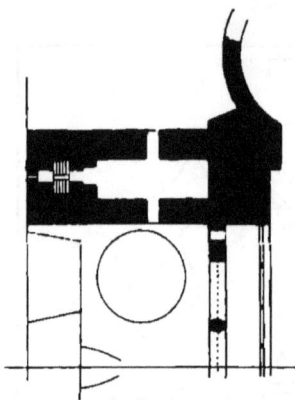

FIG. 35.—Plan of Upper Gallery as first designed.

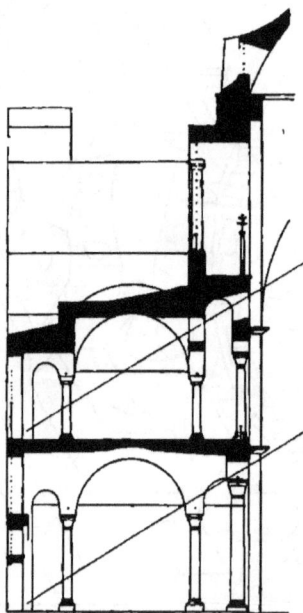

FIG. 36.—Section of Aisles and Gallery.

each of which contains twelve windows, are now filled in beneath these arches, flush with their *inner faces*, and the arches therefore do not show to the interior through the decoration (Figs, 4, 36, 38).

Now Agathias (see page 30) says that at the restoration after the earthquake in 558, at the north and south arches they brought towards the inside "the portion of the building which was on the curve." This, we think, must refer to the filling wall, in the arches of seventy-two feet span, which we suppose was formerly on the exterior, and thus left an upper gallery twelve feet wide and seventy-two feet long open to the interior. "And they made the arches wider to be in harmony with the others, thus making the equilateral symmetry more perfect. They thus reduced the vast space and formed an oblong design." That is the arches of seventy-two feet, when filled up on the inside, were no longer visible, and the dome appeared to stand over arches of 100 feet span on north and south, as already on east and west, the transverse dimension of the

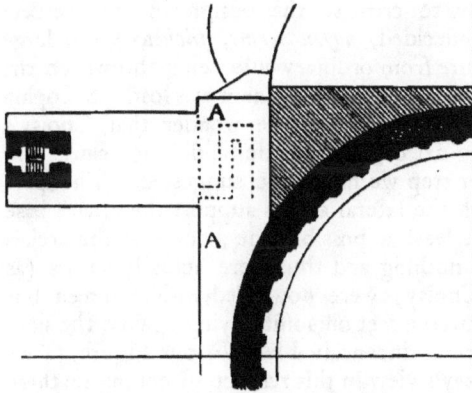

FIG. 37.—Plan of Basis of Dome as originally designed, with Additions A A containing stairs.

FIG. 38.—Section between Great and Secondary Orders.

church being lessened between these points by some twenty-four feet. Salzenberg understanding Agathias to refer to the apparent arches of 100 feet span on north and south is unable to offer any explanation.

The actual evidence in the church, we believe, fully bears out the interpretation here suggested. What we have called the secondary order of columns would pass exactly beneath the position given to this wall. These columns on the gallery floor are very strong, and a very strong row of arches runs along over them (see Fig. 38). Moreover the curtain walls in every other instance throughout the church are flush with the exterior.

That this space is not available to the interior of S. Sophia has caused Choisy to criticise the design in this respect as "a solution undecided, *moyen terme*, *fâcheux;* the large arches by a departure from ordinary rule being thrown on the outside so that the space covered by them was lost. S. Sophia Salonica redressed this error." We wonder that Choisy's views as to the original base of the dome did not cause him to take the further step we have here suggested. The present form, in which the lateral arches support the square base of the dome, is at least a possible one ; but that the arches when they carried nothing and thus were actually vaults (as before shown by Choisy) were not filled with a screen but were mere arches twelve feet on soffite, lying against the sides of the building seems inconceivable. In our Figure 34 we have amended Choisy's view in this respect. Looking on these lateral arches as vaults we have filled them with a window like the western vault, and the harmony which results between the sides and the west end amply verifies our conclusions. One point further. The upper surface of the base of the dome on the west side should not be wholly level as shown in Fig. 34, the central third *curves up* following the line of the top of semidome. In other words, the great arch of the interior pushes itself up through the base of the dome, and this treatment thus recurred at various heights— over large windows of aisles, over western and lateral lunettes, as we have shown, and over the semidome.

Originally, before the interior was narrowed in the way we have explained, there was a much clearer suggestion of a cross plan : barrel vaults at north and south being filled at their ends with large lunettes like the west vault. We suppose that the failure was mainly in the secondary order, and that the window screen and all possible weight was entirely removed and transferred to the great order. Salzenberg was satisfied that there had been great alterations in this part of the building, and Choisy's view of the window-wall, Plate xxv., entirely confirms his opinion. If it could be shown that the alteration spoken of by Agathias will not bear the interpretation we put on it, there were earlier troubles at this part mentioned by Procopius. The best proof, however, we suggest is found in the design. It has been before pointed out that Choisy and other writers have too hastily assumed that S. Sophia Salonica was built after the great church of Constantinople. That it preceded it enforces the present argument. Grelot (1680) writes that upper galleries remained in the church in these positions, but he based his assertion on the row of seven arched recesses just above the main cornice which he thought were formerly open. It is clear however from an examination of the section that the arches could only have opened to the vault of the first floor gynaeceum. That these small arches did open to the vault of the first floor, seems to be borne out by the fact that above the centre of the secondary order, where its arch is low, a similar piercing is made, through which (or the higher arches on each side) and through the seven arches, a mysterious perspective into the immensity of the dome might have been obtained by those in the gynaeceum (see Figs. 4, 36, 38). Shallow arched recesses merely used decoratively seem to have been little known to early Byzantine art, and arches on the first floor through the great piers are blocked in a similar way. Moreover such openings would explain why the vault between the two orders of columns is so much stilted up into mere darkness.

Atrium.—To explain the present confused arrangement of the exterior, we must remember that from the time of the description of the church by the Silentiary to its description by Gyllius was a thousand years—as long as from the time of Alfred to the present day—and in this time we may well expect alterations and accretions.

In Chapter IX. we have shown that the present form of the exonarthex, with its great external piers, was an alteration, made about the time the belfry was added in the ninth century. Before that time the atrium was alike on all four sides—a true *quadriporticus*—one of the most beautiful features of the ancient churches. (See Figs. 3 and 25.)

North and South Porches.—Much of the confusion at the north-west and south-west angles is the result of Turkish attachments, including the western minarets, which were built in the last quarter of the sixteenth century. The plan of gynaeceum floor furnishes the best key to the former arrangement, for where there is Byzantine work above, it must once have existed below. Comparing the first floor and roof plans in Salzenberg with the ground plan, it becomes apparent that the main block was originally finished both at north-west and south-west angles to the general square of building. The two staircases now at these angles were added as extra buttressing masses; the original stairs being the four in the piers of north and south sides. The north and south porches, with extra building above the latter on the first floor, were also additions. Besides the irregularity and inferior style of these buildings the following evidence should be noticed. The actual form of the north-west angle on the gallery floor ; and the natural reading of the three plans when laid one over the other ; broad arches, which pass across the porches ; the fact that the arch in south porch (dotted in C on Figure 24, see also Fossati, Plate i.) now has no office ; and that above the door at this end of narthex, there is a window which now merely opens into the south porch.

An examination of the exterior on the south side shows that the south-west staircase was built before the porch, or the part above it at least, because a straight joint in the walling, and the form of the roofing, here clearly make evident that the apex of the gable roof was originally over the centre of the staircase, and that the slope has been subsequently run forward to cover the part above the porch.

In considering all the other irregularly attached buildings, together with the historical evidence, it seems clear that the church as designed and first built was externally a regular parallelogram, interrupted only by the projection of the apse at the east end ; which was itself masked by a range of low chambers against the east wall, through which there were two entrances to the church as at present, and to which other two doors, in the east wall, still visible but now blocked, gave access. The other external doors, besides those from narthex, being two on the north and one in the south wall ; together with two external doors at the gynaeceum level, one of which probably gave access to the gallery along which the emperor passed to the church, and the other, to the north, may have led to the cells of the clergy.

Baptistery and Loggia.—Of early buildings detached from the church we have the round building at the north-east, which we regard as having descended from the earlier church, and the south-west baptistery, with a loggia attached to its north side. The space between the church and the baptistery on plan looks like a covered way, leading from the church with a screen in the middle, but the part next the church is, and always must have been, open. The part next the baptistery is covered with a large semicylindrical vault, arched *transversely* to the "screen," and penetrated by a less cylinder in the direction of the length of the loggia. Rebates (on baptistery side) round the doorway which stands between the pair of columns show that there was a door, and strips down the sides of the pillars, which stand above the transome, show that pierced slabs or other closures filled the arched front of the vault. If we add breast-high closures in the lateral openings, as in the portico of St. John Studius, the whole becomes an inclosed loggia against the baptistery. Salzenberg states that there was a door in the north wall of baptistery, and Labarte places another in the western compartment of south aisle of church, but for the latter there does not appear to be a particle of evidence ; and consequently the court and loggia cannot have formed a direct passage to the baptistery. 1. Salzenberg on his plan draws the transverse axis of the baptistery, and that of the western bay of the church ; these do not agree by a foot or two, but the doorway of "screen" agrees with *neither*, nor is it a mean between them, but varies by excess. 2. In the section (Salzenberg, Plate xi.) it is seen that the present level of floor in this loggia is that of baptistery, and is below that of church ; but the columns have no bases, therefore the loggia floor was beneath both church and baptistery. 3. A large arch is shown between the church and west pier of this loggia, from which it springs properly, while at the other end it is cut off incomplete by the wall of the church. These reasons together lead us to suggest that the loggia is possibly older than the church, and that it may be a part of an arcade

retained when the present church was built.   The style of the
screen would readily allow of its being twenty or thirty years
older than S. Sophia.   The capitals are not found elsewhere in
the church, while similar ones form the chief order at S.

FIG. 39.—Restoration of Loggia by the Baptistery.   Scale about eight feet
to an inch.

Sergius ; and the door is inserted between the two columns,
exactly as in the portico of S. John Studius.   We do not
however insist on its being earlier than the church so much as
on the evidence pointing to its being part of a continuous
arcade (see plan, Fig. 39).   Doubtless it might be de-

termined from a careful examination whether the loggia or the baptistery was built first.

The way by which the "Great Baptistery" was reached from the bema, as mentioned in the *Ceremonies* was probably by this cloister, which perhaps inclosed one of the courts on the sides of the church, spoken of by Procopius and the Silentiary. The portion drawn by Salzenberg still remains, although sadly plastered over and mutilated.

§ 4.—STRUCTURAL SYSTEM AND VAULTING.

The geometrical scheme of this building, which in its final form must be the result of hundreds of adjustments, modifications, and expedients, to meet newly discovered emergencies, is withal so seemingly simple, that it may be read as a bare mechanical solution of the primary conditions.

The great central area, excepting only the narrow bema, is surrounded by two stories of vaults ; the thrust of the dome over the square of about 100 feet is not only resisted by these, but by the four immense buttressing masses (or rather chambers for they are built hollow) which, pierced by arches, pass right across the aisles. East and west the dome is sustained by the semidomes of the great hemicycles, and these in turn by the vaults of the three subdivisions of the hemicycles. The thrusts are thus distributed in a regular pyramid. The external wall, which incloses the whole, being built out to the extremity of the great buttress piers of the north and south sides, and the lesser piers east and west, is thus little more than a screen, inclosing the more active parts of the structure.

One of the most remarkable expedients of this marvellously planned building is that by which the vaults of the side aisles,—which, having large spans, necessarily spring comparatively low down—are received on the secondary order of columns, standing behind the pillars of the great order. This allows of the stately colonnade on either side of the central space and those in the four exedras being only controlled by the height of the upper floor, which is forty-four feet above the area as is explained by Figs. 36, 38. These secondary pillars also transform the spaces left by the exedras into square compartments.

Arch Forms.—The great arches under the dome have their centres two feet six inches above the springing line. Those in the principal arcade appear to be semicircular. In the adjoining exedras, the porphyry columns not being nearly so long as the green ones, they were set on pedestals, and the arches are "horseshoe" in form, at least towards the nave, for they are built "winding," so as to approach a square impost on their caps. We say approach, for there is a gradual modification; the caps being an inch or two wider towards the aisles, the impost increases this by a few inches more. The openings from gynaeceum at west end are segmental, some arches to the side windows and the lateral windows of west elevation, Fig. 25, are bluntly pointed. The transverse arching of narthex is semielliptical, or rather three-centred, a segment with the curve at the ends quickened to become tangential to the wall. The pointed arch is used in the great aqueduct near Constantinople and in one of the city cisterns : both appear to be of the age of Justinian.[1]

Vaulting.—The vaulting is executed with the mastery and freedom that comes of confidence in direct methods. Certain portions are cylindrical, and others are formed by cylindrical cross-penetrations. The octagon of the baptistery, and the square compartments of the gynaeceum, are covered by domes which penetrate down into the angles with continuous pendentives. The larger compartments of the vaults of the aisles require some explanation.

Where four semicircular arches open about a square or oblong space, and it is desired to make the vault conform exactly to them, this may be accomplished by a semispherical dome, the span of which is equal to the *diagonal* of the compartment to be covered ; such a vault presents an

---

[1] There is no doubt about these arches being truly *pointed*. They were drawn so by Dr. Covel about 1675, they appear so in the careful engraving in Miss Pardoe's *Bosphorus*, and these are fully confirmed by Strzygowski and Forchheimer, *Die Wasserbehälter von Konstantinopel*, pp. 12 and 71. The use of the pointed arch in the east is probably an unbroken tradition from early days in Egypt.

-unbroken surface.   Or two cylindrical vaults may penetrate
at right angles, when the vault is broken by the intersection
into four surfaces.   At S. Sophia it was evidently desired
to keep the springing high for the sake of the monolith

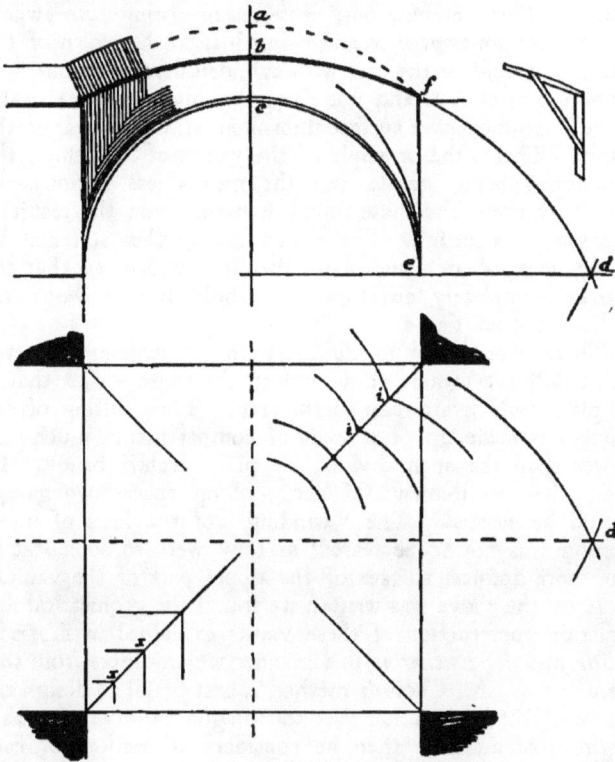

FIG. 40.—Construction of Vaults.

columns, and yet to maintain, so far as possible, a domical
surface.

Thus in Fig. 40 the dome springing out of the angle
requires the height *a*, the radius being equal to half the
diameter ; but it was wished to flatten this to *b*, and yet for

the vault to rise everywhere from the arched line *e*, *c*. Now
if the vault conforms to the surfaces generated by the
revolution of the arc *d*, *f*, *b*, about the axis *o*, *d*, intersecting
with a similarly generated surface at right angles, we get a
mean between the domed and cylindrical forms—a domical
vault. The intersections, instead of being everywhere
square on plan as at *x*, *x*, and rising just to the crown of the
vault, as would be the case with cylindrical penetrations, will
be obtuse as at *i*, *i*, and not rising so high will practically
leave a large concave surface unbroken at the crown of the
vault. This is the principle of the vaults of S. Sophia ; the
gradations being gentle and the means less obvious, the
forms are more like those found in nature, and the result is
extremely beautiful. The forms are further softened by
every edge of arch and vault being rounded, so that the
mosaic completely envelops the whole like a vast embroidered gold tissue.

There would be no difficulty in construction, for the
vault falls everywhere on an arch in the angle *e*, *f*, *b* that is
in planes which are radii to the arch. The vaulting of the
narthex is made up of a series of compartments, much nar-
rower than the span, divided by plain arched bands. To
meet the requirements of such oblong spaces two gauges
would be needed. The "winding" of the lines of intersection was not to be feared, as they were so soon lost in
the more domical surface of the upper part of the vault.

After the above was written we found the geometrical and
practical construction of these vaults explained in *L'Art de
Bâtir chez les Byzantins,* in a manner which differs from that
here given. M. Choisy's method is first of all to design the
curve of the intersection over the diagonal of the plan as a
segment of a circle : then he considers all sections of each
compartment of the vault, taken parallel to its arch, and
therefore perpendicular to its axis, to be also segments of
circles springing from a series of points on the diagonals,
their centres being on the axis of each vault.

We cannot agree with this, for, although theoretically the
vault so conceived differs immaterially from the solution we
have proposed, yet practically its erection would be full of

difficulty. M. Choisy's method is that proposed by M.
Viollet-le-Duc for the later Romanesque vaults, in which,
the materials being poor rubble, centring must have been
required.   In these Viollet-de-Duc thinks that diagonal
centres were used, and then planks were placed from them
to the generating arches, and the additional height of a
domical vault made up by a layer of earth.   It is to be
noticed that diagonal centres in this case almost immediately
produced diagonal stone ribs.

M. Choisy in his most interesting book shows that the
chief consideration in the construction of the Byzantine
vaults was to avoid wooden centring.   With this view we
entirely agree, but in the system explained in *L'Art de Bâtir*,
the lines of construction would be arrived at by an elaborate
system, which required fixed axes to the vaults and either a
diagonal centre or a rod revolving in a vertical plane over
the diagonal.   Then two rods, forming an angle with its
apex touching any given point in the diagonal curve and
the ends resting on the axis of the vault as a base, revolved
as a trammel for that course of the filling.   This had to be
repeated for a series of points.

By the method we have suggested nothing was required
except a single template to a fixed angle, the upper arm cut
to the curve from the crown of the arch to the crown of the
vault ; we may suppose this to sweep round the generating
arches like a trammel, but practically testing the work with
it at the crown, as it gradually grew forward, was doubtless
found sufficient (see Fig. 40).   Thus the vault surfaces gave
the conditions of the problem and the intersections found
themselves.

We did not notice the curious "curve of inflection" of
which M. Choisy speaks ; certainly it does not generally
exist, although according to *L'Art de Bâtir* "S. Sophia
is the most curious example which remains of this singular
conception, where the spirit of Greek logic did not hesitate
before anomalies of form" (p. 55).   We believe this curve
is deduced only by the logic with which M. Choisy's follows
up his method of geometrical projection, which certainly
generates such an inflected curve.   We cannot say this

without at the same time expressing our great admiration for
L'Art de Bâtir; its freshness of sight, clearness, vitality,
and logic are entirely delightful. Strzygowski and Forchheimer [1] follow Choisy's demonstration; and give an
elaborate and analytical explanation of the curve and its
points of inflexion. One of the cisterns they say showed
the inflected line in the axial sections of the vaults (p. 71).

Now the cistern vaults are roughly built and some of
them may have settled down; some indeed may have been
designed so that the axial section is horizontal for some
distance from the walls before the doming is commenced,
especially in the long direction of parallelogramic compartments. The essential points are two. Did these vaults
grow forward from the walls and the intersections find
themselves, or was the curve of intersection first designed?
Are horizontal sections through the intersection of two
vault surfaces just above the springing obtuse or acute?
The vaults at S. Sophia have the angles of intersection so
obtuse that this first drew our attention to the subject.

For a general view of the vaulted system of S. Sophia we
would especially refer to Choisy, whose remarks on the
construction of these vaults are most interesting. He
clearly shows how the large flat bricks made possible the
construction of vaults without centring. The extrados of
the arches from which the vaults spring being splayed to a
skew back, the large surfaces of the thin light bricks allowed
them to be stuck up against this skew back, or any part
already done, much as if they were square sheets of card-
board (see left side of Fig. 40). Indeed the bricks seem
sometimes to have been placed quite vertically, but the
better plan seems to have been to incline the beds, the vaults
were thus built in *sections* rather than in layers. To take
the simplest instance, a cylindrical vault, the arching would
begin at one end against the vertical wall, the rings of large
thin bricks being placed "on edge" in planes of say 60°
right down the vault. In other words, in a longitudinal
section of such a vault the joints instead of being horizontal
might be vertical, or a mean between the two. This method

[1] *Die Wasserbehälter*, p. 130, &c.

BUILDING FORMS AND THE BUILDERS   225

FIG. 41.—Section of Narthex and Gallery over showing Royal Doors. Scale twelve and a half feet to an inch ($\frac{1}{150}$).

Q

was known in ancient Egypt and at Khorsabad, and the immense vault at Ctesiphon is built in this way. Although
the mosaic covers most of the vaults at S. Sophia, a vast
number are exposed in the contemporary cisterns, and Choisy
seems to have found a cylindrical vault uncovered in a
chamber in one of the buttress masses (Plate ii.), he also
shows the construction of the aisle and narthex vaults (Plates
ix. and xi.), but he does not say if he had any authority
for these. We agree with him that the vaults of S. Sophia
owe much of their exceptional beauty to the fact that arches
do not break up the curving expanse of the vaulting to any
appreciable degree ; in the narthex the arches become one
with the vault, see Fig. 41.

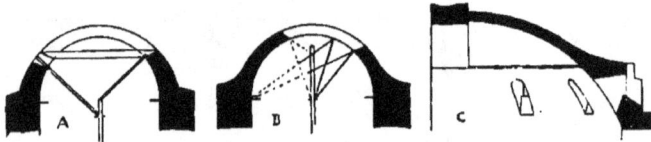

FIG. 42.—Dome Construction.

Domes.—In elaborating his theory of Byzantine dome
construction Choisy refers to a passage in Eton's *Turkish
Empire*[1] which describes domes the latter saw built without
any kind of centring. The builders put a post in the
middle about the height of the walls. To this is fixed a
pole reaching to the *inside* surface of the dome, which is
free to move in all directions. Below is attached to the post
another pole, which reaches to the outside and describes the
outside curvature of the cupola. These give the thickness
at the top and bottom and at every intermediate point.
" Where they build these cupolas of bricks they use gypsum
instead of lime, finishing one layer all round before they
begin another. Scaffolding is only required for the workmen
to close the opening at the top." Our diagram A, Fig. 42,
represents this fascinating scheme of building : with such a
rod any point in the whole curvature is defined in a moment ; it
equally gauges the horizontal courses and the rise of the dome.

[1] 1799, p. 236.

Choisy suggests a second scheme which will be made clear by B. There is no reason, he points out, why the beds of the bricks in a dome should radiate to the centre of the curve : in the Byzantine domes the beds were flattened so that they radiated more or less accurately to the springing of the opposite side of the dome. The thrusts were thus mini-mised, and the construction was facilitated. If rods forming a triangle revolve about a vertical post as shown, the horizontal curvature is gauged and the top rod will define the slope for the bed. These rods can then be raised to another position as shown in the figure. We should have supposed that little care would be taken with the slope of the beds, as from the thin bricks used the construction practically became homogeneous.

Choisy even thinks that the great dome of S. Sophia may have been built in the air without centring. c, in Fig. 42, gives his representation of the construction of the semi-domes, which he thinks were built out some way entirely without support. The outer arch was then built on a centre and the filling completed "in space" (a straight joint be-tween the arch and the dome filling is shown in the figure in Salzenberg's text). We think it more likely that in all the larger domes auxiliary support was required "to close the opening at the top," when the space had been so con-tracted that a light centring resting on the part already completed was all that would be needed.

From the importance attached to wood ties or girdles built into the small domes of Mount Athos, we may be certain that some system of chaining was applied to the great dome of S. Sophia. Choisy gives an example of the former, and also a dome constructed by interlocking semicircular bricks, " two courses of which make a circlet absolutely inextensible." See B in Fig. 45. The dome of S. Vitale at Ravenna is built of layers of earthenware pots or tapering tubes, the end of one fitting into the next and rising in a continuous spiral course, round and round from the bottom to the crown of the dome.

The question of dome construction without centring is of the greatest interest, and much might doubtless be gathered of the traditional methods still followed in modern Greece;

Egypt, Persia, and S. Italy. Our Fig. 43 represents modern
domes in Persia, the upper diagram being an ordinary type
of exterior from a photograph of Koum. The dome beneath,
Fig. 44, is from a sketch made in a Persian caravanserai by
Mr. Wm. Simpson,[1] who describes it as built of burnt brick,
square below, round above. "As I was told that centring
was never used in Persia I presume this one was constructed
without it." This beautiful form may be considered as four
conical squinches penetrating a hemisphere as at A, or as
a gradual transition from square to round, B. Ancient
Persian domes of substantially the same form, in which a
hemisphere penetrates a pyramid, are shown by Dieulafoy.[2]

Chainage and Walling.—In the East the frequency of
severe earthquakes necessitated a manner of construction
which should resist disruption. The massive walls of stone
of the Classic period are cramped together with metal. The
stone Byzantine church at Ezra has a course of interlocking
stones forming a chain around the octagon beneath the dome
(Fig. 45 a). At S. Sophia the continuous courses of stone
some feet above the floor, mentioned by Salzenberg, are
almost certainly converted into a chain by cramps ; and the
stone course at the springing of the great arches probably
has the same function. In brickwork lateral cohesion was
usually obtained by a system of continuous wood ties, which
is described by Choisy as built into the wall at every five or
six feet of height. According to the Greek architect, M.
Kouppas, ties of bond timbers were used in this way in the
construction of the cisterns, " laid not only along the outside
walls but also in parallel rows beneath the lines of pillars and
arches ; " other rows of timber were built in either as ties or
struts in continuous lines at the springing of the vaults.

At S. Sophia there was doubtless a large use made of temporary ties of this kind during the construction. In many
places at the springing of the gynaeccum vaults the ends of
such provisional ties, which have been sawn away, appear.
Besides these there is a series of wood beams which from the

[1] *Journal of Roy. Inst. Brit. Archts.*, Jan. 1893.
[2] See also p. 247, 1892, for the conditions of stability of dome of S.
Sophia.

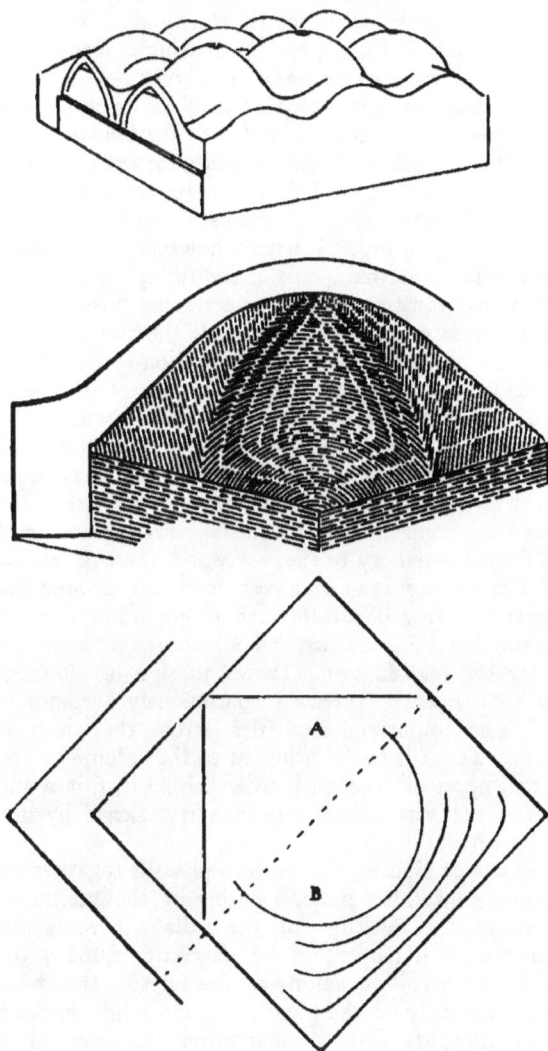

FIGS. 43 and 44.—Modern Domes built without Centring.

first were intended to be permanent, for they are richly
carved (c in Fig. 45) ; these are shown by double lines on
the right-hand side of Figs. 5 and 6, the single lines showing
the iron ties. These carved beams, as Choisy points out, are
struts rather than ties. If we take one of the columns standing in an angle in the aisles, an impost of marble connects it
with the wall to which it is nearest, and a carved wood beam
forms a strut to the other wall. The beam across the central
bay of secondary order (Fig. 5) forms a rigid strut to the
two wider arches (see Fig. 38, where, however, by oversight
the beam has been omitted ; it is at the springing of narrow
arch high above iron tie). Choisy asserts that " the architect
intended to preserve only the struts, all the ties subject to
extension were removed, but their suppression was disastrous,
and they had hastily to replace them by bars of iron which
were fixed with difficulty." We do not know what reason
Choisy had for supposing the system of iron ties to be an
afterthought, unless it is because in some cases they appear
directly above the ends of the removed wooden ties. Now
we believe they occur equally above the carved beams in the
openings from the gallery to the nave, and there is no sign
of wood ties having been removed from the ground-floor
vaults, where the iron bars fulfil such an important function.
It is certain that the iron bars to all the nave arches are
original, for the marble casing shows no sign of alteration,
and they are evidently threaded continuously through the
imposts. The important iron ties across the aisles are
shown in Fig. 45 : d is the attachment to the column of great
order, e to impost of secondary order behind it, f is a king
rod. Across the west gallery the span is lessened by stone
corbels beneath the ties g.

With a view of binding the vaults and walls together into
a homogeneous mass, the arched vaulting of the interior was
carried through the thickness of the walls : in some cases
these arches were left open, to be afterwards filled with a
screen of windows. The walling of the sides of the church
is built independently of the great piers, as straight joints on
the exterior show, and Choisy remarks that the independence
of masonry unequally charged was a leading idea in Byzantine

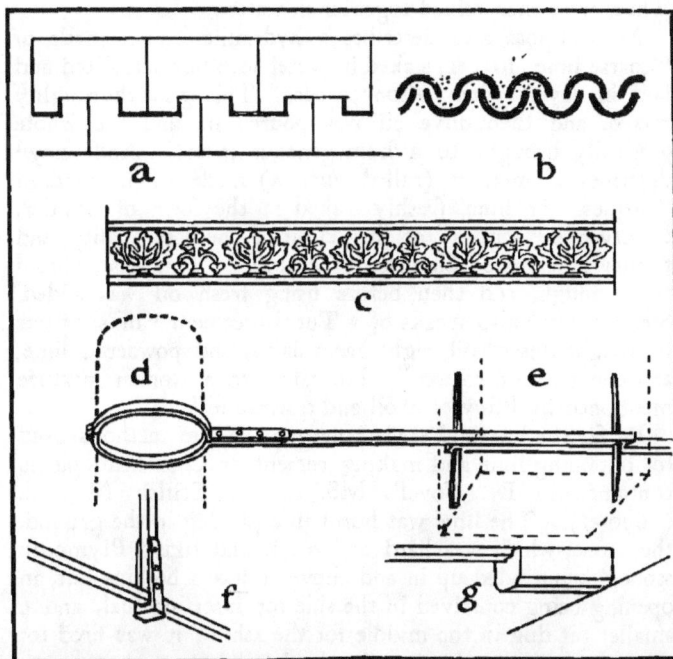

Fig. 45.—Methods of Chainage.

construction ; indeed it is obviously necessary where the quantity of mortar is so great that the brick at times becomes secondary to the joints.

Mortar and Cement.—The mortar used by the Byzantine builders was called Keramotos, from the crushed pottery or tiles which was used in its composition.   In an article in the *Transactions* of the Philological Society of Constantinople M. Kouppas [1] enters fully into the methods which have been traditionally followed in cistern building, and describes this mortar as formed of powdered unslaked lime (*asbestos*), crushed pottery, coarse sand, and tow or hair, fully a third being lime, another third the crushed pottery, about a fifth

[1] Ἑλλην. Φιλολ. Συλλ. παραρ. vol. xx., 1892.

the coarse sand, and the rest or 10 per cent. of hair or tow.
These were then mixed together in water.

M. Kouppas also describes a hydraulic cement made of
"coarse lime (*titanos*) slaked by water into powder, sifted and
laid in layers with cotton shreds. This was thoroughly
mixed, and then olive oil was poured in, and the whole
gradually brought to a homogeneous mass." Andreossy [1]
describes a mixture (called *lukium*) made of a hundred
"ocques" of lime, freshly slaked in the form of powder,
twenty-five "ocques" of linseed oil of the best quality, and
twenty drachms of filaments of cotton." This was reduced
to a dough, and then before using fresh oil was added.
Strzygowski [2] also speaks of a Turkish cement "of six parts
by weight linseed oil, eight parts slaked and powdered lime,
and one part of cotton." He refers to a Roman mixture
mentioned by Pliny of "oil and quicklime."

By far the best and earliest account of the methods used
for obtaining lime and making cement at Constantinople is
contained in Dr. Covel's MS. in the British Museum
(1670–7). The lime was burnt in a pit dug in the ground,
the stone, which was hard and black and like "Plymouth
stone," being piled up in and above it like a beehive hut, an
opening being contrived in the side for inserting fuel, and a
smaller pit dug in the middle for the ashes ; it was fired for
three days. Then he describes in detail how a cement was
made which recalls what the Anonymous says of the joints
of the piers at S. Sophia being made of unslaked lime
(*asbestos*) and oil : "To make good lukium (a strong
cement as I may call it) they take the above said calx or
burnt stone and slake it with water, and so soon as it is
moulded and turned into a meal (even while it is warm) they
work it with linseed oil and cotton till it is well saturated
and brought to the consistency of plaster, and make present
use of it, for it will not rest in its perfection above one day
or two at most, and if they use it immediately after it is
tempered it is certainly the best. In the works of their
Bagnos so soon as it is laid on [as a plastering, understood

[1] P. 485.
[2] *Die Byzantinischen Wasserbehälter*, p. 22.

here] they let the water come to it, which, by tempering the heat of the lime, hinders it from cracking. Cotton is better to be mixed amongst it than hair, it being more tenacious and apt to incorporate." He again describes a similar cement ("lukium, an excellent mortar") used in some waterworks. It is made of unslaked lime and beaten brick most finely powdered and sifted, cotton wool very thinly pulled and strewed on, and then all slaked with linseed oil and mixed together : then they use it whilst it is fresh made, otherwise it hardens immediately."[1] Such a cement must have had the hardening qualities of gesso; the oil cements or mastics used in England some fifty years ago were closely allied in their composition. Modern mortar has lost much by our neglecting the tradition of using crushed brick.

Eastern builders spared neither labour nor time in preparing and testing their materials. Tavernier tells us the waterproof terraces of the Persian houses were formed of " a layer of lime beaten for eight days, which became hard like marble." The materials used in Byzantine building were tested by long exposure, slaked lime was sealed up in pits for one or two years; and stones, bricks, and tiles they had found should not be used new, for, as Vitruvius says, " the only way of ascertaining their goodness is to try them through a summer and winter."

[1] In another place Covel gives the following. Lukium—unslaked lime, burnt brick (both in a fine powder), cotton wool very fine pulled and strewed on, linseed oil. Cistern plaister—Lime, burnt brick, cotton or flax, water [use] almost dry, smooth it and saturate with oil.

CHAPTER XI

§ I. BUILDING PROCEDURE.

THE method and sequence of the building operations as followed by the Byzantines seem to have been very much as follows. After the form of the building had been more or less decided, the first thing necessary was to collect marble monolithic shafts. At S. Sophia the eight verde-antique shafts match one another very closely ; they are all of one length, and vary from 7½ to 8 diameters in proportion. The four pairs of porphyry shafts in the exedras differ much more ; and, as we have remarked, those in the western exedras seem to be made up of separate drums. The proportions of these vary from less than 7 diameters on one side to 8½ on the other. The great monoliths are the largest known, and of nearly normal classic proportion, so we can readily see that it was necessary to have a certain knowledge where such marbles might be quarried or otherwise obtained, before even the foundations were prepared, for the columns decided the heights and points of support of the building. These once assured, the body of the structure was proceeded with as a brickwork shell without further dependence on the masons, who were only required to prepare bases and capitals, and then the cornices ; everything else was completed as a brick "carcase."

At S. Sophia the main square piers are in fact stone, but this was only for strength, not because they were to be seen finally, any more than the rough brick.

The building completed in this form we must remember was made up of vast masses of thin bricks, of which the mortar occupied probably a half of the aggregate ; this had to thoroughly settle down and dry before the rest of the marble masonry was inserted, and the wall casings applied. The marble work, however, was all the while being prepared, and, the building once ready, the windows were inserted as screens in the openings previously left ; marble jambs and lintels for the doors were placed in position also, with windows above them filling out to the brick arches. The walls were then sheeted with their marble covering, the vaults were overlaid with mosaic, and the pavement was laid down. In this way, as the bricklayers had not to wait for the masons, the carcase was completed in the shortest possible time ; and by reserving the application of the marble until the structure was dry and solid, it was possible to bring together unyielding marble and brickwork that must have settled down very considerably.

§ 2. MARBLE QUARRIES.

Much confusion exists as to the marbles of which the ancient writers speak ; this has been occasioned necessarily by wrong identifications when but few ancient quarries had been recovered, and most unnecessarily by a persistence in using antique names for modern varieties, long after the true provenance has been discovered, when the ancient marbles are not "in the market." It is the Italian names that have been corrupted in this way, and it would be a great advantage if they were discarded in England, or better still, used only in conjunction with the geographical names. In this case as the Italian names are descriptive, and, as many varieties of marble are found in the same or neighbouring quarries, we should get a safe nomenclature. Synnadan would thus be qualified as Pavonazzetto or Fior de Persico, and the banded varieties from Carystian, Proconnesian, or modern quarries might without confusion be called cipollino.

In endeavouring to identify the marbles mentioned by the

ancient writer on S. Sophia, we have made use of Salzenberg's
notes to the Poem of the Silentiary, and of the researches of
Garofalo,[1] Corsi,[2] and C. O. Müller ;[3] and we have also been
helped by the practical knowledge of Mr. W. Brindley. The
account of ancient marbles easily accessible in Professor
Middleton's *Ancient Rome*, 1892, is substantially an extract
from Corsi.

Porphyry.—The " porphyry powdered with bright stars "
of the poet is used for the columns of the exedras, and for
some of the panels on the walls. The Anonymous author
states that these columns came from a temple of the Sun, but
the Silentiary says " they loaded the boats on the bosom of
the Nile," and there seems no reason to doubt that the
columns came direct from the porphyry quarries at Mons
Porphyrites in Egypt. This porphyry mountain is at Djebel
Dochan, twenty-five miles north-east from Thebes. Lepsius [4]
seems to prove that the quarries were worked as long as· the
Nile canal remained open ; and ships still sailed on the canal
till the appearance of Islam. Letronne [5] gives details of the
method of transit. The porphyry was brought from the
quarry to the Red Sea, and then by the Nile canal to the
Lower Nile, and hence into the Mediterranean.

On this evidence we would say that the porphyry used
at Constantinople in Justinian's reign was quarried for the
purpose, and not brought from Roman buildings.

Marmor Molossium.—" The marble that the land of
Atrax yields," is called elsewhere in the poem " Thessalian,"
and, from the province in Thessaly where it was found,
" Molossian." · Corsi and Garofalo both wrongly describe
Molossian as *Fior di Persico.* The marble really is the
brecciated serpentine and limestone, now called Verde
Antico, the *Lapis Atracius* of the ancients, of which the
eight great columns in the nave and many others are formed.
Here again it has been said that these eight large columns
were taken from a building at Ephesus, but the Silentiary

[1] *Blasii Caryophili opusculum de antiquis marmoribus,* 1743.
[2] *Trattato delle pietre antiche,* 1833.
[3] *Ancient Art.*   [4] *Chronologie von Egypten,* p. 365.
[5] *Revue des deux Mondes,.* 1841.

says, "Never were such columns hewn from sea-washed
Molossis," and we can hardly doubt that they were quarried
especially for S. Sophia, together with the rest of the
enormous quantity used in the church. The quarries were
near Atrax in Thessaly, and the marble is best named as by
French writers, Thessalian green.

Lapis Lacedaemonius.—"The fresh green, like emerald,
from Sparta," was probably the porphyry quarried in
Mount Taygetus in Laconia. This green porphyry, called
by Corsi *serpentino*, is used in the opus sectile of S. Sophia.
As a green porphyry is obtainable in Egypt, the former
should be distinguished as Spartan.

Proconnesium.—"The hills of Proconnesus," according
to Paulus, " strewed the floor.". The same marble was also
used for the columns in the upper aisles, for the eight
square columns below, and for the capitals, door frames,
window lattices and other structural parts ; also for the
plating of the lower arcade and other parts of the wall-
surfaces, and as frames to the coloured marbles. It is a soft
white, or white with gray-banded streaks. The quarries
of Marmora are still worked. This marble was greatly
prized in Classic times, and Pliny mentions that it was used
at the palace of Mausolus, where, it is said, the method of
plating brick walls with marble was first applied. It closely
resembles gray Carystian but they should not be con-
founded.

" The Bosporus stone with white streaks on black,"
used for the floor, was probably the ordinary limestone—
black with white veins—used at Constantinople.

Marmor Carystium.—"The fresh green from Carystus,"
is the marble now known as cipollino ; it was quarried at
Carystus, at the foot of Mount Ocha, in the island of
Euboea. Its beautiful greenish white surface, marked with
broad wavy lines of green or purplish gray, was often
praised by the later classical writers. Its resemblance to
the markings of a sliced onion is the origin of its name.
Modern cipollino need not be confused with true *Carystian
marble*, which the ancient material should always be named.

Marmor Phrygium.—"The marble hewn from the

Phrygian land towards the Mygdonian heights," spoken
of as "many-coloured," has been identified as the marble
which came from Dokimion near Synnada in Phrygia. The
descriptions by Statius and Claudianus of the deep red-
veined marble of Synnada agree closely with the Phrygian
and Mygdonian stone as described by Paulus. It is a
brecciated marble of a rosy colour, slabs of which alternate
with verde antique in the panelling of the side aisles of
S. Sophia.

The quarries at Dokimion were visited by Leake and
Texier, and a recent examination of them by M. Leonti [1]
disclosed all shades of "violet and white, yellow, and the.
more familiar brecciated white and rose-red." This beautiful material is best called Synnadan, as the modern Italian
name Pavonazzetto is also used for the streaked marble
quarried at Carrara.

Marmor Hierapolitanum.—"The stone from the sacred
city Hierapolis." This marble has been identified by
Professor Ramsay.[2] It was found at Thiounta about ten
miles N.W. of Hierapolis in Asia Minor. It is variegated
like Synnadan, and was much used for sarcophagi ; indeed
Professor Ramsay says, "On every occasion when its use is
mentioned, it was employed to make sarcophagi." It was
called by the name of the great city which is not far distant,
"and to which doubtless orders from the outer world were
sent. Similarly the marble found at Dokimion was always
called Synnadic marble from the time of Strabo, yet Dokimion was thirty-two miles from Synnada."

Marmor Iassense.—The "Iassian, with slanting veins of
blood-red on livid white," was used for the phiale. Corsi
identifies this with Porta Santa, but Porta Santa, Garofalo
says, came from Chios, and this conclusion we believe is now
accepted. Garofalo thought Iassian to be the same as the
Carian marble mentioned by Porphyrogenitus in his *Life of
Basil the Macedonian*, and says it was quarried on the island
quite close to the coast of Caria. A "stone mingled with
streaks of red " is also mentioned by Paulus as brought from

[1] In MS. notes lent by Mr. Brindley.
[2] *Histor. Geography of Asia Minor*, p. 433.

" the Lydian Creek." Possibly the port of Iassus is again intended. The ordinary Lapis Lydius was a black touch-stone. The " rosy cipollino," in which wide bands of deep red alternate with white, used in the panelling of the aisles does not seem to be mentioned specifically by Paulus ; unless this is the Iassian marble to which his words would very well apply. A variety of rosy cipollino, the splendidly figured red and white marble, is obtained in Laconia.

Marmor Numidicum.—" The stone, nurtured in the hills of the Moors, crocus colour glittering like gold," is the beautiful warm yellow African marble from Semittu Colonia, about fifty miles from Tunis, so highly prized by the Romans, and now called giallo antico. It is used in S. Sophia in the sectile work.

Marmor Celticum.—" The product of the Celtic crags, like milk poured on a flesh of glittering black," has been identified as the Bianco e Nero Antico, quarried in the Pyrenees.[1] The black marble with white streaks, which occurs in some of the panels in the nave, is probably the one to which the poet refers.

Onychites.—" The precious onyx " mentioned by the poet is the alabastrites or onychites of the ancients. It is the oriental alabaster (aragonite) used in the horizontal bands of the nave, and some of the panels. It is a translu-cent, fibrous stalagmite formation, generally of a clear honey-colour. Some of the varieties are strongly veined with white, and others are much darker. Large ancient quarries of this Egyptian alabaster have been discovered on the east bank of the Nile.

Paulus appears to make no mention of the dusky black with dull golden veins used in the bema apse, which closely resembles the " Porto Venere " quarried at Spezzia.

The marble blocks were roughly hewn into shape with picks while still attached to the rock, and were then separ-ated by the aid of metal wedges. Many objects discovered show that they were sometimes completed at the quarry, at other times the blocks were roughly brought to the sizes and forms required. The quarries appear to have been

---

[1] See Boni, who corrects Corsi, in *La Basilica di San Marco*.

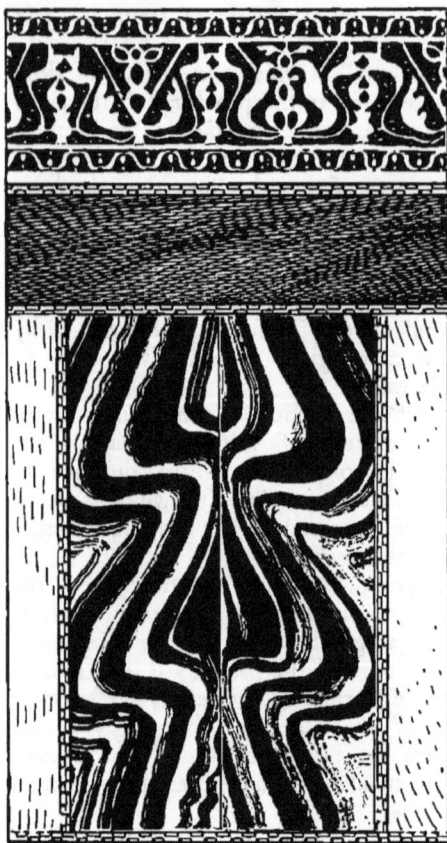

FIG. 46.—Marble Slabs and Frieze in Narthex.

officially inspected. Texier found many architectural fragments and blocks at Dokimion bearing the signs of the inspectors of the block. Professor Ramsay writes: "The route from Dokimion to the coast is commercially almost the most important in Asia Minor. The road along which the enormous monolithic columns were transported passed throughSynnada, where the central office for managing the quarries was situated."

Ephesus and Alexandria were most important centres for the working and export of marble, of which such an enormous quantity was required by the Byzantine builders. The method of slicing up the blocks into veneer is described by an Eastern pilgrim, Nasiri Khusrau, in 1047. He says : " In the city of Ramlah there is marble in plenty . . . . they cut the marble here with a toothless saw which is worked with Mekkah sand." This sand he

FIG. 47.—Portion of Marble Lining of Aisles. Scale about $\frac{1}{20}$.

tells us came from Haifa near Acre (Pal. Pilgrims' Text Soc. Compare Pliny, *Hist. Nat.* xxxvi.)

§ 3.—APPLICATION OF MARBLE.

At S. Sophia the application of the thin sheathing and incrustations (the "crustae" of Pliny) of the "delectable variety" of marbles is made in many ways. First there are the large sheets of the grayish Proconnesian, opened out side by side "so that the veining of one follows from the next." Then the richer varieties are set in bands and panels with narrow notched fillets between them, and still more precious slabs are framed round with carved margins of white. Over the doors entering the aisles at the west there are panels with especially wide and rich borders of meanders growing from chalices. The large panels are very often of two pieces with matched veining. Fig. 46 shows one of a row of strongly veined panels from the narthex with the frieze above. All the wall plating is arranged with delightful variety as to size, and in the alternate placing of light against dark, so that there is no rigidity or over-accurate "setting out."

Besides this constant change of size, colour, and arrangement, there is a great variety in the surface treatment. We have the shallow channelling into continuous mouldings of the skirtings, some portion of which has a stiff fret sunk in the surface in addition. Then there are panels on either side of the great door, and on the faces of the projections from the great piers in the aisles, coming just above the eye, (Fig. 48) of plain russet-red or brown which bear severe abstract patterns, made out by slight sinking into the surface. The centre in some cases is overlaid with an oval or square of another precious material such as red or green porphyry or the "onyx"; the whole of the sunk portions may have been filled by inlays, or in some the sinking alone may have formed the design. The upper part of the bema is incrusted with slabs patterned in this way, and here the sunk portions are entirely inlaid; several parts of this are represented by Salzenberg. In this work "casements" are

sunk into the rosso or other deep coloured field, and green
porphyry and other materials, set off by yellowish-white
lines and spaces are inlaid in geometrical panels, or friezes
of stiff foliage.

Our Fig. 47 shows the arrangement of the marble plating
on the great piers towards the middle compartment of the
aisles ; in this we have shown one of the enriched panels
now only sunk, as inlaid. Fig. 48 gives outlines of others of
these panels. The marble used in the aisles is as follows.
First comes the moulded skirting of white Proconnesian,
then a 3′·3″ band of the streaked variety of the same marble.
A band of verde antique 2′·0″ wide follows, above which is a
row of slabs alternately verde antique and Synnadan. A
second similar row of slabs comes above a band of rosy
cipollino. The frieze below the cornice is of marble sectile
work. The passages through the piers are lined with slabs
of streaked Proconnesian marble, nearly fourteen feet high.

The gynaeceum has two bands at the bottom and an
upper band of rosy cipollino ; the wall space between is
covered with a row of vertical slabs of streaked Proconnesian,
except the central space on north side where the slabs are of
rosy cipollino. In the spandrils of gynaeceum arcade at
the west are roundels of oriental alabaster.

Directly over the Royal Door is a very beautiful arrangement of decorated slabs. First there is an immense upright
piece of verde antique in the middle, ten or twelve feet high,
with two lateral horizontal pieces making a great cross,
in the quarters of which are panels with sunk and inlaid
designs. At the head of the cross is a fifth panel which
displays a still richer form of decoration. It represents
a vaulted recess or ciborium between the columns of which
hang curtains, looped back, and displaying a dark field.
Here is the matrix of a cross which was probably of silver ;
right and left of the cross are other matrices, in which were
set crowns or other objects, not to be determined from
below. The two upper lateral panels have sunk geometrical
designs. The lower pair are inlaid ; their centres are
charged with circles, above and below which are pairs
of dolphins. These inlaid designs are made out in por-

R 2

Fig. 48.—Marble Panels with Sunk and Inlaid Panels. Scale about $\frac{1}{30}$.

FIG. 49.—Inlaid Marble Slabs above Royal Door.   Scale about $\frac{1}{50}$.

phyry and green, which are separated by white lines and
spaces which shine out bright, and are probably of mother
of pearl like similar inlaid panels of this date around the
apse at Parenzo. These panels at Parenzo are so much like
those of S. Sophia that we do not doubt they were sent
from Constantinople. There are very similar panels in the
baptistery at Ravenna.

Finally we have the enriched surfaces of the two ranges
of arcade spandrils. The upper row being sectile work of
coloured morsels put together to form a pattern of scrolls
and foliage, and the lower series having the surface entirely
sculptured with the exception of discs of precious substance
which are set in them.

This uttermost splendour is quiet and soft in its result.
The surface of course has not that mechanically even,
repellently smooth, painfully fitted appearance of modern
work. The planes are waved under the hand sawing, and
the face is smooth but hardly polished. The colour in
consequence, gray and russet rising to full yellow, green
and reds, veined, waved, and flowered in all manner
of gradations and lovely combinations, *vibrates* with a
wonderful " bloom " which doubtless owes much to age ;
but it is very probable that the marble was polished with
wax encaustic which was so generally used for finishing
surfaces by ancient workers. The wax deepens and mellows
the colour and leaves a dull pleasant polish. We suppose
the method followed was that recommended by Vitruvius
for the encaustic polishing of coloured stucco walls. " Lay
on with a brush a coat of melted Punic wax tempered with
oil ; then with a brazier of hot charcoal heat all the waxed
surface, forcing the wax to melt in an even way over the
whole surface ; finally rub the wall with a wax candle and
then polish it with a clean linen cloth just in the way the
nude marble statues are treated. This practice is called γάνωσις
by the Greeks." Felix Fabri, who travelled in Palestine at
the end of the fifteenth century, describes the rows of costly
columns at Bethlehem, " and they are polished with oil so
that a man can see his face in them as in a mirror."

In regard to the wall plating we wish especially to point

out the extremely easy way in which it is applied, without
thought of disguise. The slabs of great size are placed
vertically, entirely the reverse of solid construction ; moreover the slabs of the finer panels are opened out side by
side so that the veinings appear in symmetrical patterns.
At the angles the lap shows in the most open way ; while it
is mitred where restored. The best account of the actual
methods of fixing the marble slabs to walls by metal clamps
which notch into the edges of the sheet before the adjoining
one is fixed, is given by Professor Middleton, who figures
an example of the second century from Rome which might
belong to S. Sophia.

§ 4.—MARBLE MASONRY.

After more than a thousand years of working marble
through one complete development, Greek builders, by
considering afresh the prime necessities of material, and
a rational system of craftsmanship, opened the great quarry
of ideas in constructive art which is exhaustless. In a
hundred years architecture became truly *organic*, features
that had become mere " vestiges " dropped away, and a new
style was complete ; one, not perhaps so completely winning
as some forms of Gothic, but the supremely logical building
art that has been.

If anywhere this vitalising had not been completed, it
would have been in the more decorative forms ; but here we
find no mere exercise in applying architectural orders, everything is as real and fresh as in the structure. Having the
Corinthian and Ionic capitals before their eyes and without
forgetting or rejecting them, the Byzantine builders invented
and developed an entirely fresh group of capitals fitted in
the most perfect way for arched brick construction. As
Mr. Freeman has said (*Hist. Essays*, iii. p. 61) of the new
architecture : " The problem was to bring the arch and
column into union—in other words to teach the column
to support the arch." This was done by shaping the
block of marble which formed the capital so that a simple

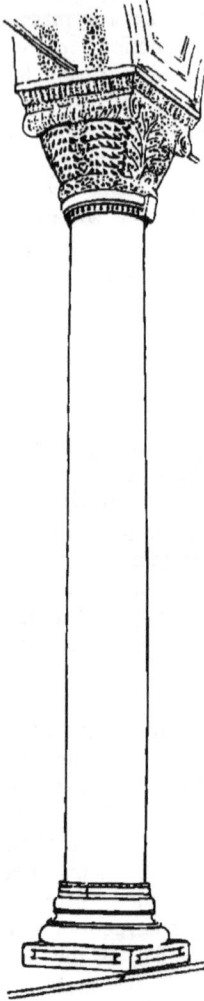

FIG. 50.—Columns of Great Order.

transition from the square block to the circle of the column was formed. When they were sculptured, and most of them are most elaborately sculptured, the general form is not altered but the carving enriches the surface only. The new "Impost capital" is found throughout the great cistern generally known as that of Philoxenus which is usually referred to the time of Constantine. In their study of the vaulted cisterns of Constantinople Forchheimer and Strzygowski have contributed much that is new to our knowledge of the architecture of the city and show that the evidence is entirely against this theory, which was propounded by Gyllius, whom more recent writers have been content to copy. This cistern, known to the Turks as Bin Bir direk (thousand and one columns), they identify with a great cistern which the *Paschal Chronicle* says was built by Justinian in 528. We believe with them that the architecture of the cistern agrees entirely with what we might expect as an outcome of the special circumstances in the time of the great building era. "Bin Bir direk exhibits the highest development of the art of cistern building, and it thus in its particular sphere resembles S. Sophia ; like it the boldness of its construction was never again equalled by the Byzantines. It would be an explanation of the bold achievement if it might be assumed that Anthemius proved his capability in this subterranean work

Fig. 51.—Capital now Outside Porch at S. Sophia.

before he made his supreme effort in S. Sophia. Technical features, however, make it seem probable that the builder was an Alexandrine."

"It is of the widest significance for the history of Byzantine art that here throughout the new 'impost capital' is employed in its plainest constructive form. It seems not improbable that the daring builder of the cistern was the first to make use of this form of capital which completely broke with classical tradition and is in such perfect accord with the exigencies of arch-architecture." This is to go too far ; for if the cistern is rightly referred to 528 it is probable, as we shall show, that the impost capital had at that time been for many years in use.

At S. Sophia the four main varieties of the new capital are all found. In the cistern the change of form is made by

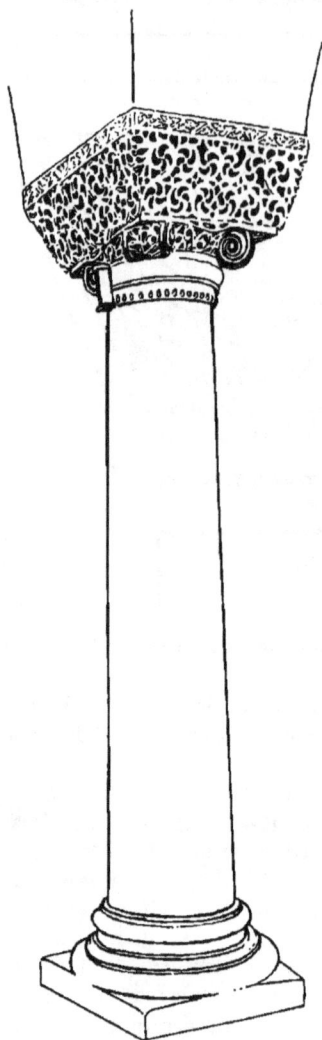

FIG. 52.—Columns in Gallery.

rounding away the angles at the bottom without reference apparently to any geometrical idea ; but in other capitals which belong essentially to this type the method seems to have been that explained in Fig. 53 which represents the form of the caps of the lamp pillars on the front of the western gynaeceum. They are most delicately carved with a network of ornament, but the general form is undisturbed as we have explained. The plain capitals of the west window and the isolated sculptured capital Salzenberg found in the north aisle are also of this form, which we shall call the Impost Capital type I. The profile can be made convex or inflected, we are only speaking of the simplest method of changing the form from a circle to a square.

Two capitals now used as mounting blocks outside the east porch, which we illustrate (Fig. 51), furnish us with a sculptured example of a similar capital in two stages of development, one of them never having been completed. We give here an outline of the blocked out capital, in which the

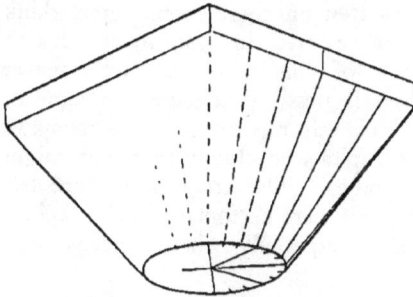

FIG. 53.—Rudimentary Form of Capital. Type I.

method of workmanship may be plainly seen. First, the block was cut away below convexly to meet the circular shaft. In this state it exactly resembles the capitals of the cistern. Secondly, on this was marked a border all round the top ; also centre lines running down each of the faces, about the centre point of each of which a circle of about seven inches diameter was drawn ; and at the bottom the width for the necking was marked off. Thirdly, the intermediate spaces were sunk about two inches ; the hollow of the abacus was formed ; the necking, and edge of the circular discs were rounded. This brings the capital to the stage shown in the diagram, the point to be observed being that the abacus, boss, and necking lie in one surface, first obtained, and the rest in another face, sunk some two inches below the former. It cannot be doubted that the style of these capitals is contemporary with the work at S. Sophia, and the finished one bears a monogram which appears to read ΘΕΟΔωΡΟΥ; it is, however, almost identical with that of Theodora, which occurs on the capitals of the interior. MM. Curtis and

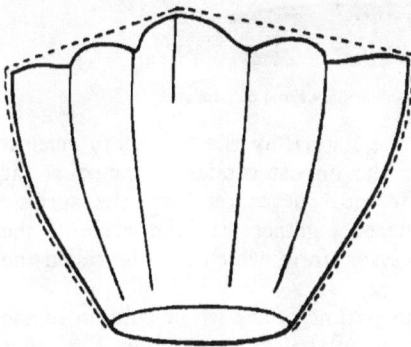

FIG. 54.—Rudimentary Form of Capital. Type II.

Aristarches,[1] who have written on these monograms, think
it belonged to a portico, restored in 409 by an eparch
called Theodoros. Work of this style was not done at
that time, and these capitals possibly belonged to some of
the outer courts of the church mentioned by Procopius.
They resemble the great capitals so closely that they might
almost be preliminary studies. The strips which are left
down two sides of the capitals were customary in the capitals
of a Byzantine colonnade, especially where screens were
inserted between.

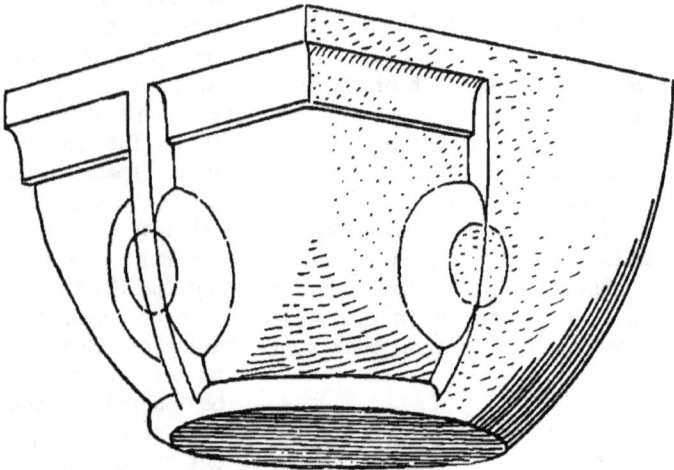

FIG. 55.—Rudimentary Form of Capital.

The two capitals in the loggia by the baptistery furnish
a well-defined variety of the impost capital. The square at
the top is here wrought into curves recalling the antique
abacus. These are gathered together into the circle of the
necking in a beautiful convex form which may be called the
Melon type II., see Fig. 54.

We give in Fig. 50 an outline of the whole column of the
great order in the interior of the church, and in Fig. 56 a
diagram of the blocking out of the capital. The columns

[1] Ἑλλην. Φιλ. Συλλ. παραρ. 1885, p. 10.

here and throughout the great church being monoliths of
fine material, the supporting area is very small compared
to the area of the arch imposts, which are of brick sheeted
with marble.   It will be seen that the projection is just
that required by the impost, which springs directly from the
outside edge.

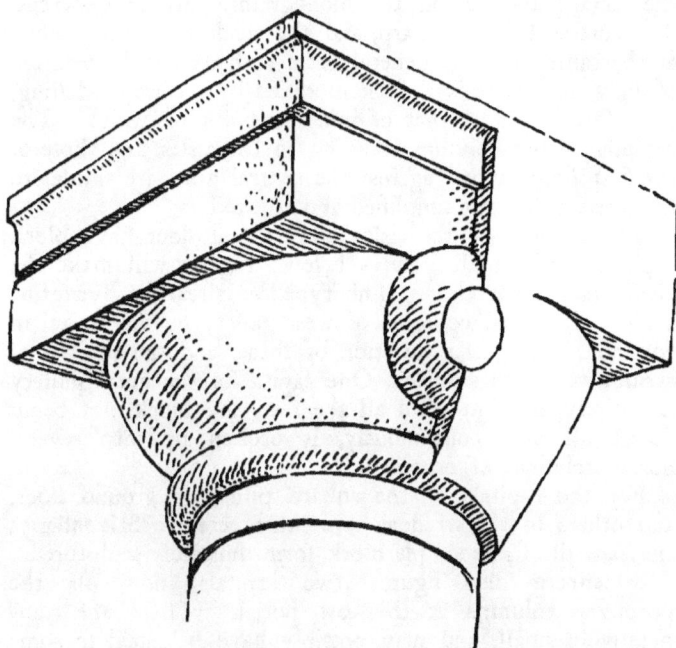

FIG. 56.—Rudimentary Form of Capital.   Type III.

The great capitals of S. Sophia are remarkable examples
of the evolution of beautiful forms on the mason's banker ;
the workman *finding form* in the stone block by the application of practical methods.   The lower half of the
capital is circular like the shaft, rising in a slightly swelling
curve of a bowl ; the upper part is square like the impost.
The basis of form is that of a bowl with a tile placed
above it, and is thus that of the Greek Doric.   This

type III. in which the circle does not pass by transition into the square impost, but changes abruptly, we may call the bowl and tile capital.

At S. Sophia the surface of the form obtained as shown in the figure is wrought into crisp acanthus and palm foliage ; and is in many places, especially at the tips of the leafage and behind the monograms, entirely undercut. The cutting being so sharp, and the shadows so deep, while at the same time the general form with its broad gradation of light and shade is so little modified by surface modelling, the effect is almost that of inlaying black on white. The capitals of the columns standing in the aisles, and those of the first floor ranged against the central area, are similar to the great order, but simplified and reduced.

The columns of the aisles on the first floor have block capitals, with small volutes below; Fig. 57 will make the elementary form clear. This type IV. is really a Byzantine Ionic. The dual columns of west gallery have a capital in common, which is a variation of these, and the capitals of atrium were also similar. One capital of the north gallery is entirely different from all the rest, the block, not being carved all over continuously, is broken up into several horizontal lines of ornament.

For the capitals of the square pillars of ground floor, and others to the windows, we must refer to Salzenberg ; they are all of the simple block form delicately sculptured.

Salzenberg also figures two capitals, now on the porphyry columns at the east porch. These are comparatively small, and may possibly have belonged to some position in the interior of the church, such as Justinian's first ambo. The form is that of a basket with four doves perched on the rim, and crosses between. Doves associated with crosses symbolized the Church. Now in St. Clemente at Rome there are two capitals of this kind which belonged to the ciborium, set up as the inscription shows while Hormisdas was pope (514–523), they are figured by Cattaneo, Fig. 7, who says they obviously were sculptured by Greek chisels. It is thus extremely possible that ours may have been late additions to the pre-Justinian church,

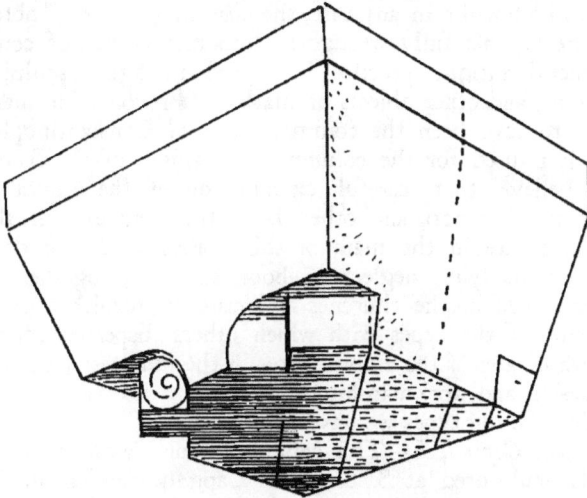

FIG. 57.—Rudimentary Form of Capital in Gynaeceum.   Type IV.

where they also may have belonged to the ciborium. Rohault de Fleury believed that this form of capital was intended to represent an offerings basket.

To these Bird and Basket capitals, type V., may be added varieties of the great class of derivatives from the Corinthian of which this is in fact one. These were in general use before the block type of capital was developed. We will here only mention two of these acanthus capitals. Those in which the leaves are set upright on the stem of the shaft we will call Byzantine Corinthian and type VI. Those in which the leaves turn over and bend round the capital we will, with Mr. Ruskin, call "Wind-blown acanthus," and type VII.

Distribution and Dates of Capitals.—We have referred before to our belief that Constantinople was a marble working centre from which sculptured marbles were dispersed to all parts of the Roman world. Having the chief types of Byzantine capitals before us it will be convenient to consider this more fully. We suppose that as white marble

256 S. SOPHIA

had to be bought in any case, the custom grew up of obtaining the capitals fully wrought. Importation was, of course,
a general antique practice in regard to figure sculpture,
columns, and other objects of marble. Proconnesian marble
seems to have been the common stone of Constantinople so
that it is used for the columns and capitals of the cisterns.
We believe that careful examination of the capitals at
Ravenna, Parenzo, and other Byzantine centres will show
that they are in the main of this material. As to design
the capitals lying neglected about the city, together with
those *in situ* in the churches and cisterns, furnish a perfect
museum of the types with which others dispersed through
the whole area of the empire agree in the minutest particulars
of design and workmanship.

To take the types we have mentioned:

Impost Capital, I.—This capital is found with the surface
richly sculptured at S. Sergius. Capitals identical in form
and decoration with the isolated capital of S. Sophia
(Salz. Pl. xx., fig. 8) are found at Parenzo and in
Jerusalem. The splendid examples of this type at S. Vitale,
Ravenna, are well known ; here the fretwork of sculpture is
almost entirely relieved from the ground. We found an
example absolutely similar at Constantinople. Mr. Ruskin's
"Lily Capital" which belongs to this group is found at
S. Mark's, at S. Vitale, at Parenzo, and at Alexandria.
Another variety is covered all over with horizontal bands of
zigzag fillets ; an example rests in the Tchenli-Kiosk
Museum, others are found at Athens, at Mistra, and a
third now at S. Mark's is figured in the *Stones of Venice*.
The capitals at S. Sophia, Salonica, figured by Texier are
probably the earliest of type I. to which an approximate
date can be given ; it was certainly in general use at the end
of the fifth century.

Melon Form, II.—These magnificent eight-lobed capitals
form the great order at S. Sergius, and are found at the
church usually called Agia Theotokos. Similar capitals
belong to the upper order at S. Vitale, and others are found
at S. Mark's. Some of the nave columns of S. Demetrius
at Salonica have fine capitals of this type which although

evidently derived from the last probably also originated in the fifth century.

Bowl Type, III.—These, the great capitals of S. Sophia, seem to have been especially designed for the metropolitan church : the beautiful palm foliage, however, with which they are sculptured is found again at Parenzo and on a capital in the Ravenna museum said to have been brought from Pomposa. The church at Parenzo was begun in 535.

Byzantine Ionic, IV.—These occur in their perfected form of block capital fully sculptured in S. Sergius and at the palace of Hormisdas in Constantinople, also in the upper order at S. Sophia, Salonica. Examples are also found at Venice.

In their earlier form of transition from the "Ionic with a plain dosseret" an immense number are found in the sub-terranean structures of Constantinople. An example has been found in Chalcis.[1]

Bird and Basket, V.—S. Sophia furnishes two examples, but there is no proof that they originally belonged to the building. Another example is in Cairo. That at S. Clemente, Rome, is signed with the name of John Mercurius; Piranesi figures a capital of this kind from the Palazzo Mattei, bearing a monogram which is indecipherable in his plate. Period, end of fifth century and beginning of sixth.

Byzantine Corinthian Type, VI.—These are of great variety; we will only mention one. In the portico of John Studius the acanthus leaves are doubled, one leaf lying over and within another, so that a double row of serrations is shown around the margins (see figure in Salz.). Similar capitals are found in S. Demetrius, Salonica, and at S. Mark's, Venice. This particular form is probably nearly concurrent with the last, possibly a little earlier.

Wind-blown Acanthus, VII., is represented at Constantinople by two examples forming bases for the posts of a wooden porch to a house near Gûl Jami, and another is found in the cistern usually called after Arcadius or Pulcheria. Absolutely similar capitals are found in S. Sophia, Salonica (*circa* 490) and one occurs at S. Demetrius. At Ravenna fine examples are dated by bearing the monogram of Theodoric.

[1] *Mittheilungen, etc., Arch. Inst. Athens,* 1889, xiv. 286.

S

Others at S. Apollinare in Classe resemble the last so closely that we doubt their having been made specially for the church built in 534–549. An example was found in Chalcis with the Ionic capital just referred to and De Vogüé figures one from Syria. Period, say 425 to 525.

The seven most typical Byzantine orders were thus being wrought concurrently at the end of the fifth century, and it seems that the three last did not long outlast this century. The others in their central types probably did not continue in use much beyond the sixth century. After this time somewhat coarse varieties of Byzantine Corinthian, or Type I., were mostly used.

The evidence of the original block in the fully sculptured finished work which we find in the most characteristic examples of the Byzantine capitals is of primary importance in all marble sculpture, and differentiates the work of the chisel from being a mere stone model of a clay model which is practically what most modern sculpture has become. In many of these capitals the vertical strip shown in Fig. 55 left in the finished work furnishes a further suggestion of the block from whence they were hewn.

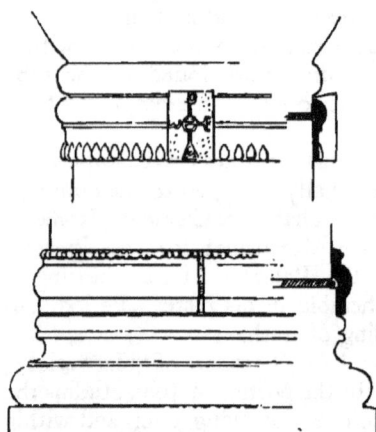

FIG. 58.—Bronze Annulets of Columns.

Shafts and Bases.—The usual theory that the Byzantines wrought but few new marble shafts does not bear scrutiny. Byzantine shafts have neckings of very slight projection, thus obviating the waste of labour and material of Roman work.[1] The shafts of the baptistery loggia at S. Sophia,

Mr. Brindley has shown us a photograph of a half worked Byzantine column with a flat necking, still attached in a horizontal position to the rock on its underside while the upper part is rounded.

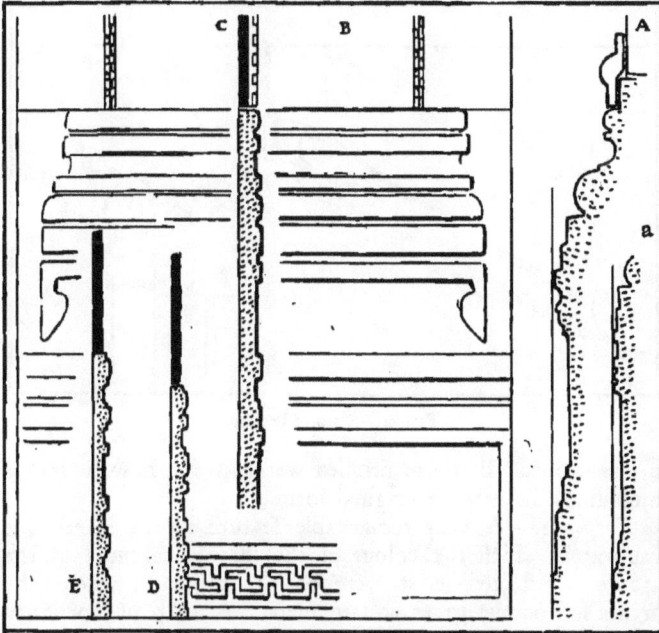

FIG. 59.—Marble Pedestals and Skirting Slabs.

figured by Salzenberg, furnish good examples; sometimes
the necking, as to the square marble pillars, is a simple broad
fillet of about a quarter of an inch projection.   The hundred
round shafts of S. Sophia exhibit a remarkable and beautiful
structural expedient by which the necking is entirely sup-
pressed, and bronze annulets surround the shaft under the
capital and above the base ; which prevent the shafts from
sliding or splitting, and retain the lead beds from being
forced out by the weight (see Choisy, p. 15). Large
monolithic shafts were the more apt to split, as they
had to be set up contrary to the direction of the quarry
strata.

Fig. 58 represents these bronze zones in association with
the great capitals and bases. The pedestals of the exedra
columns A *a*, next figure, are worked together with the bases

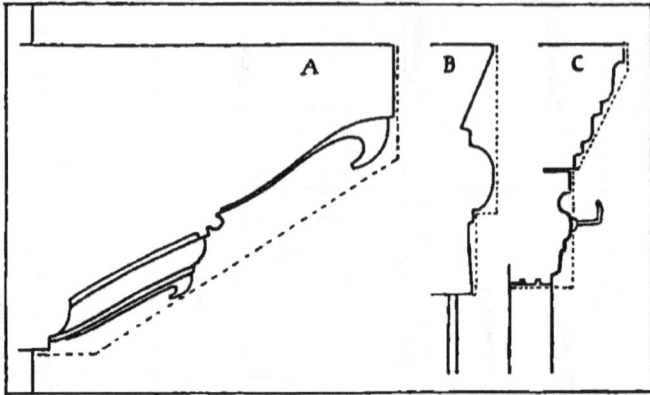

FIG. 60.—Cornice Profiles.

in one stone. In these profiles we again see how little the mouldings disturb the original form.

Responds.—A very remarkable feature in the interior, is the way in which the colour of the marble columns of the arcade is reflected as it were on the responds, where the arches fall on the great square piers. A strip of porphyry or verde antique, the width and height of the free shafts, is inlaid into the marble casing of the piers absolutely flush, the edge being only defined by a line of the notched fillet. A flat sculptured slab at the top echoes the capital, and a base slab of mouldings worked in a vertical plane ranges with the bases of the columns. Salzenberg's plate does not render this feature properly, the "capital" is flat and has straight sides and instead of the "base" he shows a portion of the wall skirting. Fig. 59 shows this base in elevation (B), and section (C), ranging with the pedestals of the exedra, Columns (A). The way in which the sculptured and inlaid spandrils of the arcades stop against the plain veneering of the great piers is also most noteworthy.

Cornices and Skirtings.—We give here (Fig. 59, D and E) two profiles of the skirtings where the principle of working out of thin veneering-slabs is applied to moulded work. The parapet slabs of first floor are worked in a very similar way ; Salzenberg shows design of front, and they bear flat lozenges between two crosses at the back. See Fig. 61.

The cornices of the interior, which really formed walks for the lamplighters, are made up of no regular combination of curves ; they project steeply forward, the general slanting plane being little disturbed (A, Fig. 60) ; they are decorated with rows of acanthus, the curved tips of which catch the light in bright points. The cornice of aisle is given at B. We also give a profile of the door-head, which shows how the mouldings conform to a plane of least labour (C). By the jambs and heads being mitred together, the difficulty of working stop ends was also obviated. The mouldings

FIG. 61.—Closures between Pillars, Front of Gynaeceum.

are not sharp and accurate, as is suggested by Salzenberg's engravings.

We may mention here that all the doors entering the church from the narthex have raised marble thresholds, that of the Royal Door being a magnificent piece of verde antique which rises some seven inches above the level of the floor ; the others are of white marble.

Windows, &c.—The pierced lattices of the windows also furnish examples of another beautiful method of marble slab construction. The large windows are subdivided by marble posts, between which the pierced lattices make a mere screen. Salzenberg, who found a store-room full of broken fragments, gives a section of a bar. Windows over the western entrances,

FIG. 62.—Marble Window Lattice.

and another at the foot of the south-west stair, which are similarly pierced out of sheet marble, have a simple meander carved on the bars (Fig. 62); this we suppose to be of the ninth or tenth century. The lower part of the window openings going down to the floors are filled with marble closures, some of which bear flat sculptured devices, such as a fish in a lozenge, and on the outside a cross; above this came a second tier of slabs pierced with square openings, which were possibly covered by marble slabs as opening casements.

Some of these closures are translucent; one in the West Gallery over narthex is the well-known "Shining Window" which is mentioned by Grelot. These transparent slabs of "Phengites" were much used in Byzantine architecture. The transparent marble slab windows of S. Miniato are well known. At Ravenna there is a sculptured slab altarfront, through which shone the light of candles placed behind.

Placed against the east side of the marble screen now in south gynaeceum

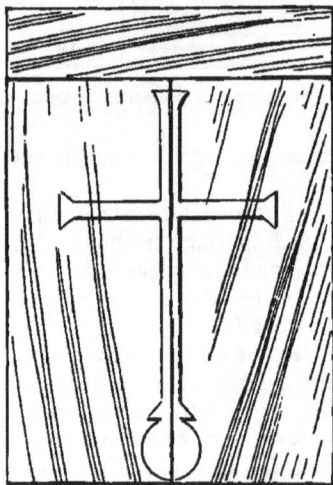

FIG. 63.—Cipollino Slabs with Cross.

are slabs of cipollino, which bear large crosses standing on
circles ; the relief being very slight and the edges softened
these show in the faintest way ; each cross extends over two
slabs, the joint being down the middle. A similar slab with
a cross is now placed in the opening on south side of
bema. These cross
slabs some seven feet
high are beautiful
examples of the
proper use of marble.
(Fig. 63.)

Carving.—Of the
carved ornament we
can only stay to re-
mark on the large
use made of the
drill in obtaining
points and chains of
sharp shadow : and
that in the design new motives and old—the acanthus and
the vine are found side by side, both equally alive. The
acanthus has been redrawn from the leaves which tracery
the stones along the shore ; and even the archaic lotus, for
centuries degraded into "egg and tongue," buds once again
into leaf.

FIG. 64.—Forms on Carved Impost Moulding.

CHAPTER XII

§ I. BRONZE WORK.

ONE of the most interesting facts in connection with the building is the lavish use of bronze in construction and decoration. There is every reason to suppose that the bronze casing of the Royal Doorway entering the church from the narthex, was applied long subsequent to the building of the church. We give in Fig. 65 a sketch of the bronze cornice of this door, with its hooks for the door hangings ; the left hand shows the form towards the narthex, the right hand the interior. The deep-splayed casing of the cornice resembling a sarcophagus may have suggested the story quoted by Buzantios,[1] that the body of S. Irene reposed above this doorway. By comparing it with the adjoining marble door-ways, it is apparent that the bronze must be laid over similar marble forms, and that this deep-splayed casing simply covers a marble cornice hacked back to one slanting face. Salzenberg gives a detail of the panel at the centre, and the inscription has already been quoted. Such inscriptions were general at the entering in of ancient churches. For instance, a small church[2] in Palestine has the legend, " This is the gate of the Lord, the righteous shall enter in thereat," and a similar inscription is on the lintel of the early church at Corfu.[3] An isolated lintel at Constantinople has "Open

---

[1] H. Κωνσταντινουπολις, p. 500.
[2] *Survey of Western Palestine*, vol. iii., p. 357.
[3] Walsh, *A Residence at Constantinople*, "Errata" to p. 80.

FIG. 65.—Bronze Casing to Royal Doorway.   Scale ₁⁄₂₀.

me the gates of righteousness, that I may enter and praise the Lord." Paulinus says that at the door of his church at Nola was written, " Peace be to thee with peaceful heart and pure, who comest within the secret place of Christ."

In a paper on the inscriptions at S. Sophia, by C. G. Curtis and S. Aristarchês in the *Transactions* of the Philological Society [1] of Constantinople the authors point out that S. Sophia was greatly injured by earthquake on the 25th of October, 975, and restored six years afterwards, and say that the form of the letters of the inscription suggests that it was written at this time. Possibly an earthquake gave a very sufficient reason for such a casing, by fracturing the great marble lintel, but there appears to have been a whole series of additions and alterations at this end of the church before this period, and it might very well have been done at the same time as the mosaic above it.

All the doors opening into or from the narthex, with one exception, are cased in bronze on a wood foundation about five inches thick, formed into panels. They are all hung in two leaves, and the back edges against the frame are rounded continuing top and bottom as pivots on which they revolve. The nine doors entering the church are comparatively plain, each leaf being divided into three panels.

The central doors entering the narthex are two panels high, each of which bore a large cross ; these were applied separately, the upper one under a round arch on pilasters, and

[1] Ἑλλην. Φιλ. Συλλ. παραρ., vol xvi., 1885, p. 34.

FIG. 66.—Central Bronze Door entering Narthex. Scale about three feet to an inch.

the lower beneath a gable also supported by pilasters.   The lower cross is planted on a rock, from which flow the four rivers, symbol of the Gospel preached to the ends of the earth.   Part of a verse in the mosaic of the apse at Nola as given by Paulinus makes this symbolism clear.

> "Christ the rock
> Of all the church, the base of rock sustains
> From which as living streams four fountains flow ;
> The four evangelists, whose words are gone
> Through every land."

The margins, framing the panel of this pair of doors, are decorated with elliptical hollows and pairs of small rosettes alternately (see Fig. 66).

The two doors right and left of this central door are less in size ; here each leaf is again divided into two panels. The top one has a relief of a chalice from which rises the stem of a cross with crisp acanthus foliage on either side. The lower panel has a large plain cross.   These reliefs are all applied to the panels, the crosses being made up of four arms, which are separately inserted into a central boss.   The horizontal arms, and in many instances the whole crosses, have been removed by the Mahommedans.   The styles and rails of these doors are inlaid with strap-like forms and gammidae in silver, and engraved with a representation of a setting of gems (see Fig. 67).   These inlaid straps, with seal-like ends, exactly repeat the forms found on door-hangings.   See Fig. 13. At S. Sophia the forms have certainly been taken from similar veils.   The large simplicity of the design of these beautiful bronze doors suggests that they may be of Justinian's time.

The doors still further from the centre, right and left, that is to say the two end doors of the five entering the narthex, have each leaf divided into three panels.   The top and bottom panels are charged with crosses ; and the centre one, which is smallest, bears an annular boss ; the styles are studded with discs.   The south door of narthex, and also the end doors in the west wall of the nave are similar to these ; the others in this wall, including the great central door from the narthex, have the big panel in the centre and two smaller ones with circular boss top and bottom (see Fig. 68).

The outer doors of the porch at the south end of narthex are still more remarkable. The panel margins are made up of cast bronze decorated with meanders, frets, and leaf mouldings, very delicately modelled in high relief. These are evidently of antique workmanship, possibly they may be as late as the fourth century, but they can hardly have been wrought later. The ancient doors have been enlarged by adding outer margins, consisting of later relief work, and flat metal studded with little leaf ornaments which form the heads of pins. The panels have been filled with plates of bronze, which bear an inscription ingeniously made up of monograms, arranged on crosses in circles ; these are deeply engraved into the metal plates and filled with silver. It is interesting to find here an example of the damascened work of which some of the doors in Italy brought

FIG. 67.—Bronze Door of Narthex. Scale about four feet to an inch.

from Constantinople are such remarkable specimens.[1] The letters are beautifully designed, and in all cases the horizonal arm of the cross is above the centre of the circle in which it occurs.

Good engravings of these doors are given by Salzenberg,

[1] See Bayet, *L'Art Byzantin.*

who however incorrectly transcribes and arranges the inscription on the panels. Of this we here give a corrected version, Fig. 69. (The top line in the figure is actually above the right-hand monograms.)

The inscription has been deciphered in the previously mentioned *Transactions* of the Greek Syllogos at Constantinople.

[ΘΕΟΦΙΛΟΥ ΚΑΙ]	ΜΙΧΑΗΛ ΝΙΚΗΤΩΝ
ΚΥΡΙΕ ΒΟΗΘΕΙ	ΘΕΟΦΙΛΩ ΔΕCΠΟΤΗ
ΘΕΟΤΟΚΕ ΒΟΗΘΕΙ	ΘΕΟΔΩΡΑ ΑΥΓΟΥCΤΗ
ΧΡΙCΤΕ ΒΟΗΘΕΙ	ΜΙΧΑΗΛ ΔΕCΠΟΤΗ
ΕΤΟΥC ΑΠΟ-ΚΤΙCΕΩC	ΚΟCΜΟΥ STMΘ ΙΝΔ. Δ

(of Theophilus and)	Michael Conquerors
(1) Lord, help	(2) Theophilos Emperor
(3) Mother of God, help	(4) Theodora Augusta
(5) Christ, help	(6) Michael Emperor
(7) Year from the creation	(8) of the world 6349. Ind. 4

The sixth and eighth monograms show evidence of having been altered. The silver has been removed from the earlier form, and the grooves having been filled up with bronze fresh letters were inlaid : the lines stopped out however show a different colour from the original ground, and so the palimpsest can be read. The revision was made "after the birth of Michael the first son of Theophilus in 839 and his coronation in the year 840.[1] Before this time the monogram of John the patriarch, which may still be traced, occupied the position of Michael's monogram: and instead of 6349 Indiction 4, the date was 6347 Indiction 2, thus giving the year beginning September 838, when John the Sixth was Patriarch of Constantinople."[2] The inscription "Michael Conquerors" (which is formed by piercing a bronze plate, not by damascening, as shown by Salzenberg) occupies the top of the right-hand leaf of

---

[1] A.M. 5508 of Byzantine chronology coincides with A.D. 1 up to September 1st. Indictions were cycles of fifteen years commencing in 312 A.D. Both the years of the world and the Indictions began on September 1st.

[2] Ἑλλην. Φιλολ. Συλλ. παραρ., vol. xvi., p. 30.

the door : that on the left corresponding to it is lost.
MM. Curtis and Aristarches have restored this as above.
The existing words, it is evident, must have been added after
Michael's birth and with the alteration of the monograms
probably form a memorial of his coronation. *Murray's
Handbook* 1893 sug-
gests that the word
Nikêtôn refers to the
restoration of images;
but the revision of the
inscription was made
during the lifetime of
Theophilus, who was
the last of the icono-
clastic emperors. Ac-
cording to Muralt [1]
Theophilus died Jan.
20 A.M. 6350 (842).
Just before, feeling
himself to be dying,
he made the empress
swear not to re-
establish images, and
not to depose the
patriarch John. Three
weeks however after
the emperor's death,
Methodius was named
patriarch. " The vic-
tory of the image-

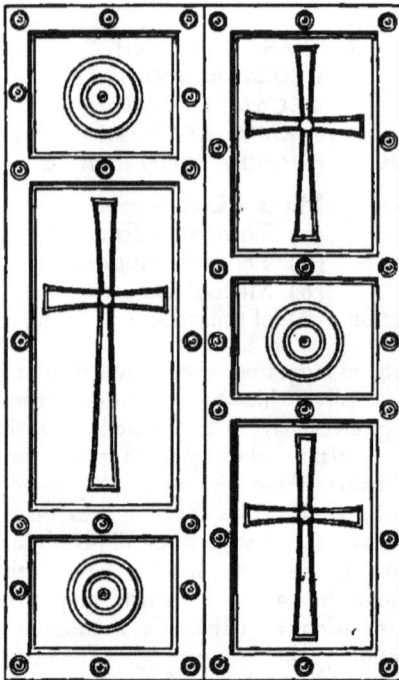

FIG. 68.—Bronze Doors in Narthex. Scale about
four feet to an inch.

worshippers was cele-
brated by the instal-
lation of the long-
banished pictures in S. Sophia on the 19th of February 842,
just thirty days after the death of Theophilus." [2]   It is
almost certain that the conjectural restoration is correct for
Theophilus and Michael are thus associated in a mural

[1] *Essai sur la Chronologie Byzantine.*
[2] Finlay, vol. i., p. 165.

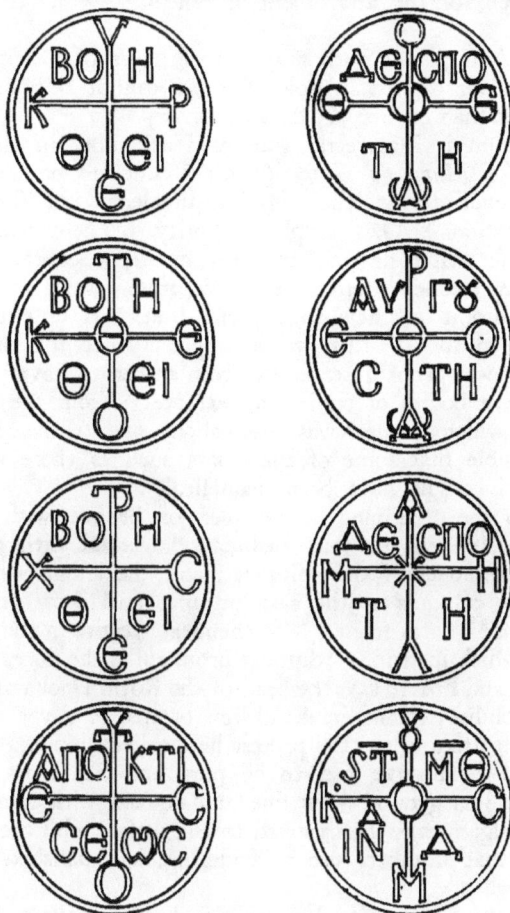

FIG. 69.—Inscription Damascened in Silver on Bronze Door.

inscription [1] and Niketes was a common title from Constantine downwards. On the panels are certain pin-holes [2] placed symmetrically between the monograms; these must have been for the attachment of reliefs.

The Anonymous author speaks of doors of "elektron" and of silver dipped in gold, but we cannot rely on this any more than on his 365 doors of ivory.

Electrum is incorrectly translated as amber in the last edition of *Murray's Guide* (1893). Labarte pointed out that enamel forms the right equivalent, and for this interpretation he has ample authority. Theophilus, the Byzantine writer on the arts, continually uses the word for glass enamels, either set as separate jewels, or fused as translucent enamels to a metal base. A note in the English edition of this writer explains that this use of the word was probably extended from amber to cover other transparent bodies of similar appearance. From the lavish way in which enamel was used about the tenth century it is possible that some of the doors such as those in the iconostasis might have been enamelled.

As to the "dipping" of silver or bronze with gold the Silentiary tells us that Justinian "overlaid with gold" the bronze zones of the columns; and the annulets of the porphyry columns at the east entrance still show gilding. Buzantios [3] quotes from a MS. chemical treatise in the Paris library which mentions "dipping bronze like the doors of S. Sophia," and Fossati says the head of the Royal Door was gilt.

Theophilus explains in detail how bronze or silver might be gilt by fire-gilding, the process here called dipping. The copper in the bronze had to be pure and free from lead. The gold was ground very fine and cooked with mercury. This amalgam was then applied to the surface with a copper bit, like that plumbers use in soldering, and polished with a wire brush.

We have given sketches of the bronze collars which surround the columns, at the junction of capital and shaft,

[1] Mordtmann, p. 36.   [2] Shown in Salzenberg's plate.
[3] H. Κωνσταντινουπολις, vol. i. p. 500

and just above the bases.   The porphyry columns in the two western exedras have many intermediate annulets at unequal heights; these in some cases were doubtless intended to bind up longitudinal fractures in the shafts, which show in many places ; but in other instances they appear to cover the junction of separate drums of porphyry.   These are all shown in Grelot's interior view.   The principal collars are certainly of the time of Justinian ; those under the capitals have square metal bosses or boxes covering the point where they meet and are pinned together.   These "seals" of the great order bear the monograms of Justinian and Theodora.

The annulets at the base are made continuous at the joint, and have the appearance of being brazed : those of the main order are now kept brightly polished.   One of the base annulets in the north gallery is signed by a monogram as the work " of Stephen." [1]

Besides the hooks, in the form of upturned fingers, for the hangings at the bronze door, similar hooks occur in the marble lintels of the doors in the narthex and the exonarthex.

§ 2.—MOSAIC.

The mosaics of figures exposed at the time of Fossati's repairs are many of them figured by Salzenberg, although his harshly coloured diagrams can but very inadequately represent the beauty of the originals.   We give here his descriptive text in a slightly condensed form as a basis for our own remarks.   Dethier [2] asserts that only a part of the mosaics discovered were published by Salzenberg, and that Fossati preserved others inedited in his portfolios.[3]

The mosaics are formed of glass of various colours cut into small pieces and applied to the vaults with a cement. The gold mosaic was made by laying leaf gold on the glass, which was then covered by a thin film of glass to protect the surface.   Silver mosaic was made in the same way.   The gold

[1] Curtis, *Broken Bits of Byz.*, part ii.
[2] *Le Bosphore et Constantinople*, 1873.
[3] See below, p. 287.

T

was used, in spite of its apparent abundance, with great economy. For instance, in vertical spaces high up and only visible from almost immediately beneath, the tesserae are arranged in horizontal rows at a distance of two or three tesserae from each other with their upper edges projecting. The projecting edge of the lower row hides the bare space between it and the row above. There is thus a saving of more than half the material, and great play of light is obtained. The tympana of the aisles are covered in this way. The coloured tesserae are set in the usual way, as the difficulties involved by the other method in the curves of the ornament would outweigh the saving of material.

Besides gold and silver, red, blue, and green are the principal colours ; though others are used in the heads of the figures. The vaulting throughout was covered with a background of gold, on which are conventional patterns that follow the forms of the construction. Some of the spaces have representations of figures.

In the bands of ornament are gamma-crosses [*swastikas*], hearts, leaves, and crosses, placed in circles, squares, and other figures. There are no sharp arrises to the vaults, but patterned bands are placed on the rounded edges.

The vault of the narthex has its wide transverse bands adorned with gamma-crosses. In the domed portions between the transverse arches are diagonal bands which culminate in a circle inclosing a cross.[1]

The vaults of the gynaeceum, perhaps because they were visible from the nave, are more elaborate than those of the aisles below.[2] Salzenberg's Plate xxv. shows the western dome on the south side, on which is represented the descent of the Holy Spirit : the arches have the same ornament as those below.[3]

Details of the dome are given in Salzenberg's Plate xxvi. The edges of the ribs and window openings are

---

[1] See Salz., plate xxiii. Fig. 2 is one of the tympana, the centre one has figures : fig. 3 transverse arches ; fig. 5 soffite of a window.

[2] Salzenberg's plate xxiv. gives details of the lower aisles.

[3] Fig. 2 is the barrel vault near the window ; fig. 3 arches and vault adjoining ; fig. 6 the intrados of the arches opening to the nave; fig. 7 a pattern of the west gynaeceum.

covered with bands of ornament. The faces of the ribs have alternate squares and crosses, which decrease in size as they get higher. The central space has lost its figure subject, but it is surrounded by a wide border.[1] The sides of the window openings are lined with silver mosaic. The lower part of the dome is not decorated, as the projecting cornice hides it from below.[2]

The edges of the exedra-conchs have bands similar to those on the great arches, and the same pattern occurs again on the edges of the eastern barrel vault, and the bema apse.[3] The rest of the decoration of the surface of the apses has disappeared.

Over the centre door from the narthex to the nave is represented Christ on a throne, holding a Gospel open at the words, " I am the Light of the world : Peace be with you." A monarch is prostrate before him, and in medallions on either side are Mary the Intercessor, and Michael the Protector.[4]

The nimbus of Christ has three rays, and His hand blesses in the Greek manner, by which the fingers represent the initial and final letters of Jesus Christus. The undergarment has broad gold stripes worked on it, and the lights are given in silver ; it seems to be of silk, the upper garment appears to be of a white woollen stuff.

The great western arch has a medallion of the Virgin at the crown, and full lengths of Peter and Paul at the sides, Peter on the south ; however, only a few remnants of these figures are now left. The border which surrounds the medallion of the Virgin has colours of the rainbow, the circle of her halo is red ; the flesh colour is fair, and the eyes are blue. The veil is blue, with a gold cross, and the cloak is also blue. Under the veil is a kind of band round the head, like that which the Spanish Jews of Constantinople wear ; it is of a blue green colour with dark stripes ; the hair is not visible. Her nimbus has three silver rays on a gold ground; her hands

[1] Plate xxvi., fig. 6.
[2] See fig. 3 for this cornice, the band beneath, and the edges of the great arches.
[3] Fig. 7 gives the borders of the windows in semidomes.
[4] Salz., plate xxvii.

T 2

rest on the shoulders of the Child, whose right hand blesses, while the left holds the book of the Gospel.

Peter's face is dark, the nimbus is blue, the garment is bluish green, and the gold rod, surmounted by a cross, has red and blue bands. He thus has the same insignia as the St. Peter on the Ciborium Curtain, and it is this which, in the mosaic, identifies the figure as Peter, for there is no inscription. Porphyrogenitus, in his life of Basil, mentions that when the western arch was restored the pictures of the Virgin, and the Apostles Peter and Paul were placed there by that emperor. The figure of Paul has an upper garment of green with silver lights, and the undergarment is a greenish yellow. The whole figure is about seventeen feet high, but the head is wanting.[1]

On the large semicircular walls beneath the northern and southern dome-arches are a number of figures in mosaic. The seven arched recesses were filled with representations of martyrs and bishops; above, between the windows, were six smaller figures of prophets, and a larger figure at each end. At the height of the upper row of windows were probably the archangels, but of these only the feet remain.

The figures that now exist are the following. In the recesses on the south side, the second from the east is Anthimos, Bishop of Nicomedia, martyred in 311 : in the third is Basil, Bishop of Caesarea, martyred in 379.[2]

The fourth recess from the east has Gregory Theologos, Patriarch of Constantinople from 378 to 383. The next figure is Dionysius the Areopagite; who was converted by St. Paul, and became, tradition says, Bishop of Athens. In the sixth recess is Nicholas, Bishop of Myra, who died in 330. This figure is partly destroyed. The seventh is Gregory, Bishop of Armenia, who died in 325.[3]

The figure of Isaiah, which is to the east of the row of windows, had been covered up (when Salzenberg made his drawings), but it was described by Fossati as having an undergarment of green with silver lights, and over it a cloak of a white woollen stuff. The right hand pointed towards

[1] Salz. xxxii., fig. 4.   [2] Salz., plate xxviii.
[3] Salz., plate xxix.

the bema, and in the left was an open scroll with the inscription, "Behold, a Virgin shall conceive and bear a son." Under the figure was a monogram.[1] Higher up again on the same wall was the inscription :—

ΑΙΓ . . . . ΤΗCΑΘΑΝΑΤΟΥ CΟφΙΑC
ΗΡΑ . . . . ΤΟΥΚΕΑΚΗΡΑΤωΝ . . . .

The recesses of the north wall have no mosaics [see below, p. 287.]

At the height of the windows, the first figure beginning from the east is Jeremiah.[2] The undergarment has stripes of blue and red, and the upper represents a russet-coloured woollen stuff. The right hand blesses, the left has an open roll [with the inscription shown in the plate, "This is our God ; no other shall be compared to Him."].[3]

The figure between the first and second window is probably Jonas, as ΑC still remains on the right side of the head, and there is only room for three letters on the other side. The undergarment is a greenish blue with silver lights, and has broad red stripes. The nimbus is blue.

Over the head of this figure is found the remnant of an inscription ΝΤΙΔΟC. This may have belonged to one of the figures above, of which a sandaled foot and edge of a garment alone remain. The foot does not stand upon green earth, like the prophets below, and therefore probably belonged to an angel. Only a part remains of the third prophet from the east, which was inscribed Habakkuk.[4]

The mosaics on the soffite of the eastern arch were covered before drawings were made. At the crown is a medallion with a white ground. In this is a low throne of gold, with two green cushions upon it ; over them is thrown a blue cloth with a white hem, and upon that is placed a golden book. Above is also a gold cross with three arms ; the middle one is the longest, and at its intersection with the upright member is a circle. On the south face of this

---

[1] Reading ΚΥΡΙΕ.   [2] Salz., plate xxx.
[3] The figure of Jeremiah at S. Clemente, Rome, bears the same inscription.
[4] Salz., plate xxv., fig. 3.

eastern arch is the figure of John the Baptist, with long hair, and a brown shaggy garment ; his right hand blesses, and his left holds a cross with three arms. Opposite, on the north side is the Virgin, with uplifted hands in the attitude of prayer. She has a white undergarment, bound with a golden girdle, a red upper garment, and a veil of a green-blue, with a gold hem. Under her is John Palaeologus, who restored this part, and to whose time these figures and designs certainly belong. The emperor wears a crown, with strings of pearls on either side. He has a closely fitting undergarment of gold, decorated with pearls and embroidery. A magnificent cloak hangs down from the left shoulder, and round the neck and breast is a kind of broad gorget richly embroidered. In his right hand is a sceptre, and in his left a roll.

The archangel on the south side of the bema vault [1] has a globe in the left hand, and a staff in the right. He is clad in white, with imperial red shoes. The arch of the apse bears an inscription, which ends with the letters CЄIЄ ΠΛΛIN.

On the conch of the apse is the Mother of God upon a throne, holding the Child between her knees ; her upper garment, which is blue, conceals the whole figure, except that at the breast, under the arm, and above the feet, the white and gold garment beneath is visible. The Child has his right hand uplifted, and his left against his breast. He wears a white garment, with a gold girdle. His hair falls down freely, and the nimbus has three streams of light. The throne is gold with red ornaments, but is without a back, and the footstool is of green silk.

In the dome pendentives are Cherubim with six wings. Each head is four feet two inches high. The upper feathers of the wings are a light green, and the under feathers brown.[2] The great centre-piece of the dome, which, according to Du Cange, represented Christ as Judge of the World seated upon a rainbow, no longer exists.

Only one of the domes of the gynaeceum preserves its mosaic ornament of figures. This[3] represents the descent of

[1] Salz., plate xxii. [2] Salz., plate xxxi.
[3] Salz., plate xxxi.

the Holy Spirit. Only a part remains of the throne in the centre; on it is a green cushion, and a blue cloth with gold patterns. Groups of spectators fill the pendentives of the vault.

Above the doorway which leads from the western gynaeceum to the chambers over the south porch, are remains of figures, which can no longer be identified.[1] In the ceiling of the chamber over the stairway is a design of green tendrils on a gold ground.[2]

The small dome in the chamber which opens out of the western buttress of the south side on the first-floor level has four angels with uplifted hands, supporting a medallion in the centre. This design is similar to that in the side chapel at S. Prassede at Rome.

"The figure representations belong to the time of Justinian, though the Silentiary, otherwise so accurate, does not describe them."

First Scheme.—A reading of Salzenberg's notes on the figure mosaics will show how little ground there was for his impression that these belonged to the time of Justinian, which the last sentence expresses. Several of these mosaics are dated as being parts of restorations. Thus he shows that Basil I. placed figures on the arch of the great western hemicycle, and that those of the great eastern arch are the work of Palaeologus.

The subject has been much obscured by insecure assumptions and inexact assertions. Labarte, who was one of the first to doubt that Justinian was intended by the figure of the kneeling emperor before Christ over the Royal Door, thought that the Silentiary described figure-mosaics as covering the interior.[3] Gerspach in *La Mosaïque* calls the emperor 'Justinian' and appears to mistake the Pentecost cupola for the great dome. In regard to the date of the lunette containing the emperor, Labarte suggested that it was a work of the seventh century, and that the emperor was Heraclius.[4] Woltmann and Woermann placed it still later

---

[1] Salz., plate xxxi., fig. 7.   [2] *Ibid.* fig 8.
[3] *Arts Industriels.*   [4] *Hist. of Painting*, vol. i., p. 234.

and write, " There is no kind of resemblance between
the beardless portrait of Justinian at Ravenna and this
bearded, gray-headed man.   It is more likely to be Basil I.
the restorer of the western apse, and this opinion is supported
by the miniatures of his time."   The pilgrim Anthony seems
to refer to it as Leo the Wise, but the Russians ascribe so
many works to this emperor without reason that this is in-
conclusive.   The forms of the letters in the inscriptions,
however, show that the mosaic is late.   Bayet,[1] who has
considered the mosaics afresh, and thinks the silence of
Paulus is conclusive as to the absence of figure-mosaics
when the poem was written, about 562, himself seems
to misread some parts of the poet's description ; thus
he thinks patterns in mosaic are intended in lines 607—612.
The animals of the atrium may possibly have been of glass
mosaic : but we think it more likely that inlaid marble
like the dolphins of the interior (Fig. 49) is intended.   The
baskets of fruit, branches with birds, and the golden vine
in the church, spoken of in lines 668, &c. seem to refer to
the carved and gilt surfaces of the spandrils of the arcade,
not to the mosaic, as Bayet supposes.

The figure scheme, so far as it can be traced, closely
agrees with the Byzantine Manual of Painting : and the
subjects and treatments can be associated with work in other
churches of the ninth and tenth centuries which have in
several cases almost identical designs.   Altogether it
may be doubted if a single figure belongs to a time anterior
to the iconoclastic period of the eighth century.

We believe the original scheme of decoration is best
accounted for without figures, and even if this were not
so, we can hardly believe that in the Patriarchal Church at
the door of the Palace figures would have lasted through
the reigns of the iconoclastic emperors and patriarchs,
as they may well have done in remoter churches where
the clergy were on the other side.   Leo issued his first
decree against images in 726.   Its purport was not, as is
often stated, that pictures should be hung higher in the
churches in order that people should not adore them

[1] *Recherches.*

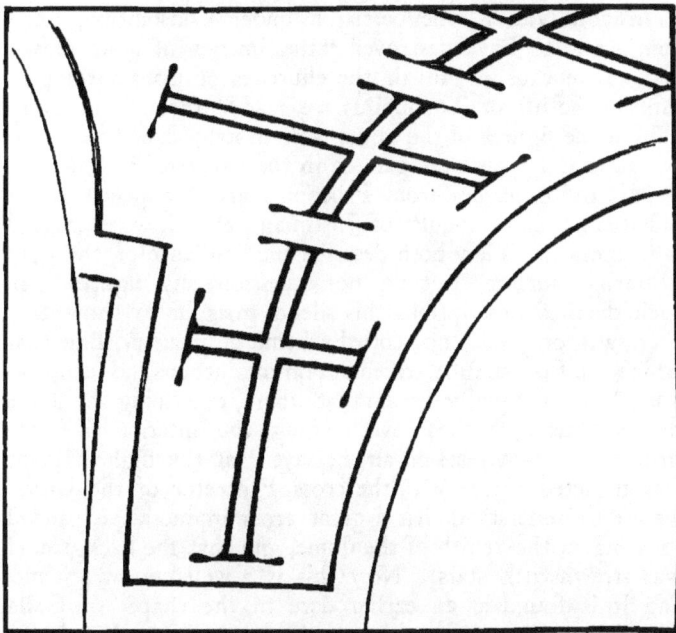

FIG. 70.—Mosaic of small Vault Compartment next the Bema.

by kissing : "it commanded that they should be totally abolished."[1]

It is well known that a figure of Christ over the entrance to the palace was destroyed by Leo the Isaurian. Dr. Walsh, who was chaplain to our embassy at the Porte about 1820, writes, "There stood till very lately in Constantinople an inscription over the gate of the palace called Chalces. Under a large cross sculptured over the entrance to the palace were the following words :—

" ' The emperor cannot endure that Christ should be represented (*graphes*) a mute and lifeless image graven on earthly materials. But Leo and his young son Constantine have at their gates engraved the thrice-blessed representation of the cross, the glory of believing monarchs.' "[2]

[1] Bury, vol. ii. 432.
[2] R. Walsh, *Essays on Ancient Coins, &c.*, 1828, gives the Greek.

In 768 Nicetas, the patriarch under Constantine, Leo's son, is said to have destroyed "the images of gold mosaic and wax encaustic" in all the churches of Constantinople.[1] And in the life of Theophilus we read, "throughout every church the figures of the saints were destroyed, and the forms of beasts and birds were painted in their places."[2]

It is quite certain from Procopius and the poem of the Silentiary that the vaults of Justinian's church were covered with mosaic. They both describe the brilliance of the gold glittering surface, but do not mention any figures. In such detailed descriptions this silence goes far to show that there was originally no storied scheme of imagery, like that which the Poet so fully traced out on the curtains and iconostasis. It seems equally certain that where, describing the dome on the strong arches, overhanging the interior like the firmament which rests on air, he says, "at the highest point was depicted (*epigraphe*) the cross, Protector of the City," we are to understand that a great cross in mosaic expanded its arms on the zenith of the dome, and that the background was strewn with stars. Now this is a well-known scheme, and it is found at an earlier date in the chapel of Galla Placidia at Ravenna, and later it is mentioned by Porphyrogenitus in a description of a domed apartment in the palace. The stars on the dome are more than once referred to in the poem (page 36), and it is probable that the surfaces between the ribs as well as the central circle had gold stars set in azure, the ribs being of gold; nothing less would seem to justify "the firmament of the roof its rounded expanse sprinkled with the stars of heaven."

It is evident that, however easily figures and pictures might be added here and there at various dates, the church, being once incrusted with mosaic, would at no subsequent time have had the enormous areas of tesserae removed to be again renewed.

It follows that the ground, and any patterns evenly distributed in every part of the vaults, are assuredly of the first work. First among such designs is a jewelled

---

[1] *American Journ. Archæol.*, iv. 143.
[2] Theoph. Cont. ed. Bonn, p. 99.

cross thirteen feet high, which is blazoned on both ground floor and gallery vaults, and which must have been repeated some twelve times twelve. We give an outline of one of the smallest vault compartments in the church, the irregular space to the east directly south of the bema : here three of the crosses can still be seen through Fossati's colouring, their interlocking arms spreading over the whole field. This form of cross, with lobed ends, is found set in a circle of stars, in the mosaic apsoid of S. Apollinaris in Classe. (Fig. 70.)

A similar argument applies to other forms which occur with equal frequency. A square panel of ornament which alternates with the crosses, certain diapers, the bands up the edges of the aisle vaults, and the small circles each containing the six-armed cross or monogram at the centre of these compartments, would all seem to be parts of the original work, and these simple elements we believe formed the first scheme of decoration. Texier figures a mosaic from Salonica made up of crosses. The splendid simplicity of such a scheme seems entirely in harmony with S. Sophia, for even figures would disturb the beauty of the expanse which at each movement glitters like a web of golden mail swayed by a breeze.

Later Mosaics.—For the mosaics displaying figures we refer back to Salzenberg's description. Much further information might have been gathered if he had given copies of the inscriptions which exist, in however incomplete a state. His section (Plate x.) shows that a long inscription surrounded the arch of the apse, but in his text he only gives the last few letters CEIE ΠΑΛΙΝ; this possibly belonged to the words ἀνεστήσειε πάλιν, "Set up again," and the whole may have contained the name of the emperor under whom this restoration was effected. (See below, p. 287.)

On the great lunette of the wall of the south side also, where the tiers of saints and prophets seem a part of a scheme representing the Church triumphant, or a *Benedicite*, two monograms occur (see Salzenberg's Plate ix.) ; only the first, which reads KYPIE, is figured in the text ; it is evidently a part of the well-known invocation, 'Lord, help,' which requires the name of an emperor or artist to complete it.

An inscription between these monograms is partly given
in the text ; and supposing it to be correctly rendered the
whole probably read "Lord, help" (*name* who painted this
wall) "of the Immortal Wisdom" (with the figures) "of
the saints ".

The entire later scheme of the mosaics must have
corresponded closely to that in the New Church in the
palace built by Basil, which is described by Porphyrogenitus.
Here, at the centre of the dome, was the human form of
Christ embracing the whole world in His regard ; below were
ranges of angels. In the apse was the figure of the Virgin
with arms uplifted in prayer,
"a choir of apostles, martyrs,
prophets and patriarchs filled
the other spaces of the whole
church." This in turn resembles very closely the icono-
graphy at S. Luke's.

FIG. 71.—Restoration of Throne at
Crown of Pentecost Dome.

The following instances may
be given of the agreement of
the mosaics at S. Sophia with
the instructions of the Painter's
Manual. For example, it directs
that over the door of entrance
from the narthex Christ be
represented throned, holding
the Gospel open at the words, "I am the Door : by me, if
any man enter in, he shall be saved." At each side the
Virgin and the Prodromos are to be represented. The figure
to Christ's left at S. Sophia, called Michael by Salzenberg,
Grelot tells us was the Prodromos and he probably followed
the traditional ascription, although the type seems to agree
better with an archangel.

Again, "Inside the Sanctuary at the centre of the vaults
draw the Virgin seated on a throne holding Christ as a
little child." [1] This exactly describes the apsoid mosaic at
S. Sophia. The cupola of the gynaeceum, representing the

[1] A composition of this kind at Parenzo appears to go up to the sixth
or seventh century.

descent of the Holy Spirit, is also in close agreement with
the directions given in the Manual :—" The Holy Spirit
is seen in the form of a dove, twelve tongues of fire go out
from it and rest on the apostles." This subject is treated
at S. Luke's in a manner almost identical to that at S.
Sophia, and it is also found in a dome at S. Mark's.

Diehl in his examination of the mosaics at S. Luke's
has pointed out that the central circle of the Pentecost
cupola at S. Sophia as shown by Salzenberg in Plate xxxi.
is quite insufficient to have contained the figure of Christ
as shown in the restoration given on Plate xxvi., and that
consequently the Holy Spirit as a Dove really occupied this
position as at S. Luke's. In Fig. 71 we give an amended
restoration of this centre ; it will be seen from Salzenberg's
text that he had no evidence for a figure. The two angels
above the sanctuary are described by Salzenberg as bearing
lances or banner poles ; these were doubtless surmounted
                              ΑΓΙΟϹ
by Flabella bearing the words ΑΓΙΟϹ as at S. Luke's and
                              ΑΓΙΟϹ
Nicaea.[1] There is a very similar angel holding a flabellum
of this kind in the tenth century Menologium ; and the words
Holy, Holy, Holy, are directed to be put on flabella in the
manual.

Again the Manual says, "At the summit of these vaults
(opening from the dome) draw the holy Veil to the east
and opposite to it the holy Cup." Now in Grelot's view
of the interior, made when many of the mosaics were still
visible, he shows a large square mosaic at the crown of
the bema vault directly over the altar, which he says was
"the picture of Christ's face upon a napkin called Veronica."

The representation of the throne at the centre of the
soffite of the eastern arch (see p. 277) is one of the most
beautiful symbolisms of Byzantine art. At Nicaea the same
design occurs in a similar position on the triumphal arch,
and it is inscribed ΕΤΟΙΜΑϹΙΑ ΤΟΥ ΘΡΟΝΟΥ. This
"Preparation of the throne" referred to the second coming
of Christ. Our figure represents a throne of this kind

[1] See Diehl in *Byz. Zeits.*, 1893.

which we offer as an illustration of that at S. Sophia ; it is based on a throne inscribed H ETHMACIA which appears on the cover of a Byzantine Gospel book at S. Mark's.[1] The small dome of the little chapel on the first floor, Salzenberg says, resembles a dome at S. Prassede. The latter is a work of the ninth century.[2]

Salzenberg's description seems to account for all the figured mosaics mentioned by Grelot (1680) except the "Veronica over the sanctuary." When Grelot made his drawing there was no figure at the crown of the dome but only the bands rising to the central wreath. Clavijo how-

FIG. 72.—Restoration Throne at Crown of Great E. Arch.

ever writes, " The vault of the square is covered with very rich mosaic work, and in the middle of the vault high over the great altar the image of God the Father very large is wrought in mosaics of many colours ; but it is so high up that it only looks the size of a man or a little larger though really it is so big that it measures three palmos between the eyes." This must be the Pantocrator of the Manual— " draw near the summit of the cupola a circle of different colours like a rainbow seen on clouds in rainy weather. In the centre represent Christ with the Gospel and this inscription, Jesus Christ, the Almighty."

Since the above has been in type we have found a pamphlet published by the brothers Fossati in 1890,[3] describing a collection of drawings of S. Sophia, shown by them at Milan. From this we gather the following additional particulars of the mosaic subjects.—Over the door of the south porch " was a remarkable mosaic representing the Virgin and Child, to whom Justinian presents the Church and Constantine the City."—A representation of Christ, the Virgin, and S. John,

1 Il Tesoro.   2 Pératé, Archéol. Chrétienne, with figure, p. 265.
3 Relievi storico artistici sulla architettura Bizantina.

forming the Trimorphion (Pantocrator, Pantochrante, Pante-
popte.)—Two groups of the Fathers of the Church, thirteen
altogether: Ignatius Oneos, Methodius, Ignatius Theophorus,
Gregory Thaumaturgus, John Chrysostom, Cyril, and Atha-
nasius.   [These must occupy the seven recesses on the north
window-wall, as the six others agree with those given by
Salzenberg on the south side].—The Pantocrator on a throne
[? supposed centre of Pentecost dome].—John Palaeologus
[? with the Virgin on north side of great east arch, p. 278].—
John Comnenus and Irene with the Virgin between them.—
Constantine XI. and Zoe with Christ between them.—
Alexius Comnenus X. or XI.—Alexander, the brother of
Leo [some of these also were doubtless on the great east
and west arches].—Three Virgins.—S. John with six apostles
surrounded by cherubim [? in higher part of one of the
window-walls, p. 277].—Prophets [? of window-wall, p. 276].
—A circle with colossal Pantocrator [? the destroyed centre
of the great dome].—Different emblems with Greek and
Latin descriptions.   Besides these, a drawing of Cherubim
" saved from the Atrium Portico " is mentioned ; and the
inscription on the arch in front of the apse is given as
follows, and may be compared with Salzenberg's Plate x. :—

HIANIPCEIAP HPANΘEOHAPIHAP ΘECICHNANEAICEIE
ΠAPIN.

The earliest description of the mosaics entering into any
particulars is that of Dr. Covel's MS. 1670-7 in the British
Museum.   " In those cupolas [of gynaeceum] are imagery of
Saints and the story of the Bible which the Turks have in
many places quite defaced and plastered them all over ; in
other places only scratched out or disfigured their faces as
the cherubims in the corners under the great dome."   He
then enters into details of the pentecost dome which was the
only figured vault entire ; and then describes mosaics in the
western gallery not otherwise mentioned.   " In the sides of
the second window [from the south], is Christ coming up
from Jordan and the Descent of the Holy Ghost with these
words, Matt. iii., 17 :—OYTOCECTIN, &c., on one side and
over against it, Christ between Moses and Elias with these

words, Matt. xvii., 5 :—OYTOC, &c." The window jambs of the western gallery are now plastered, it is probable that a series of mosaics of the life of Christ covered them. Up to 1840 every visitor seems to have been offered tesserae, which for better assurance were broken out before his eyes. The Italian MS. of 1611 also in the British Museum (Harl. 3408), after saying that the walls of the church were lined with marble adds, "the porch as well, except that this is all worked in mosaic with growing leaves of great beauty down to the pavement of the porch."[1]

Signor Boni has noticed that some of the gold tesserae at Parenzo are inserted at an angle of 30° to the plane of the wall, so as to be normal to the line of vision, just as Salzenberg describes at S. Sophia; the same thing occurs at the Dome of the Rock. This, besides saving the material, aided in flashing the light, a property of the gold tesserae which was much valued, as several inscriptions from the mosaics show.[2] In S. Maria in Domnica, the apse—" *Nunc rutilat jugiter variis decorata metallis*," again in S. Maria in Trastevere the vault " *divini*

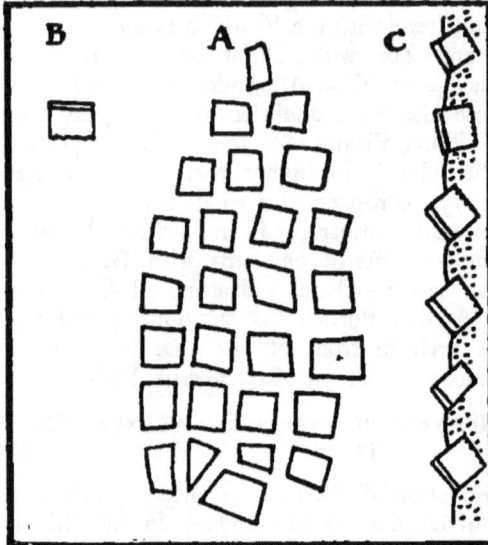

FIG. 73.—Mosaic Tesserae, actual size.

[1] See note above the index.
[2] *Il Duomo di Parenzo*, p. 26.

rutilat fulgore decoris," and at S. Paulo fuori le Mura the
mosaic—*"fulget fulgente decore."*

We have examined a handful of gold tesserae from S. Sophia
through the kindness of Mr. James Powell. The cubes
average a quarter of an inch in size, the glass is yellowish,
slightly amethyst or dark green. The surface layer equals
stout paper in thickness. At the back of the tesserae a
dusty red appears, which under a glass proves to be of
powdered tile. This roughens and adheres to the surface
of the glass, which was evidently sanded with the powder
while in a molten state, and of course before it was broken
into morsels. The first purpose of this without doubt was
to increase the hold of the cubes to the cementing material,
but the reddening—almost like a coat of vermilion paint—
may probably have assisted the gold to show out better than
if the tesserae had been fixed without it into the perfectly
white stucco which forms the bed. The cementing material
was an inch or more in thickness, formed of lime with broken
reed for binding, and a considerable amount of crushed white
marble, in the part next the mosaic at least.

§ 3. GLASS, PLASTER AND PAINTING.

The Romans probably largely used coloured glass for
windows. The lattices were sometimes bronze or thin slabs of
marble pierced into a pattern.[1] Sidonius († 484), describing
the basilica of Tours, clearly mentions the patterned windows
of green and sapphire glass.[2] It has been suggested that some
of the windows at S. Sophia were filled with glass of brilliant
colour. Theophilus, in his preface to the section of his work
dealing with coloured glass, says, "I have approached the
atrium of Holy Sophia, and beheld the chancel filled with every
variety of divers colours." He proceeds to describe windows
of painted glass in which the pieces are united by leads :
but assuredly, if coloured windows did exist in the apse of
S. Sophia, the glass was inserted in pierced marble, like

[1] Middleton, *Anc. Rome*, i. 31.
[2] See Labarte, *Arts Indust.*, vol. iii., p. 331.

U

the plaster lattices of the Orientals. Beautiful windows of
brilliant-hued glass exist in the mosques and turbehs. The
Arab lattices show us what beautiful mosaics of jewels may
be formed in this way ; the singular charm of them is the
spreading and blending of the colours, by reflection from the
sides of the thick dividing bars ; lumps of crystal seem to
have been used occasionally in place of glass. Most beautiful ' braided ' Byzantine lattices of marble are to be found
at S. Mark's which would be well characterised as θύραι
δεδικτυομέναι which according to Lenoir was the name of
these windows. If coloured glass was used in S. Sophia,
we think it can only have been in small windows of this
kind in the apse and conchs. Labarte thought, from the
descriptions of Procopius and Paulus, that the windows were
of white glass which allowed the rays of the sun to shine
through unaltered. It is hardly possible to conceive of the
great windows being of anything else than white glass.

A fragment of " ancient crystalline " glass from S. Sophia
was exhibited at the Society of Antiquaries in 1876. It is
described as only "one sixteenth of an inch thick, and
nearly colourless except for iridescence."

Grelot remarked that the plain glazing was "of round
panes set in plaster," but this must refer to the gradual
filling round of the panes by repairs, as may at present be
seen in the baptistery windows ; although circular panes in
a plaster setting were much used in Byzantine work, the
glass being spun in separate discs of slightly varying sizes
was inserted in marble or plaster slabs in different combinations. Windows of this kind remained in the apse of
the Theotokos church twenty years ago. Dr. Covel is
precise as to S. Sophia in 1676; he says the windows were
" cut out of entire stone into quarries exactly square," 10
by 12 or 14 inches. " In the first window of the west
gallery (coming in on the south side), are several pieces of
white transparent stone which I take to be Indian alabaster."

Modelled stucco work was much used by late Greek,
Roman, and Byzantine builders. Paulinus tells us that
at Nola " a cornice of gypsum " separated the mosaic and

FIG. 74.—Plaster Friezes of Gynaeceum.

marble of the apse. A large number of examples from the fourth to the sixth century are found in Rome, Parenzo, and Ravenna. "About the middle of the fifth century Galla Placidia built the church of S. Croce in Ravenna 'of very precious stones, and with stucco (gypsea) modelled with the tool' (Agnellus. *Lib. Pontif.* i. 283). Decorative stuccoes in the apse of S. Ambrose at Milan were destroyed thirty years ago, as they were supposed to be 'Baroque.' Dartein analysed the material and found that it contained 85 per cent. of plaster (gesso), a little lime, sand and brick-dust or pozzolana." "The rich decoration of the Chapel of S. Maria at Cividale (eighth to tenth century), and the Arab-Norman modelled stuccoes of Sicily show that the traditions of this kind of ornament were not lost at a later time." [1] In the churches of Greece this material is largely used, and its application in Arab work was due to Byzantine example. At S. Sophia an ornamental plaster frieze runs along both sides of the south porch : this is a scroll throwing out acanthus leaves and fruits like poppy seed-vessels. The background is coloured blue.

The flat frieze-like cornice of the first floor ornamented with two patterns of leafage appears to us to be of stucco ; we figure these here, but we have not been able to verify the material. If of stucco, as we suppose, it is cast or stamped in small square panels as shown : certainly some of the Byzantine plaster-work, as for instance that forming the cornice of the apse at S. Apollinare in Classe, was cast in short sections and then applied.

---

[1] Boni, *Il Duomo di Parenzo*, pp. 4, 5.

The blue background of the plastered frieze just mentioned may remind us of the decoration of the beam above
the columns of the ambo with gold ivy leaves on a background coloured ultramarine as described by the poet.
(The spade-like leaves which occur in several places in the
mosaic must be ivy.) This decoration of gold and
" sapphire " seems to have been general in Byzantine work.
The sculptured beam of the iconostasis at St. Luke's has the
blue background nearly intact, and here and there the gold
is visible (Diehl, p. 26).

Traces of the blue ground may also be noticed in the
sculptures of Mone tes Choras at Constantinople. The
notched fillet, which separates the marble panels in S. Sophia,
is used so extensively at Venice that Mr. Ruskin called it
the Venetian dentil ; the complete intention of this fillet,
he writes, is now only to be seen in pictures, " for like most
of the rest of the mouldings of Venetian buildings it was
always either gilded or painted—often both, gold being laid
on the faces of the dentils and the recesses coloured
alternately red and blue."[1] It is clear from Paulus that at
S. Sophia the sculptured capitals were all gilt (Part II., lines
129 and 244), as apparently were also the carved surfaces
filling the spandrils of the lower arcade (line 236). The
red colouring which Salzenberg notices was probably the
preparation for the gold. It is thus almost certain that the
notched fillets and carved frames of white marble surround-
ing the marble wall panels were gilt, as the Anonymous says,
and coloured, thus reflecting as it were from the wall
surfaces the brighter hues of the mosaic vaults.

§ 4.—MONOGRAMS AND INSCRIPTIONS.

The poet Paulus speaks of the iconostasis as bearing the
names of the emperor and empress, combined in a monogram
—" one letter that means many words."

Such ciphers or monograms had been in use for some
centuries, and at the end of the fifth century they were used
as signatures in discs left in the capitals. They appear at

[1] *Stones of Venice*, I., xxiii., 13.

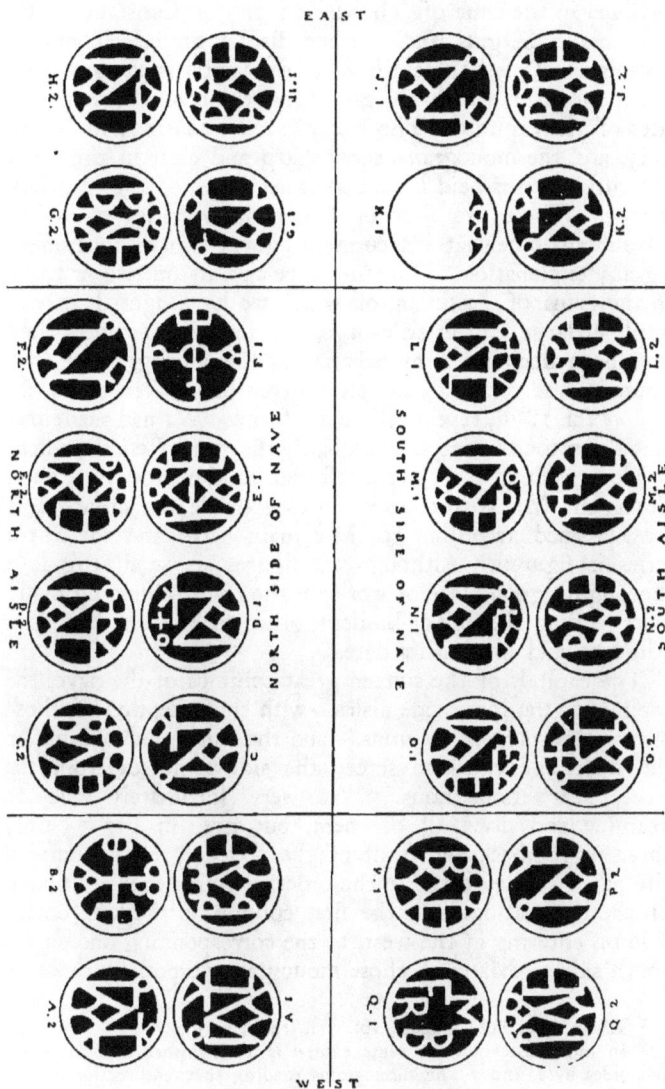

FIG. 75.—Monograms on Capitals of Nave.

Ravenna in the time of Theodoric ; and, in Constantinople,
S. Sophia, S. Sergius, and S. Irene display similar ciphers of
Justinian. At S. Sophia almost every capital is charged with
two monograms which are carved on the bosses on opposite
sides of the capitals. The background is entirely hollowed
away, and the monograms show sharp and clear in the nest-
like cup which is held by the serrated edges of the acanthus
leafage. There are four or five main varieties of which
Salzenberg somewhat inaccurately figures two without offer-
ing any explanation. The first type appears on two or three
of the coins of Justinian, of which we have figured an example at large on the title-page, and in these instances they
have been deciphered by Sabatier as the monogram of that
emperor. A ceramic inscription given in the *Revue Archéo-
ogique* for 1876, repeats the same form. We had made out
that the second variety was probably the word *Basileos*, when,
at Constantinople, we were referred to the paper by Canon
Curtis and M. Aristarches.[1] In this article the monograms
are classified according to their main types and the whole
series is figured. Although the figures are small, this is a
thoroughly good piece of work, in the result obtaining many
pairs reading Justinian, Basileos, other pairs with Theodora
Augusta, and one with a date.

The capitals of the sixteen great columns of the nave, the
capitals of the lower side aisles—with the exception of those
on the eight square columns,—and the thirty-six columns on
the floor above, which screen the side gynaecea from the
nave, bear monograms. We were fortunately able to
examine and draw all of them, but give in Fig. 75 only
those on the back and front of the sixteen great columns of
the nave. They occur in the order in which they are placed
on the illustration from the first column on the left (north)
side on entering at the west, to the corresponding one on the
south side.[2] Many of those monograms, especially those of

---

[1] Ἑλλην. Φιλ. Συλλ. παραρ., vol. xvi., 1885, p. 13.
[2] In our illustration the same capital is distinguished by a letter, the
two sides by 1 and 2, the monograms reading in the direction of the
reference to their position. Those of " N. Aisle " for instance read from
left side of page.

the galleries, bear evidence of having been restored. We
may recollect that the capitals were said to have been
restored by Romanus (p. 123). It is possible that Fossati
tampered with them ; the Italian MS. of 1611 in the
British Museum states that " the Turks have destroyed some
figures which were anciently carved (*intagliarsi*) on the
capitals."

There are fifty-six examples on the capitals which Curtis
and Aristarches give as being monograms of Justinian ; in
all these the letter N forms the main lines, to which additions are made, so that the letters IOVCTINIANOV can be
traced out. Some of these have crosses in addition.

The next monogram is that read BACIΛEWC. It occurs
in all on fifty-five columns, the examples of it in our
illustration are B.1, E.2, H.1, P.1, C.2, P.1, G.2, J.2, L.2, N.2,
Q.2, the remnant of K.1, shows that this was similar. This
monogram is found also on the capitals of S. Sergius and
Bacchus, and on three beautiful Basket Capitals at S. Mark's.[1]

Several of the fifty-six, classed together as Justinian,
furnish varieties from the clearest typical form. In some a
letter appears which may be read either as E or B, also an W
and a sign of contraction : see M.1 and O.1 ; possibly this is
a combination of Justinian and Basileos or only a variant
spelling : this form occurs in the church of S. Sergius as well
as at S. Sophia.

On twelve capitals is carved the monogram ΘEOΔWPAC.
This is either designed on the cross form as B.2 F.1, another
in the side aisles, and three in the gynaeceum above, or else
as in E.2 it approximates to Basileos. Two of this latter
type also occur in S. Sergius, which shows how early Justinian associated his wife with him in his architectural labours.

---

[1] Two varieties of monograms on capitals at S. Mark's have been the
subject of much study which Cattaneo sums up in Boito's text of the
great monograph on S. Mark's, but they have never been deciphered. One
(see Photos, vol. ii., p. 127) is a perfect example of Justinian ; three
which show in capitals of the upper stage south side are perfect examples
of Basileos—if corresponding monograms probably on the hidden sides of
these capitals are examined, they too may be found to contain the
Justinian monogram. For monograms at S. Sergius see *Byz. Zeit.* for
1894.

Finally from S. Sophia, and from there only, we have twelve examples of ΑΥΓΟΥϹΤΑϹ. Typical ones are shown in G.1, and A.1—A.2 ; possibly some of these, as A.1, may have been read Augustus, if any care was taken in their distribution. The letters on the last capital Q.1 have been read by Curtis and Aristarches as ϜΜΒΒ. They take Ϝ to be a capital form of the obsolete letter which is used for 6 or 6,000, Μ is as usual 40, and Β is 2. Hence they get 6042 for the year of the world. The lower Β is then explained as the year of an Indiction, reading it as ΙΒ, or 12. One Indiction period of fifteen years would have ended in 522 A.D., and the twelfth year from that would be 534 A.D. equalling 6042 A.M. Therefore this gives a date, two years after the church was begun, when they suggest that this capital was put in its place. This ingenious explanation requires too much adjustment for it to be conclusive, and the Ϝ form is at least unusual. This monogram looks very white, as if it had been made up in plaster ; if we were assured as to how much is ancient we might perhaps, if it proved different from the others, find here the inserted monogram of a later emperor who made repairs.

Salzenberg gives some monogram signatures from the closures under the great west window, which are carefully carved and entirely different from rough masons' marks, although some of the forms occur amongst those. We were unable to examine them, and taking Salzenberg's representation, we can only suggest that they may be the signatures of master-workers ; one appears to be Phocas.

M. Choisy [1] has investigated the masons' marks of S. Sophia ; besides the ordinary signs, he makes out a system of numbering in the pavement slabs of the galleries.

Strzygowski [2] pursues the subject of Byzantine marks in general, much further. He points out the same signs on the columns of S. Vitale, of Pomposa, and of Parenzo, and in the cistern Bin-Bir-direk at Constantinople. From this we gather that not only " the columns of Ravenna, but also the similar architectural features of Constantinople, Salonica,

[1] In *L'Art de Bâtir* and *Revue Archéologique*, 1876.
[2] *Die Wasserbehälter von Konstantinopel*, p. 245.

Parenzo, in fact along the whole coast of the Mediterranean " were taken from the quarries of Proconnesus, and in the lettering on the different members we can recognise the working signs of the quarrymen or masons belonging to the guild, which sprang into existence there at the founding of New Rome, and which even as early as the end of the fourth century was exporting to the islands of the Ægean.

A few other inscriptions on the marble may be briefly noticed. On the inner border of the marble parapet of the north gallery is scratched, " Place of the most noble Patrician Lady Theodora," ending with an abbreviation that may mean S. Sophia,[1] and again on a panel of the parapet of the north gallery at the west end is seen, " Timothy, keeper of the vessels." Coteler in his *Monumenta Ecclesiae Graecae* finds mention of one Timothy, who was skeuophylax of the Great Church at the time of the Monothelite heresies about 622.[2]

On a column in the southern gynaeceum occurs the word Teodorus, but the fact that it is spelt with the Latin T and D proves it to have been written during the Western supremacy, 1204–1261.

In the south gallery is a slab forming a part of the paving ; " marks in the face of which seem to suggest that a railing inclosed the space within which a sarcophagus used to stand, supported by pillars." This is inscribed with the name of the blind Doge who led the Venetians against Constantinople in 1204, and died the following year, " HENRICUS DANDOLO."

[1] Curtis, *Broken Bits of Byzantium*, pt. ii.
[2] Ἑλλ. Φιλ. Συλλ. παραρ., vol. xvi. p. 29.

NOTE

The following additional inscription from the mosaics is given in Clarke's *Travels* (1812). It was taken, he says, in one place, "from the ceiling of the dome," but in another place he seems to associate it with the eastward semidomes :—

OCKAIXPYCOY
ΠΕΝΤΗΚΟΝΤΑ
ΤΑΛΑΝΤΑΘΕΟΚ
. . N . . . OICNE
. EKEI . . . . .

INDEX

A

Abdul Mesjid, restoration by, 148
Acacius, S., church of, 129
Acanthus, 46, 166, 167, 254, 257, 261, 263
Acropolis, 1, 2, 7, 10, 11, 12, 17
Additions to church, 154, 155
Adoration of Cross, 98
Agathias (6th c.), 30, 33, 159, 204, 212, 214
Agatho the Deacon, 182
Agora of Milion, 179, 181
Aisles, 27, 43, 44, 151 ; lamps in, 51 ; marble, 171, 243 ; mosaics, 247 ; vaulting, 160, 220, 221
Aix, 116, 192
Akoimetoi lamps, 118
Alexandria, 6, 249 ; capital of S. Mark's at, 255
Alexius, S., 181
  „   Comnenus (1081), 100, 105, 181
Altar, 16, 29, 48, 68, 69, 100 ; cross placed on, 92 ; cloth, 71. See also Holy Table
Ambo, 18, 29, 53, 57, 94, 98, 124, 130, 139, 140 ; candelabra round, 111, 118 ; singers in, 79, 104 ; coronations in, 61, 63
Amiens, Knight of ; see Robert de Clari
Amurath III., 127
Anastasia, S., church of, 21
Anastasius, 116, 117, 119
Ancyra, church at, 203

Andreossy, 232
Andronicus, S., 129
  „   Palaeologus, 124, 152
Anemodulion, 178
Anna Comnena (12th c.), 183, 186
Anna, Empress, 124
Annulets round shafts, 259, 273
Anonymous Author (12th c. ?), 24, 26, 28, 30, 36, 43, 204, 248, 270
Anthemius, 24, 26, 28, 30, 36, 43, 204, 248, 270
Anthony of Novgorod ; see Novgorod
Antioch, 6, 17, 44, 181, 203
Antux, 37, 41, 43, 45, 47, 49, 57
Apollinaris, S., 258, 283
Apostles, church of, 14, 15, 18, 74, 85, 205
Apse, 19, 22, 24, 29, 32, 37, 67, 69, 132, 150, 216
Apsides, 25, 28, 30, 41, 43, 133, 180, 182
Apsoid, 22, 25, 209, 210
Arcadius (395), 16, 180 ; baths of 11 ; cistern, 257
Arch, 210, 213 ; western restored, 123 ; forms, 220
Architraves, marble, 138 ; bronze, 264
Arculf (7th c.), 92, 95, 98
Ark of Noah, 109, 138, 147
Arrises of vaults, 244
Arsenius, 86, 109, 124
Asbestos, 27, 132, 136, 231
Athos, Mt., 98, 115, 118, 119, 189, 227

x

T.

Technitai, 24, 206
Tektonikos, 133, 206
Temples at Byzantium, 1—4
Tesserae, 45, 274, 288
Texier, 10, 149, 193, 203, 283
Theodora, wife of Justinian, 70, 86, 88, 294; wife of Theophilus, 122, 269
Theodoric, 86, 88, 257
Theodosius I. (379), 16, 129, 177, 180; Code of, 206
Theodosius II. (408), 6, 16
Theophanes (9th c.), 14, 20, 29, 72, 100, 207, 209; Continuator (10th c.), 71, 87, 90
Theophilus, Emperor (829), 175, 269; writer, 272, 290
Thessaly, marble of, 32, 37, 40, 44, 58, 59, 130, 164, 236
Thomaites, 65, 181, 186
Throne, 62, 105; of bishop, 68; in mosaic, 277, 279
Thusiasterion, 18, 28, 67, 130, 132, 136
Tiberius (578), 174
Titanos, 27, 232
Tombs in S. Sophia, 102
Tralles, 24, 204
Transparent slabs, 262
Trees of light, 51, 57, 118, 119
Tribunal with porphyry steps, 11
Triconcha, 175
Turks capture city, 126, 127, 147
Turrets at west end, 163

U

Ultramarine, 60, 291
Undercutting in carving, 254
Unger, 8, 78
Urns, marble, 84

V

Varangi, 64
Vaults, 69, 150, 160, 161, 199, 200 207, 219; mosaic on, 274
Vela, 65, 86, 87
Venice, 71, 72, 99, 175, 193
Verde antique, 67, 81, 82, 164, 165, 166, 167, 170, 172, 242, 260, 261
Veronica, 286
Villehardouin, 107
Virgin, figure of, 83, 109, 123, 275, 278, 284
Vitale, S., at Ravenna, 88, 227
Von Hammer, 145, 152

W

Walls of church, 155, 157, marble casings, 285
Wax, encaustic, 246
Well, Holy, 78, 91, 95, 105, 130, 139
West front, 192
Windows, 42, 43, 158, 168, 209, 261
Wood, Holy, 94, 95, 97, 105
Wood tie beams, 161, 162, 168, 227, 228, 230

Z

Zeno, building laws of, 6
Zenobia, city of, 206
Zeuxippus, baths of, 3, 4, 11, 179
Zonaras (11th c.), 29, 160, 179, 209
Zosimus (5th c.), 4, 5

THE END.

www.ingramcontent.com/pod-product-compliance
Lightning Source LLC
Chambersburg PA
CBHW020458270326
41926CB00008B/657